HOLDON

Locks a file so that other users cannot wri[...]
HOLDOFF command.

LARCHIVE [*path* | **SYSTEM**]

Backs up files and NetWare attributes to a local hard or floppy disk.

LISTDIR [*path*] [*option ...*]

Displays a list of all the subdirectories in a directory, along with other information.

LOGIN [*server/[user]*]

Permits a network user to access a file server and invoke the system and user login script.

LOGOUT [*server*]

Terminates access to one or more file servers.

LRESTORE

Restores files and attributes backed up with the LARCHIVE command.

MAP [*drive:*]
MAP *path*
MAP *drive:* = [*drive:* | *path*]
MAP [INS] *drive:* = [*drive:path*]
MAP DEL *drive:*

Displays and allows changes to drive maps.

NARCHIVE [*path* | **SYSTEM**]

Backs up file and NetWare attributes to another network drive.

NCOPY *filespec* [TO] [*path*] [*filename*] [/V]

Copies files from one network directory to another.

NDIR [*path*] | [*filename*]
NDIR (*path* | *filespec*) *option* [*...*]

Displays information about subdirectories and the files within subdirectories.

MASTERING
NOVELL
NETWARE

MASTERING
NOVELL®
NETWARE®

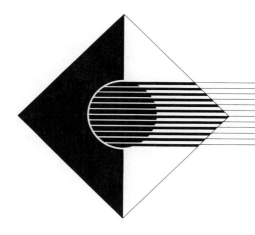

CHERYL C. CURRID
CRAIG A. GILLETT

SAN FRANCISCO • PARIS • DÜSSELDORF • LONDON

Acquisitions Editor: Dianne King
Editor: Judith Ziajka
Technical Editor: Walter Albers
Word Processors: Deborah Maizels, Chris Mockel
Series Designer: Julie Bilski
Chapter Art and Layout: Joe Roter
Technical Art: Jeffrey James Giese
Screen Graphics: Delia Brown
Typesetter: Winnie Kelly
Proofreader: Ed Lin
Indexer: Ted Laux
Cover Designer: Thomas Ingalls + Associates
Cover Photographer: David Bishop
Screen reproductions produced by XenoFont

Library of Congress Card Number: 89-63317
ISBN 0-89588-630-8
Manufactured in the United States of America
10 9 8 7 6

To Ray, Tray, and Justin.

—C. C.

To Mom and Dad

—C. G.

ACKNOWLEDGMENTS

WE OFFER OUR SINCERE APPRECIATION TO ALL OF the people providing support to this project. Judy Ziajka's editorial expertise and patience transformed an often rough manuscript into a cohesive (and grammatically correct) final product. Walter Albers, the technical editor, provided a constructive constant challenge to our approach to help ensure that we didn't overlook any technical details.

We also are indebted to the World's Greatest Network Manager, Mr. David Ellerbe, for allowing us to disturb more than a few of his evenings and weekends when we needed to dig a little deeper into NetWare techniques. We often marveled over the quick response time and precision of his answers.

Of course, our families endured the most inconvenience while we worked on this project. Ray, Tray, Justin, Connie, and Ashley Gail: Thanks again for your understanding. We promise this will be the last book (until next time).

Thanks to our professional colleagues: Ann, Ed B., Randy, Merryl, Karen, Louis, Jeff M., Jan, Cheryl H., Laura, Tish, Ralph, Steve, Frank, and the others who didn't give us a hard time about writing another book. Next weekend, we'll learn how to play golf.

And finally, thanks to all the others, too many to mention, who by stretching their intellect, pushing the edge, and reaching for their dreams, provide constant inspiration.

CONTENTS AT A GLANCE

INTRODUCTION   xxiii

PART I NETWORKS AND NETWORKING

1: What Is a Network?   5
2: Network Components and How They Work   15
3: Network Options   31
4: Planning for NetWare Installation   43

PART II INSTALLING AND CONFIGURING YOUR NETWARE NETWORK

5: An Installation Checklist   53
6: Preparing the Hardware   65
7: Installing NetWare   75
8: Creating User Access Programs   97

PART III CREATING THE USER ENVIRONMENT

9: Laying the Foundations for the User Environment   119
10: Adding Users and Groups   137
11: Creating Login Scripts and Batch Files   149
12: Establishing Network Security   171
13: Defining Printer Options   195
14: Creating User Menus   211

PART IV TAKING THE NETWORK FOR A TEST DRIVE

15: Logging In and Printing from the Network   221
16: User Utilities   233

PART V NETWORK MAINTENANCE AND FINE TUNING

17: Maintenance Techniques   255
18: Monitoring System Performance and Troubleshooting   267
19: Backing Up and Archiving the Network   283
20: Expanding Your Network Communications Options   303

PART VI NETWARE COMMANDS

21: Introduction to NetWare Commands   325
22: NetWare Commands   333

APPENDICES

A: NetWare 386   387
B: Glossary of Networking Terms   399

INDEX   409

TABLE OF CONTENTS

INTRODUCTION   *xxiii*

P A R T   I *NETWORKS AND NETWORKING*

C H A P T E R   1: *WHAT IS A NETWORK?*   5
Types of Networks   5
Benefits of Using a LAN   8
Building a Local Area Network   9
Summary   10

C H A P T E R   2: *NETWORK COMPONENTS AND HOW THEY WORK* 15
File Servers and Workstations   15
Workstation Operating Systems   17
Topology   17
Shared Resources   18
Communication with Other Systems   19
   Bridges   20
   Gateways   21
Summary   25

C H A P T E R   3: *NETWORK OPTIONS*   31
Network Data-Passing Schemes   31
   Performance Considerations   31
Network Systems   32
   Ethernet Networks   34
   Token Ring Networks   34

ARCnet Networks   35
Cabling Options   35
    Coaxial Cable   36
    Unshielded Twisted-Pair Cable   36
    Shielded Twisted-Pair Cable   37
    Fiber-Optic Cable   38
Summary   38

C H A P T E R   4:   **PLANNING FOR NETWARE INSTALLATION**   **43**
What Is NetWare?   43
Choosing a NetWare Version   43
    Choosing NetWare for a Small Network   44
    Choosing NetWare for a Medium-Sized Network   45
    Choosing NetWare for a Large Network   46
Other Startup Considerations   46
    Determining the File Server Location   46
    Determining Cable Placement   47
    Determining Where to Locate Network Printers 48
Summary   48

P A R T   II   **INSTALLING AND CONFIGURING
YOUR NETWARE NETWORK**

C H A P T E R   5:   **AN INSTALLATION CHECKLIST**   **53**
Preparing for the Installation   53
An Installation Checklist   54
Preparing the Hardware   55
Configuring and Installing NetWare   55
Creating the User Access Programs   56
Setting the Directory Structure and Loading Applications   57

Setting Up Login Scripts and User Groups   57
Adding Security Features   58
Configuring and Testing Network Printers   59
Creating Menus   60
Planning Network Administration   60
Summary   61

C H A P T E R   6: **PREPARING THE HARDWARE**   **65**
Preparing the File Server Location   65
    Protecting against Static Electricity and Heat   65
    Protecting against Electrical Noise, Power Surges, and
    Power Outages   66
Preparing Your Hardware to Run NetWare   66
    Checking Computer Requirements   67
    Preparing Network Computers   68
    Preparing Network Printers   68
Cabling the Workstations   68
    Documenting the Cable Layout   69
Installing the Network Printers   69
Summary   70

C H A P T E R   7: **INSTALLING NETWARE**   **75**
Configuring the Operating System   75
    Preparing Working Copies of NetWare Disks   76
    Selecting a Configuration Method   76
    Selecting Operating System Options   77
    Defining and Configuring the File Server Hardware   82
    Generating the Operating System and
    Communications Utilities   83
Installing the Network Interface Cards and Preparing the
Hard Disk   85
    Setting and Installing the Network Interface Cards   85
    Preparing the Hard Disk   86
Installing the Operating System   88
Booting the File Server   92
Summary   93

C H A P T E R 8: **CREATING USER ACCESS PROGRAMS**   **97**

Getting Ready for Work   97
    Preparing a Master Disk   97
    Selecting a Configuration Method   98
Generating the Workstation Shell Files   98
Creating a Master Shell Desk   100
Logging In for the First Time   102
Creating a Custom Login Program   104
    Generating Message Screens   105
    Writing the Login Batch File   108
Booting from a Hard Disk   110
Diagnosing Problems   112
Summary   113

P A R T III **CREATING
THE USER ENVIRONMENT**

C H A P T E R 9: **LAYING THE FOUNDATIONS
FOR THE USER ENVIRONMENT**   **119**

Using Directories and Subdirectories   119
    Using NetWare Directories   119
    Using System Directories   121
    Creating Directories   121
Using Drive Maps   122
    Using Local Drive Maps   123
    Using Network Drive Maps   124
    Using Search Drive Maps   124
    Using NetWare Default Drive Maps   124
    Adding or Changing Drive Maps   125
Developing a Directory Structure   126
    Creating the Directories   127
    Creating the Subdirectories   129
    Viewing the Directory Structure   130

Loading Files into Directories 130
   Loading DOS Files 130
   Loading Applications and Data 132
Summary 133

CHAPTER 10: ADDING USERS AND GROUPS **137**
Defining Network Users 137
Defining Network Groups 138
Adding, Changing, and Deleting Users 138
Creating Groups 142
Getting Online Help 144
Security Considerations 145
Summary 145

CHAPTER 11: CREATING LOGIN SCRIPTS AND BATCH FILES **149**
Types of Login Scripts 149
Login Script Commands 149
Creating the System Login Script 151
   Setting Up the Drive Maps 152
   Defining the Environmental Parameters 155
   Displaying a Welcome Message 156
   Testing the System Login Script 157
Creating a User Login Script 159
Copying User Login Scripts 161
Writing Program Batch Files with Dynamic Drive Mapping 164
   Preparing the Batch File 164
   Writing the Batch File 166
Summary 167

CHAPTER 12: ESTABLISHING NETWORK SECURITY **171**
Developing a Network Security Strategy 171
   User Restrictions 172
   Directory and File Restrictions 172

Adding Password and Login Security   173
    Limiting Concurrent Sessions   174
    Implementing Intruder Detection and Lockout   175
    Restricting LAN Access Times   176
Adding Trustee Security   177
    Granting Trustee Rights to Individuals   178
    Granting Trustee Rights to Groups   180
    Granting Rights through Security Equivalences 181
    Deleting Trustee Rights   183
Adding Directory Security   184
    Using the Maximum Rights Mask   184
    Determining Effective Rights   185
Adding File and Directory Attributes Security   186
    Setting File Attributes   187
    Setting Directory Attributes   189
Summary   190

CHAPTER 13: DEFINING PRINTER OPTIONS   **195**
Using Print Queues and Servers   195
Using the NetWare Printer Default Settings
versus Customization   196
Using the Printer Definitions (PRINTDEF) Utility   197
    Importing Print Device Definitions   197
    Editing Device Options   198
    Defining Forms   200
Using the Printer Configuration (PRINTCON) Utility   202
    Creating a Printer Configuration   202
    Copying Printer Configurations   203
    Selecting the Default Print Job Configuration 204
Using the Printer Console (PCONSOLE) Utility   205
Summary   206

CHAPTER 14: CREATING USER MENUS   **211**
Planning the Menus   211
Using the NetWare Menu Utility   212

Creating the Menus   214
Summary   216

P A R T IV **TAKING THE
NETWORK FOR A TEST DRIVE** ———————

C H A P T E R 15: **LOGGING IN AND PRINTING FROM THE NETWORK** **221**
Preparing for Network Use   221
  Recruiting Test Pilots   221
  High-Level Network Training   222
  Start-Up Support   222
Preparing for the Network Users   223
Logging In for the First Time   223
Printing from the Network   225
  Printing from Applications   225
  Printing with PCONSOLE   225
  Working with Print Queues   227
  Printing from the Command Line   228
Summary   229

C H A P T E R 16: **USER UTILITIES**   **233**
Using the System Configuration (SYSCON) Utility   233
Using the Session Management (SESSION) Utility   236
  Changing and Displaying Drive Map Information   237
  Using Group and User Options   239
Using the File Maintenance (FILER) Utility   240
  Displaying Volume Information   241
  Displaying Directory Information   242
  Displaying File Information   243
  Changing FILER Options   246

Using Command-Line Utilities   246
    Sending Messages   247
    Listing Users   248
    Changing a User Password   248
    Displaying User Information   249
Summary   249

P   A   R   T   V   *NETWORK*
                    MAINTENANCE AND FINE TUNING

C H A P T E R   17:   *MAINTENANCE TECHNIQUES*   *255*
Monitoring Disk Space   255
    Displaying Specific Disk-Use Information with NDIR   256
    Reviewing Users' Disk Space with SYSCON   257
    Recovering Space from Deleted Users   257
    Monitoring Common File Area Space   259
    Monitoring Duplicate Files   259
Monitoring File Server Statistics   260
Performing Other Maintenance Checks   261
    Performing Security Checks   262
    Checking the Root Directories   262
    Recovering from File Server Failures   263
    Monitoring Network Use   263
Summary   263

C H A P T E R   18:   *MONITORING SYSTEM*
                      PERFORMANCE AND TROUBLESHOOTING   *267*
Monitoring Key System Performance Areas   267
    Using Novell's PERFORM Utility   267
    Using FCONSOLE Information   270

Troubleshooting   272
   Troubleshooting Software Problems   273
   Troubleshooting Hardware Problems   273
Summary   278

C H A P T E R 19: **BACKING UP AND ARCHIVING THE NETWORK**   **283**
Determining Who Backs Up the System   283
Backing Up versus Archiving   284
Choosing Hardware and Software   285
   Using NetWare Utilities   285
Establishing Procedures   285
   Backing Up Files Daily   286
   Backing Up the Entire System Weekly   286
   Archiving Files Monthly   287
Using NetWare Backup and Archiving Utilities   288
   The NARCHIVE and NRESTORE Utilities   288
   The LARCHIVE and LRESTORE Utilities   294
Summary   298

C H A P T E R 20: **EXPANDING YOUR**
NETWORK COMMUNICATIONS OPTIONS   **303**
Expanding Single-Site Communications   303
   LAN-to-LAN Bridging   303
   Modem Sharing   304
Expanding Remote Communications   306
   Using Remote-Control Software   306
   Using Novell Remote-Access Products   306
Expanding Wide Area Network (WAN) Communications   310
   Using Dial-Up Lines   310
   Using Public Data Networks   310
   Using Leased Lines and T-1   311
   Using Satellite Communications   311
   Effecting LAN-to-LAN Communications   312

Expanding LAN-to-Host Communications   314
    Effecting Single-User Connection   314
    Using SNA Gateways   317
Summary   317

P   A   R   T   VI   ***NETWARE COMMANDS***

C H A P T E R   21:   ***INTRODUCTION TO NETWARE COMMANDS***   *325*
Types of NetWare Commands   325
Commonly Used Commands   326
    File Server Commands   327
    Workstation Controls   328
    Printer and Print Queue Commands   328
    Status Information Commands   329
Summary   329

C H A P T E R   22:   ***NETWARE COMMANDS***   *333*
Command Conventions Used in This Chapter   333
NetWare Commands   334

A P P E N D I X   A: ***NETWARE 386***   *387*
NetWare 386 Design Philosophy   387
Differences between NetWare 386 and Previous Versions   388
    Increased Capacity   388
    Dynamic Resource Allocation   389
    More Flexible Printer Connection   390
    Enhanced Security   390

Upgrading to NetWare 386   395
   Building a New Server   396
   Using the UPGRADE Utility   396
Summary   397

A P P E N D I X B: **GLOSSARY OF NETWORKING TERMS**   *399*

INDEX   *408*

INTRODUCTION

IF YOU ARE A MICROCOMPUTER MANAGER—OR even a noncomputer professional—facing the task of installing, maintaining, or using a NetWare local area network (LAN), this book is written especially for you. *Mastering Novell NetWare* is a concise, easy-to-follow guide to configuring, installing, and operating a personal computer network using Novell NetWare.

Mastering Novell NetWare helps you wade through the 15-plus manuals that come with the NetWare 286 software. Unlike systems documentation that focuses on functions, *Mastering Novell NetWare* demonstrates the process of actually setting up a network from start to finish. This book also addresses the important topics of maintenance and troubleshooting and includes a reference to NetWare commands.

Nearly every important function, command, and utility available in NetWare is demonstrated step by step. As you follow the examples in this book, the mystery of local area networking will diminish, and your ability to exploit the full potential of NetWare will increase significantly. Moreover, you'll find several techniques and tips gathered from successful network administrators and not discussed in the NetWare documentation.

STRUCTURE OF THE BOOK

This book is divided into six parts. Part I, composed of the first four chapters, reviews networking fundamentals. This part explains LAN terminology, how networks communicate data, and the various components used in a typical local area network. It also discusses network size and its implications for your choice of NetWare software.

Part II, Chapters 5 through 8, focuses on preparing for the installation and actually configuring and loading the network operating system. An installation checklist outlines the steps necessary to successfully activate a local area network. This part also presents helpful tips for preparing the hardware. Then the installation of the network software is described step by step.

In Part III, Chapters 9 through 14, the network's user environment is developed. Again, the emphasis is on showing both the basics and advanced techniques that can enhance the functionality of the LAN. Among the topics discussed in these chapters are creating the directory structure, adding users and groups, writing login scripts, establishing security provisions, setting up network printers, and building custom menus.

Part IV, Chapters 15 and 16, shifts the focus to the user of network. Chapter 15 illustrates the process of logging in for the first time and describes the process of printing on network printers. Chapter 16 explores the NetWare utilities designed for the network user.

The next four chapters, Part V, discuss ongoing maintenance and network expansion. This part emphasizes where to look for problems and how to correct them. This part also demonstrates several of the important troubleshooting utilities available in NetWare.

The final two chapters, Part VI, summarize the NetWare command-line utilities for quick reference.

Appendix A describes NetWare 386—the most recent and powerful release of the Novell operating system—and compares it to the 286 version. Appendix B is a glossary of networking terminology.

PART I

NETWORKS AND NETWORKING

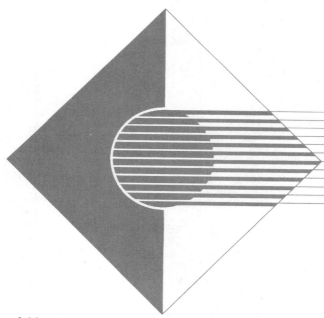

Successful local area network design and implementation requires planning and preparation. The chapters in this part review the concepts and definitions that underlie Novell networks. This background will help you make better decisions about the physical layout of your network and the components the network uses.

CHAPTER 1

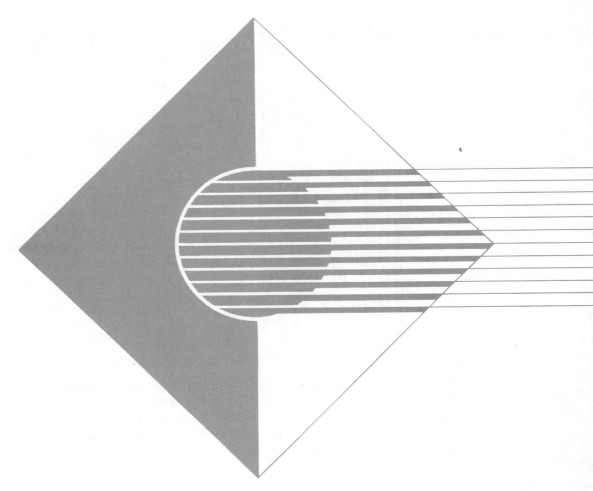

WHAT IS A NETWORK?

Fast Track

Networks can be either   5

- Hierarchical networks, as often found in a mainframe or minicomputer installation, or
- Peer networks, as are local area networks (LANs).

The benefits of a LAN from a hardware cost standpoint include   8

the capability to share peripherals, such as expensive printers, high-capacity disk drives, specialty devices, and communications devices.

The benefits of a LAN from the user's standpoint include   8

the capability to link people and groups together. Improved communications among people often results.

The benefits of a LAN from a maintenance standpoint include   8

the capability to share data-processing maintenance services, such as backup services and software installation services.

To set up a network,   9

1. Select the hardware and topology.
2. Install the hardware and network operating system.
3. Configure the system and load application software.
4. Create the user environment.
5. Set up procedures for ongoing network administration.

CHAPTER 1

IN THE PAST SEVERAL YEARS, PERSONAL COMPUTER networks, called local area networks, or LANs, have arrived in the mainstream.

In 1988, the Democratic National Party installed ten local area networks, consisting of over 300 workstations, to support its national convention. These LANs were used for functions ranging from counting delegate votes to keeping track of party invitations. In addition to the main network, candidates set up their own separate networks. These separate networks were connected to the main network, thus allowing the candidates and the party to easily share information.

In Seoul, Korea, in 1988, the National Broadcasting Company, Inc. put together a 126-workstation LAN for its coverage of the summer Olympic games. This multipurpose network helped NBC officials coordinate travel arrangements, inventory a 20,000-tape video library, and maintain Olympic statistics and trivia for on-air use.

Why did these organizations choose local area network technology in lieu of other data processing approaches? This chapter looks at some of the reasons why increasing numbers of organizations are building LANs. This chapter also outlines the simple steps that allow you to easily connect your computers and information resources to a network operating system such as Novell NetWare.

TYPES OF NETWORKS

In the not so distant past, when computers were expensive and large, organizations could not give employees entire computers for their personal use. Instead, the central processing unit (CPU) had to be shared. Thus, networks emerged.

The first networks were hierarchical. In this scheme, shown in Figure 1.1, the center of computing activity, where the CPU is located, is

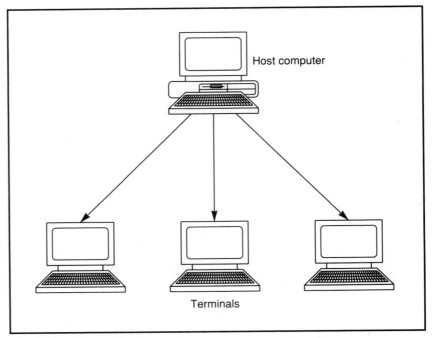

Figure 1.1: Hierarchical network

the host hardware unit. This host is usually a mainframe or minicomputer. Users access this host through satellite terminals, often called dumb terminals because they cannot perform any processing themselves. The basic purpose of dumb terminals is to provide an interface between the host and the users.

Hierarchical networks provide centralized computing, but they are limited in important ways. The users of the central processor are limited to the applications on the host computers. The user's ability to perform custom analysis is therefore limited, because changes to host programs are often costly and time consuming, and because the host program must meet the needs of all users on the network.

With the advent of silicon technology and the corresponding drop in prices of computer processors, computing capability, in the form of personal computers, or PCs, could be placed on individual desktops.

Personal computers allow each user to customize software and to perform data analysis to meet his or her particular needs. However, standalone, unconnected computers do not offer direct access to the organization's data, nor can information and programs be easily shared.

Local area networks provide a solution to the limitations of both standalone and centralized processing environments. As Figure 1.2 shows, LANs are peer networks, which means that all devices on the network can communicate with each other. Instead of dumb terminals, LANs use smart terminals—microcomputers with their own central processing units. LANs provide a bridge not only between people and information, but also between individual users.

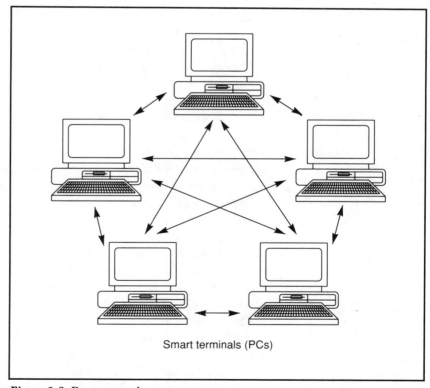

Smart terminals (PCs)

Figure 1.2: Peer network

BENEFITS OF USING A LAN

Often, the installation of a local area network is initially justified as a means of sharing peripheral devices. For example, a single hard drive can be used to support an entire work group. Expensive output devices, such as laser printers, can be shared, as can other specialty devices, such as PC-FAX boards, high-speed modems, and color printers.

But as the network grows and becomes integrated into the organization, device sharing usually becomes insignificant in comparison to the other advantages of networking. Local area networks link people as well as computer hardware. The result is both an electronic network and a human network. LANs provide an effective tool for communicating through the use of electronic mail (e-mail) and other work-group software. Messages can be sent instantaneously throughout the network, work plans can be updated as changes occur, and meetings can be scheduled without placing half a dozen phone calls.

Networking can also help reshape the way a company conducts certain business activities. The use of work-group software reduces the need for face-to-face meetings and other time-consuming methods of information distribution. At the same time, networking allows increased interaction among workers from their workstations. Networking can also enhance the effectiveness of communication, because people tend to put more thought into written communications than into informal conversation.

Because LANs provide direct access to work-group information from each desktop, productivity is also enhanced. Everyone has access to the data and, by using the tools available on the network, can manipulate it and share the results with others. Efficiencies can also be gained by putting on the network any process that depends on input from many members of the organization. LANs reduce, or in some cases eliminate, the need for one person to finish working on a file before another can use it.

An important side benefit of local area networks is that software and data are much easier to maintain and protect than in a standalone environment. Critical data can be backed up daily, or even hourly, if necessary. When software needs to be upgraded, the job can be done at a single source rather than at every personal computer that runs the program.

BUILDING A LOCAL AREA NETWORK

Building a local area network is not difficult, but it does require thoughtful planning. Networks are inherently modular, so once the right base is established, functions can be added later.

There are five basic steps to building a network:

- Select the topology and hardware.
- Install the hardware and network operating system.
- Configure the system and load the applications.
- Create the user environment.
- Set up ongoing LAN administration.

The first step in building a network is to design the physical architecture. Working with a network installer, you must decide which offices will be cabled for the network and where key components (such as the file server) will be located. You must select the types of computers to use as the terminals and the network scheme itself.

Your next step is to install the equipment and link the computers together with network interface cards and cables. At this point, the operating system can be loaded onto the hard drive in the computer you select as the file server and configured to recognize other devices (such as printers). You can now set up the subdirectory structure and organize the hard drive in preparation for loading the application software and other data.

Next, you create the user environment—the look and feel of the system—through the screens that appear when a user logs in and the menus that help guide the user through the available options. Security schemes also need to be established to protect the integrity of the data stored on the network.

Finally, since LANs require ongoing administration, you need to set up procedures to support the network.

Future chapters discuss these steps in detail.

SUMMARY

This chapter acquainted you with some of the history and concepts of local area networks. The advent of inexpensive microprocessors allowed computer resources to be shared in new ways. Using LANs, many companies now are moving away from hierarchical networks made up of dumb terminals to peer networks made up of smart terminals.

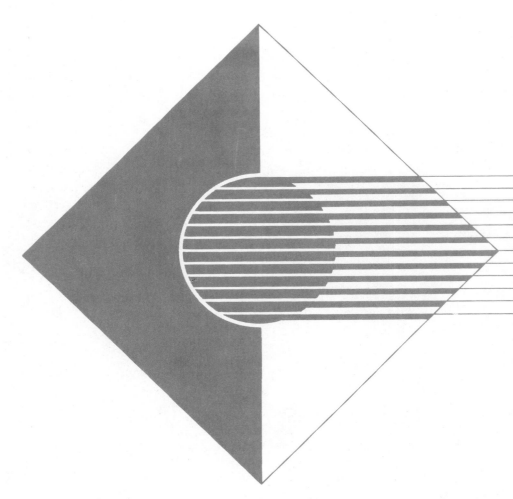

NETWORK COMPONENTS
AND HOW THEY WORK

FAST TRACK

A file server is   15

the core of the LAN. It is the microcomputer that runs the network operating system and that controls the activities of the network.

A network workstation is   16

a personal computer that has a network interface card installed and is physically attached to the file server through cables. In addition to the card and cables, the network workstation must run a special program, called a network shell, for it to communicate with the file server.

A network topology is   17

the route data travels along the network. Three popular types of topologies are bus, star, and ring.

Network bridges can be   20

either internal or external. External bridges are almost always faster (and more expensive) than internal bridges.

Gateways are microcomputers that are   21

configured with hardware and software that enables communications with other systems, such as mainframes and minicomputers.

CHAPTER 2

NOVELL NETWARE ALLOWS YOU TO CUSTOMIZE THE LAN architecture to meet the specific needs of your organization. This flexibility applies not only to the applications you run on the network, but also to the hardware and functions you use.

A LAN can consist of a single file server supporting a small number of workstations or of multiple file servers and communications servers connected to hundreds of workstations. Some networks are designed to render relatively simple services, such as sharing an application and file and providing access to a single printer. Other networks support communication with mainframes and minicomputers, shared modems, a variety of output devices (such as plotters and thermal printers), and high-capacity storage devices (such as WORM drives).

This chapter discusses some of the major options to consider as you plan your network's architecture. We'll begin by exploring the basics: the file server and workstations. Then we'll look at how these computers communicate with one another through the personal computer and network operating systems. Next we'll briefly examine the physical layout of the network—its topology—a topic we'll explore in more detail in Chapter 3. Finally, we'll investigate some of the alternatives available for sharing peripheral devices and for communicating with other systems.

FILE SERVERS AND WORKSTATIONS

The file server is the core of the local area network. This computer—typically a high-speed microcomputer—runs the operating system and manages the flow of data through the network. Individual workstations and any shared peripheral devices, such as printers, all are connected to the file server.

Each network workstation is an ordinary personal computer running its own disk operating system (such as DOS or OS/2). Unlike a standalone personal computer, however, a workstation contains a network interface card and is physically attached to the file server through cables. In addition, a workstation runs a special program, called the network shell, that permits it to communicate with the file server, other workstations, and other network devices. This shell allows the workstation to use files and programs on the file server as easily as it can those on its own disks.

Figure 2.1 illustrates a simple local area network. This LAN consists of two workstations and a printer connected to a file server. All of the network files (both programs and data) can be stored on the hard disk in the file server, as opposed to on the workstation hard disk or on floppy

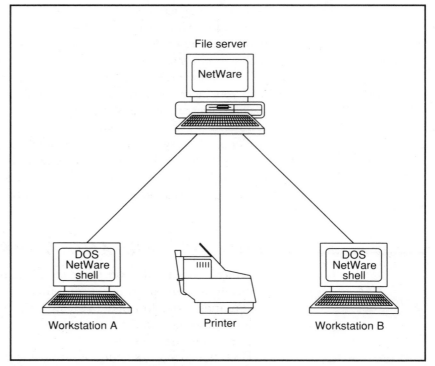

Figure 2.1: Simple local area network

disk drives. As the regulator of the network, the file server manages access to network files, printer use, and other network activities.

For example, when the user of workstation A wants to run an application, such as the network version of Lotus 1-2-3, the program is transferred through the network to this workstation. The application then runs the same as if it had been loaded from a disk drive in the workstation computer. If the application files for this version of Lotus 1-2-3 are designated for sharing, then these files can be also be used by workstation B at the same time. Thus, both users can load the program from the same location on the server. If workstation A is updating spreadsheet data in a nonshared file, however, then the file cannot be accessed by another user until workstation A releases it. The options of making files shared or nonshared are discussed more fully later in this book.

WORKSTATION OPERATING SYSTEMS

Each workstation computer runs under its own operating system (such as DOS or OS/2). To make each workstation a part of the network, a network operating system shell is loaded on top of the computer operating system. The shell preserves most of the operating system commands and functions, thus letting the workstation retain its familiar look. The shell merely adds more functions and flexibility to the local operating system.

TOPOLOGY

Network topology refers to the route data travels along the network. There are three basic types of topologies: bus, star, and ring.

In a bus, or linear, network (see Figure 2.2), each workstation and the file server is connected to a central cable called a bus or a trunk. In a star network (also called a distributed star network; see Figure 2.3), each workstation is connected to the file server, but not to each

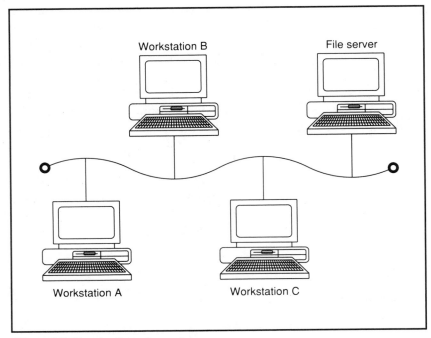

Figure 2.2: Bus (or linear) topology

other. In a ring network (see Figure 2.4), the cabling runs from workstation to workstation (and to the file server) without any endpoint.

Generally, networks with bus and ring topologies can extend over longer distances. You should seek the advice of a network consultant or installer to determine the best topology for your situation.

SHARED RESOURCES

Linking an organization's personal computers lets users share peripheral devices and other resources. Often, the efficiency of sharing resources allows an organization to use more expensive, higher-quality output devices than might be attached to a standalone personal computer. For example, laser printers, color plotters, film

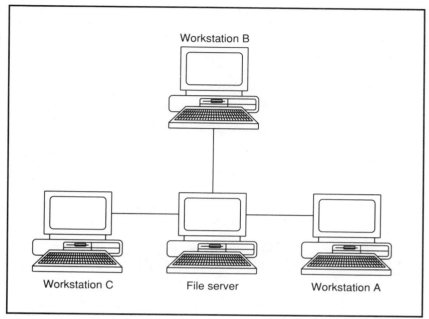

Figure 2.3: Star topology

recorders, and specialized computer-aided design (CAD) output devices can be shared efficiently and economically.

Resources can also be shared through what is known as a value-added process (VAP). These applications can be linked to the operating system to expand the capabilities of the network. The program code of a VAP is written to run on top of the operating system to enhance its functionality without interfering with the network's regular operation. Some typical VAPs are printer servers, database servers, and archive servers.

COMMUNICATION WITH OTHER SYSTEMS

An entire LAN can be connected to other LANs and to an external host computer such as a mainframe or minicomputer. Connection is

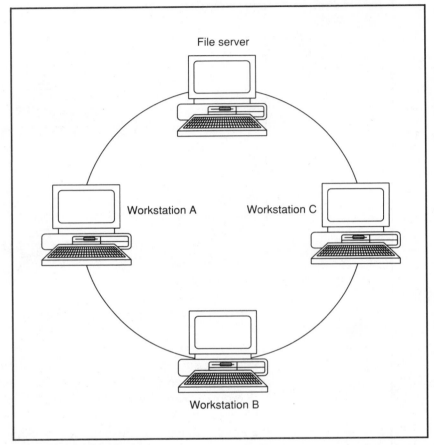

Figure 2.4: Ring topology

accomplished through the use of bridges and gateways. These devices can be purchased from third-party companies and added as needed.

BRIDGES

A bridge is a combination of hardware and software that connects networks that use similar communication methods. With NetWare, bridges can connect networks with different topologies, such as ARCnet and IBM Token Ring networks, as well as other NetWare networks.

Local bridges are either internal or external. Both function the same way, but performance differences can be considerable: external bridges almost always result in better performance; however, they are more costly to implement.

Internal bridges reside within a file server and consist simply of an additional network interface card. Communication between the bridged networks is managed by the operating system. Using internal bridging, NetWare can be bridged to up to four other local area networks from one file server. This simple and effective approach to creating an expanded network is illustrated by Figure 2.5.

An external bridge requires the use of a bridge workstation and bridge software. In addition to offering better performance, external bridges also permit bridging when a file server has no available slots, and through strategic placement on the network, external bridges can help overcome wiring limitations. Like an internal bridge, with NetWare an external bridge can also connect up to four additional local area networks. Figure 2.6 shows an example of the external bridging of two networks. Notice how a bridge is required for each network.

Remote bridges are also available when the distance between networks makes it impractical (or impossible) to physically connect them with cables. In this case, telephone lines or public data networks (PDNs) are used to provide an intermediate transmission medium. Connecting geographically separated networks is accomplished by having a bridge on each network and communication passing through modems, as shown in Figure 2.7. Chapter 21 discusses the transmission options available for remote communcation.

GATEWAYS

Communication gateways connect dissimilar systems. They can connect networks to mainframes and minicomputers. Similar to bridges, gateways can be either local or remote, depending on whether the physical distance dictates an intermediate transmission medium.

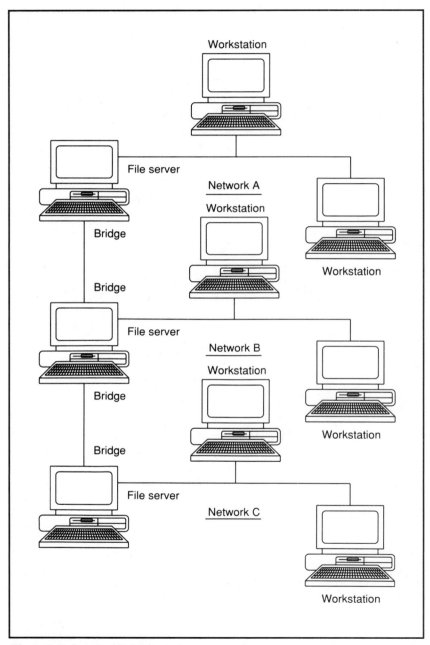

Figure 2.5: Internal bridging to two networks

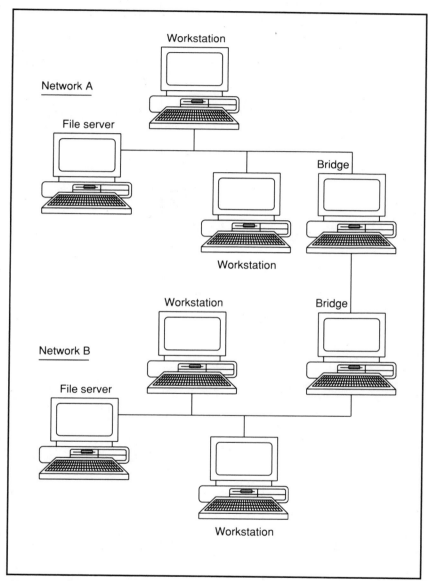

Figure 2.6: External bridging

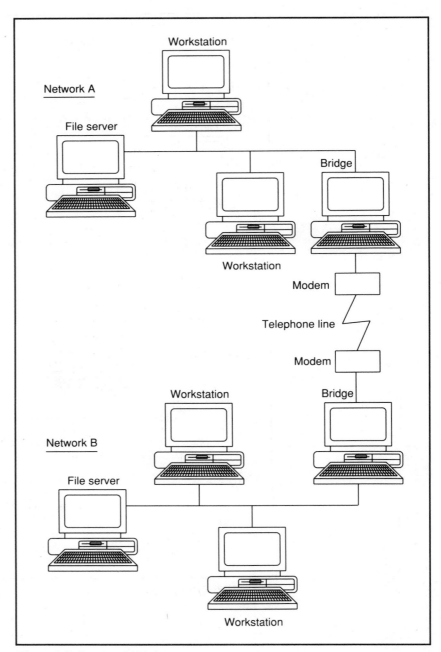

Figure 2.7: Remote bridging

Gateways have become a popular, cost-effective means of giving everyone on a network access to a mainframe computer. Instead of installing an interface card and cable for mainframe hookup in each personal computer, one gateway computer can be installed. This computer gives everyone on the network access to the mainframe computer. With NetWare, depending on the gateway used, 16, 32, or 64 users can access the mainframe computer at the same time.

Gateways can be used in many ways. Although a detailed discussion of each is beyond the scope of this chapter, let's look at how a local area network can be connected to a mainframe computer via a 3274 cluster controller. For example, the NetWare SNA gateway software can be run on the network on a gateway computer that has a specially designed interface board. A coaxial cable connects this interface board to the cluster controller. This architecture, illustrated in Figure 2.8, allows any workstation on the local area network both to emulate a mainframe terminal and to transfer files to and from the host computer.

SUMMARY

This chapter provided an overview of the basic components of a NetWare local area network and how they operate. Although your LAN may not incorporate all of the options discussed, it is important to know the alternatives available as you design your system. Like ordering a la carte at your favorite restaurant, NetWare allows you to select from a mix of topologies, peripheral devices, and connections to other data resources.

Perhaps the most important consideration in designing a network, however, is its physical design. The next chapter explores in more detail the technical and topological design of a local area network.

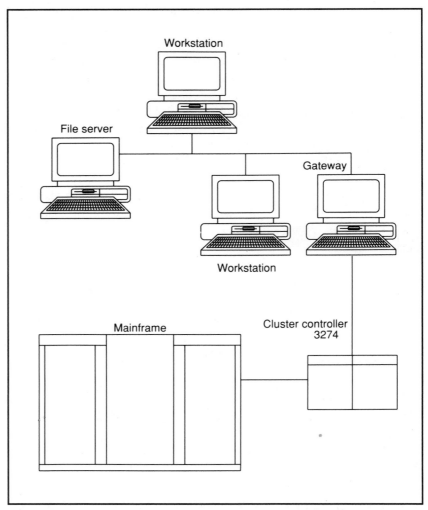

Figure 2.8: Connecting a LAN to a mainframe computer via a gateway

CHAPTER *3*

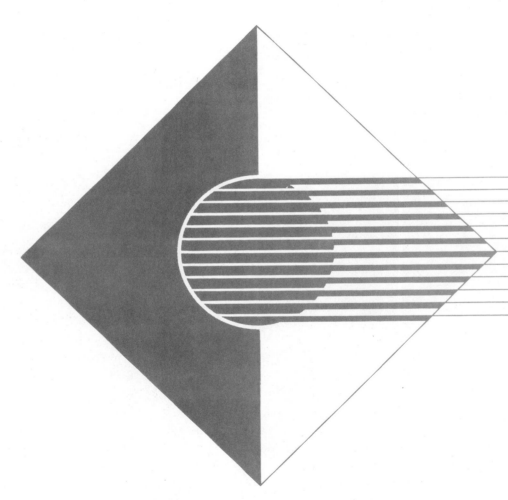

NETWORK OPTIONS

FAST TRACK

To pass data on the network,   **31**
two basic schemes can be used:

- Contention
- Token passing

Communicating data over the network involves six components: **32**

- Source computer
- Protocol engine
- Transmitter
- Physical cabling
- Receiver
- Destination computer

Ethernet networks use   **34**
the contention data-passing scheme. Depending on the
requirements and brands used, Ethernet networks can be wired
in either bus or star topologies. They can use coaxial, twisted-
pair, or fiber-optic cables.

Token Ring networks use   **34**
the token-passing data-passing scheme. Token Ring networks
are wired physically like a star, but they behave like a ring.
They can run on unshielded twisted-pair, shielded twisted-pair,
or fiber-optic cables.

ARCnet networks use   **35**
the token-passing scheme. They can be wired like a bus or a
star. They can run on coaxial, twisted-pair, or fiber-optic cable.

Networks use four main cable types: 35
> coaxial, unshielded twisted-pair, shielded twisted-pair, and fiber-optic cable.

Coaxial cable is popular   36
> in buildings with IBM 3270 terminals. Several types of co-axial cable (but not all) are compatible with local area network topologies.

Unshielded twisted-pair (type 3) cable   36
> is commonly used as telephone wire. Most buildings have an abundance of this wiring. Although inexpensive and commonly available, it may not be the best cable for your local area network.

Shielded twisted-pair (type 1) cable   37
> is similar to unshielded twisted-pair except it uses thicker wires and is shielded from interference.

Fiber-optic cable   38
> transmits data as light pulses over glass cables.

CHAPTER 3

ONE OF THE STRENGTHS OF NOVELL NETWARE IS ITS ability to run on a variety of networks. This gives the network manager much flexibility in deciding which network architecture to install.

This chapter reviews the key elements of popular networks. Its purpose is not to provide an exhaustive technical discussion, but to offer an overview of network data-passing schemes, network systems, and cabling options.

NETWORK DATA-PASSING SCHEMES

Two basic schemes are used to send data along a network: contention and token passing. Networks that use contention schemes wait for the line to go quiet before sending out messages. If two computers happen to send messages at the same time, chances are good that the messages will collide and be destroyed. When this occurs, the messages are resent. Ethernet systems use contention.

Networks that use token-passing schemes send data in a more orderly way. Messages are held at the local workstation until the token comes around to pick them up and deliver them to their destinations. The ArcNet and IBM Token Ring systems use token passing.

PERFORMANCE CONSIDERATIONS

There is a considerable debate regarding which scheme—contention or token passing—is more efficient. However, networks that use token-passing schemes usually are slower but more predictable than those that use contention. As more users join a network, systems that use token-passing schemes degrade more slowly than those that rely on contention.

Network performance depends on the total amount of network traffic, which is not necessarily related to the number of active workstations. With a contention scheme, collisions occur when numerous workstations attempt to send data simultaneously. Thus, if most processing within a network is performed locally (for example, if workstations are used largely for local word processing), network performance will be good, even if the network includes a large number of users.

With a token-passing scheme, performance is directly affected by the number of active workstations, not the total network traffic. Each additional user adds another address that the token must pass by, whether or not the workstation needs to send data.

NETWORK SYSTEMS

The process of communicating data through a network is managed by six components: the source computer, the protocol engine, the transmitter, the physical cabling, the receiver, and the destination computer. The source computer can be a workstation, a file server, a gateway, or any computer on the network. The protocol engine consists of the chip set and software driver for the network interface card. The protocol engine is responsible for the logic of network communication. The transmitter initiates the electronic signal through the physical topology. The receiver recognizes the network signal and captures it for translation by the protocol engine.

As Figure 3.1 shows, the data tranmission cycle begins with the source computer submitting raw data to the protocol engine. The protocol engine arranges the data into a message packet that contains the appropriate request for services, information about how to process the request (including the destination address, if necessary), and the raw data to be transferred. The packet is then forwarded to the transmitter for conversion into a network signal. The packet flows through the network cable until it is delivered to the receiver, where the signal is decoded into data. At this point, the protocol engine takes over. The protocol engine checks for errors, sends an acknowledgment of packet receipt to the source, reassembles the packets, and passes the packets on to the destination computer.

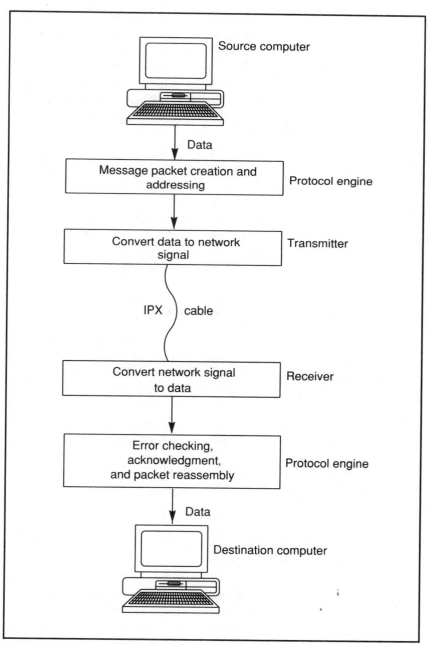

Figure 3.1: Network communication

During this process, the protocol engine controls the logic of network communications through the access scheme. Depending on the type of network system—the electrical topology—packets are either transmitted randomly via a contention scheme or systematically via a token-passing scheme. The NetWare operating system works in conjunction with the network system to manage the flow of data.

The three most important systems for local area networks are Ethernet, IBM Token Ring, and ARCnet. The standards for two of these schemes, Ethernet (802.3) and Token Ring (802.5), are published by the Institute of Electrical and Electronics Engineers (IEEE). The standardization of these schemes helps maintain consistency among the sundry software and hardware manufacturers that use them. Standards for ARCnet, originally created by Datapoint Corporation, are not presently published by IEEE. The various ARCnet vendors, however, closely monitor the compatibility of their implementations to ensure that the cards of different vendors work together.

ETHERNET NETWORKS

Ethernet uses the contention data-passing scheme for managing data transmissions on the network. Ethernet networks can be wired in either bus or star topologies using coaxial, twisted-pair, or fiber-optic cables. (Cabling options are discussed later in this chapter.)

A key advantage of Ethernet is speed. With transmissions occurring at 10 megabytes per second (mbps), Ethernet is one of the fastest local area networks available. However, this speed can also lead to problems. Because the limit of thin copper cable is only slightly greater than 10 mbps, even a small amount of electromagnetic interference can significantly degrade network performance.

TOKEN RING NETWORKS

As indicated by its name, IBM Token Ring networks use the token-passing scheme for data transmissions. A Token Ring network is wired physically like a star, but the network behaves like a ring (see Figures 2.3 and 2.4). In other words, the packets of data flow from workstation to workstation in sequence (as in a ring network), but continually pass through a central point (as in a star network). Token

Ring networks can run on either unshielded twisted-pair, shielded twisted-pair, or fiber-optic cables. (Cabling options are discussed later in this chapter.)

Token Ring networks are available in two versions, supporting transmission speeds of 4 mbps or 16 mbps. However, although an individual network runs at either 4 mbps or 16 mbps, networks operating at different speeds can be bridged together.

Token Ring networks are reliable, fast (particularly the 16-mbps version), and easy to install. However, compared to ARCnet networks, Token Ring networks are expensive.

ARCNET NETWORKS

ARCnet uses a token-passing scheme and can operate as either a bus or a star. The star will usually provide a better performance because this topology yields fewer transmission collisions. ARCnet is compatible with coaxial (RG-62), twisted-pair, and fiber-optic cables. (Cabling options are discussed in the next section.)

ARCnet systems are relatively slow. Transmissions occur at only 2.5 mbps, which is significantly slower than in other types of systems. However, in at least one respect, slowness is an advantage. Because its speed does not challenge the capabilities of any of the cables, ARCnet is not especially sensitive to electromagnetic interference. Therefore, it is the best candidate for running on existing unshielded twisted-pair cables or existing RG-62 coaxial cables (used by IBM 3270 terminals), which can be susceptible to electrical interference.

Despite its slow line speed, ARCnet remains a popular choice. Its slow speed is somewhat offset by its efficient method of passing signals. ARCnet is relatively inexpensive and flexible and is easy to install, expand, and reconfigure.

CABLING OPTIONS

Four types of network cables are commonly used today:

- Coaxial (or coax) cable
- Unshielded twisted-pair cable

- Shielded twisted-pair cable
- Fiber-optic cable

The first three conduct an electrical signal through copper wiring. Fiber-optic cables convey light through glass.

Cabling is a more serious consideration than is often perceived. The cable you select for your network affects your future expansion options. Most networks allow several cabling options. You should, however, understand the consequences of using a particular cable type for a network. For example, if a Token Ring network uses unshielded twisted-pair (type 3) cable, only 96 devices can be connected to a ring. In contrast, if you use shielded twisted-pair (type 1 or type 2), 255 devices can be connected to a ring.

Although the cable in your building can be replaced later, doing so is often disruptive, cumbersome, and expensive. Thus, you should consider your future plans as well as your present needs in choosing cable.

COAXIAL CABLE

Coaxial cable is a popular cable in buildings with IBM 3270 terminals. Coaxial cable consists of two conductors surrounded by two insulating layers. The first layer of insulation encloses a central copper conductor wire. This first layer has an outer shielding conductor braided over the top of it.

Several types of coaxial cable are compatible with local area network topologies. If the building in which you are installing the network has mainframe terminals, then many yards of IBM 3270 cable probably run through the ceilings. Other common coaxial cables are thick and thin Ethernet cables.

Some types of coaxial cable are thicker than others. Thicker cables offer greater data capacity, can be run longer distances, and are less sensitive to electrical interference. However, thick cable is more expensive and harder to pull through conduits.

UNSHIELDED TWISTED-PAIR CABLE

Most buildings have an abundance of unshielded twisted-pair cable. It is commonly used as telephone wire. Twisted-pair cables are comprised of two wires twisted together at six turns per inch to provide shielding from electrical interference plus consistent impedance, or electrical resistance. Another name commonly used for this wire is IBM type 3. Because existing buildings usually contain plenty of this wire, there is often a great temptation to save expense and time by using it.

However, using telephone wire, especially when it is already in place, can lead to several major problems. First, unshielded twisted-pair cable is sensitive to electromagnetic interference, such as the electrical noise created by fluorescent lights and passing elevators. The ring signal on phone lines running alongside the network cable can also cause interference. In addition, poor-quality twisted-pair cables may have a varying number of twists per inch, which can distort the expected electrical resistance.

Also important to note is that telephone wires are not always run in straight lines. Cable that appears to run a relatively short distance between two offices might actually run through half the building. A misjudgment could cause you to exceed the maximum cable length desirable.

In short, unshielded twisted-pair cable is inexpensive, easy to install, and may work for small networks. But be careful: The money that you save may be more than offset by additional costs later if the network doesn't function properly because of cable problems.

SHIELDED TWISTED-PAIR CABLE

Shielded twisted-pair cables are similar to unshielded twisted-pair cables except that they use thicker wires and are shielded from interference by a protective coat of insulation. The most common type of shielded twisted-pair cable used in local area networks is IBM's type-1 cable. The standard developed for type-1 cable calls for a shielded cable with two twisted pairs of solid wire. For new buildings, type-2 cable might be a better option because this cable includes data wires as well as four unshielded pairs of solid wires for voice telephone transmissions. Type-2 cable thus permits the use of a single cable for both voice and network data communications.

The shielding and close attention to the number of twists per inch make shielded twisted-pair cable a reliable cabling alternative. However, with this reliability comes additional cost.

FIBER-OPTIC CABLE

Fiber-optic cables transmit data as light pulses through glass cables. The major network systems now support fiber-optic cabling.

Fiber-optic cable has significant advantages over all of the copper cable options. Fiber-optic cables provide the fastest transmission speed and are more reliable because they are not susceptible to packet loss through electromagnetic interference. Fiber-optic cable also is very thin and flexible, making it easier to move than the heavier copper cables. Perhaps most important, only fiber-optic cable has the data capacity that tomorrow's faster networks will require.

Unfortunately, even though the price of fiber-optic cabling is declining, it is usually still more expensive than copper. Installation of fiber-optic cable also can be more difficult than copper cables because the ends must be precisely polished and aligned in order to make a solid connection.

SUMMARY

This chapter discussed some of the options for the physical layout of the network. It examined the important network systems—Ethernet, IBM Token Ring, and ARCnet—and reviewed their requirements and relative advantages. It evaluated the cabling alternatives available and discussed the strengths and weaknesses of coaxial, twisted-pair, and fiber-optic cables.

The following chapters put this information to use as they discuss how to begin installing and configuring a Novell NetWare local area network.

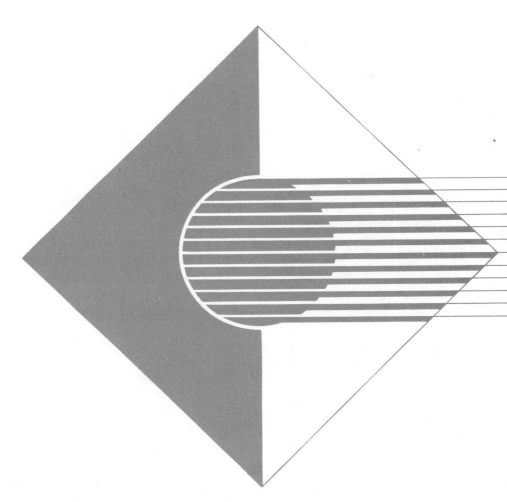

PLANNING FOR
NETWARE INSTALLATION

Fast Track

NetWare is a network operating system   43

just as DOS is an operating system for standalone computers. Individual computers on the network run DOS under NetWare control. NetWare can be used with any of the popular physical networks: Token Ring, Ethernet, or ARCnet.

There are four basic types of NetWare: 44

the entry-level system (ELS), Advanced NetWare 286, Advanced NetWare 286 SFT, and NetWare 386. Table 4.1 summarizes the NetWare versions and uses.

A very small network   44

should choose the ELS version of NetWare. However, the functions and growth opportunities of such a network are limited.

A medium-sized network   45

should choose one of the Advanced NetWare 286 versions (with or without SFT). These versions can run on either 80286- or 80386-based microcomputers.

A large network   46

should choose NetWare 386. This is the most robust version of the operating system and contains a number of advanced features not available in other versions.

The file server location   46

should be an area that is well ventilated and has ample electricity. With Advanced NetWare 286 or less powerful versions, the network printers must be attached to the file server. You should, therefore, keep the server close to its users.

Cable placement considerations include   **47**

routing all cables back to a central wiring closet. This approach may be expensive, but it helps reduce maintenance and debugging problems. Also, every cable should be labeled as it is installed.

The location of network printers   **48**

should be carefully planned for maximum accessibility to frequent users. NetWare 386 has a special print server utility that facilitates sharing local printers over the network.

CHAPTER *4*

THE PREVIOUS CHAPTERS PROVIDED AN OVERVIEW of networks in general and device, topology, and cabling options. This chapter discusses how to choose among NetWare versions and factors you should consider in setting up the NetWare network operating system.

WHAT IS NETWARE?

NetWare is a network operating system, much like DOS is an operating system for standalone personal computers. The primary difference between NetWare and an operating system like DOS is that NetWare is designed to manage the communication of data among several computers instead of just one.

A NetWare LAN can be a Token Ring, Ethernet, or ARCnet network and can have a bus, star, or ring topology. The network access scheme (Token Ring, Ethernet, or ARCnet) provides the electronic highway for transporting data; NetWare provides the intelligence for controlling system resources and the data processing.

As you'll see when we configure the NetWare operating system, NetWare can accommodate a variety of network configurations.

CHOOSING A NETWARE VERSION

Because the network operating system controls the file server actions and provides services to each of the workstations connected to the network, your choice of an operating system is critical to the effectiveness of the network. Novell NetWare is available in several different forms. The one right for you depends on the size and complexity of your network. In general, the version you select will be determined by the number of workstations you expect to connect to the network. In some cases, however, you may want to consider such factors as the number of gateway units you expect to use and whether your network will ultimately be part of a wide area network.

Remember when selecting a NetWare version that networks grow, and often they grow quickly. For this reason, you should estimate the total number of workstations that might eventually connect to the network, and then prepare for connecting all of them. Because networks are so flexible and easy to add on to, you should also plan for an increasingly complex network. Generally, network users find they expand their software applications well beyond traditional spreadsheets and word processing programs. Because users often store critical company data on the network, security is another important factor in selecting the operating system.

Table 4.1 summarizes the NetWare versions and their uses. The primary criteria in your selection will be the number of users and the overall complexity of the network as determined by the need for such features as inter-LAN bridging, sophisticated backup procedures, and multiple servers.

Table 4.1: NetWare Versions

NETWARE VERSION	NUMBER OF WORKSTATIONS ON THE NETWORK	COMPLEXITY
ELS NetWare	3–6	Simple
Advanced NetWare 286	6–30	Simple
Advanced NetWare 286 SFT	6–30	Complex
NetWare 386	30–250 +	Simple or complex

CHOOSING NETWARE FOR A SMALL NETWORK

For very small, simple networks, those that will probably never exceed six workstations, Novell's entry-level system—ELS—is the proper choice. This version of NetWare is relatively inexpensive.

It can be configured to run in nondedicated mode, so that the computer configured as the file server can at the same time be used as a workstation.

Because it is the most basic NetWare version, ELS does have important limitations. The workstation that doubles as a file server is likely to have limited memory and may not be able to run all software. Also, ELS does not have many of the rich features offered by other versions. For instance, ELS cannot mirror, or make simultaneous copies of, network drives, an important feature of other versions that protects data by letting you set one drive as an exact duplicate of another.

Thus, ELS is suitable for very small, simple, noncritical networks. It is not recommended for any network that is likely to grow, contain important data or company processes, or become a part of a wide area network.

CHOOSING NETWARE
FOR A MEDIUM-SIZED NETWORK

Networks that may include up to 30 workstations should use the Advanced NetWare 286 or Advanced NetWare 286 SFT (system fault tolerance) operating system. These versions run on file servers that use an 80286 or 80386 processor. However, an 80386-based file server is preferable, even for these 80286-based versions. The extra speed and horsepower of the 80386 processor, plus the upgrade potential, makes this a wise investment for this critical computer.

Advanced NetWare 286 without system fault tolerance is a good choice for a moderate-sized network. It contains a full suite of operating options, and security is built in.

The SFT version of Advanced NetWare can mirror disk drives. This ability allows you to set up one disk drive that is an exact duplicate of another, a process called duplexing. Then if your primary network disk drive fails, you will have a copy instantly available. The transfer takes place so smoothly that system users do not even know they are operating on the alternate drive.

CHOOSING NETWARE FOR A LARGE NETWORK

Networks of 30 or more workstations, or those with a potential for complex applications, should choose NetWare 386. This product is the most powerful and most expensive version of NetWare. It also is the easiest to install and, potentially, least expensive to maintain over time. NetWare 386 requires a file server that uses an 80386 processor. The workstations on the network, however, do not have to be 80386-based computers.

NetWare 386 has a number of advanced features not available in the other versions. Among them are

- Enhanced security
- Ability to support a greater number of users per server
- Enhanced file system
- Ability to support large database files
- Optional file flags to immediately purge erased files
- Enhanced printer-sharing capability
- Dynamic resource configuration

For large, complex networks, the extra functions of NetWare 386 usually offset the price difference between it and the less expensive versions. This product provides the powerful functions and operating platform required for important company applications.

OTHER STARTUP CONSIDERATIONS

Once the version of NetWare is selected, a number of other startup decisions must be made. You must determine where to put the file server, the cables, and the network printer.

DETERMINING THE FILE SERVER LOCATION

Depending on which version of NetWare you choose, the location of the file server can be important. No matter where you place the file server, however, make sure the space is well ventilated. The file server will likely run continuously, 24 hours a day, so it should be located in an area that does not get too hot or too cold. You should also be sure to check the available electricity. The file server will likely have extra disk drives and printers attached to it, and these will require extra power beyond that for an ordinary personal computer. If you will be using a laser printer, which requires extra power, having a qualified electrician check the power supply to ensure adequate and consistent current is especially critical.

If you are using ELS or Advanced NetWare 286, you should locate the file server near the users. This location is for the users' convenience, especially in getting their work from the network printer. If the server is located far from the users, determine where printers will be required. You may be able to attach a long cable to the printer or to connect a third-party printer server.

Users of NetWare 386 can locate the file server either close to the users or several floors away. Advanced printer services are available that allow special queuing of printers. These services also allow local printers to be configured as network printers. Because NetWare 386 users are likely part of a larger LAN, the file server should be located in the very best place from a climate and physical security perspective.

DETERMINING CABLE PLACEMENT

The network topology you select will most likely determine the cable type the network uses. You will, however, likely have some options regarding cable placement in wire closets or hubs.

Where possible, you should route all cables back to a common area, such as a wire closet. Your office or building likely has a central closet for telephone wire, and this area makes an excellent place for LAN cables too. Although this method is more expensive than stringing cables in long, bus fashion, it is much easier to maintain later on. Locating a cable problem is much easier when all wires come to a common area.

You also should start a cable numbering scheme even before your network is installed. To facilitate debugging, you should label every cable on the network. This can be done easily as the network is installed. Once the network is in place, however, determining what cable goes to what location is nearly impossible.

Remember that installing cables for a LAN can be disruptive for everyone in the office. Therefore, be sure to do it right the first time.

DETERMINING WHERE TO LOCATE NETWORK PRINTERS

Make sure you adequately plan the printer location for your network. Not doing so can cause problems later. Unlike most other peripherals, printers are utilized regularly by every user of the network.

As a general rule, place the best printers as close as possible to the frequent users. Doing so may require the use of extra long cables or of a printer server.

All versions of NetWare except NetWare 386 require printers be physically attached to the server. When this is not practical, you can purchase third-party printer software. The most reliable of this software also requires you to dedicate a personal computer as the printer server. This may or may not be practical.

NetWare 386 has special printer service functions that allow you to configure local printers as remote printers. This procedure requires running special software on the workstations that share the printers. Because this software runs as a terminate-and-stay-resident (TSR) function, it may cause memory problems for the users who share the printers. These memory problems may surface as conflicts with other software or as a constraint in the amount of memory available to load an application.

SUMMARY

As this chapter has discussed, careful thought and planning is necessary before NetWare is installed. The next part of this book tells you how to actually get a NetWare network up and running.

PART II

INSTALLING AND CONFIGURING YOUR NETWARE NETWORK

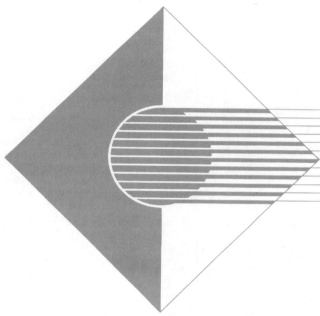

In Part I, we reviewed the basics of local area networks and the NetWare operating system. In the next four chapters, we'll roll up our sleeves and begin putting the pieces together.

CHAPTER 5

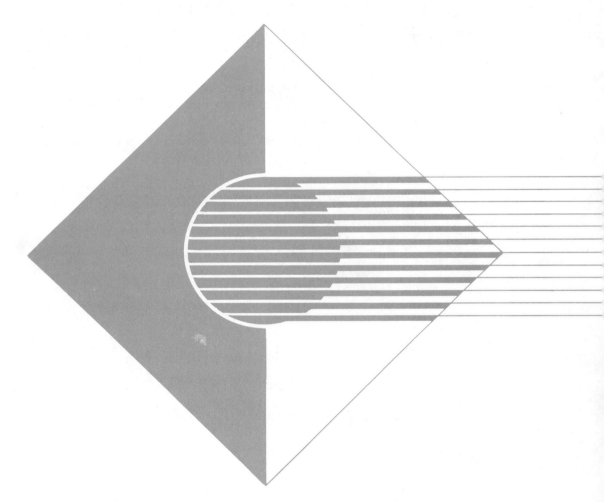

AN INSTALLATION CHECKLIST

FAST TRACK

Basic site preparation includes   53

    finding a well-ventilated, dust-free environment with ample power. Cable installation should be performed by a reliable cable contractor.

Hardware preparation includes   55

    setting up and ensuring that ample memory is installed and key information is recorded.

NetWare installation is managed by   55

    a program called NETGEN.

Preparing the file server's hard disk   55

    is accomplished by using the COMPSURF NetWare utility. This surface analysis program tests the file server drive for defects.

User-access programs are created by   56

    the SHGEN NetWare utility.

Special login scripts can be set up   57

    to direct workstations to perform a number of functions upon entering the network.

Security features can be set up   58

    to limit users' reading, writing, and opening of files and directories.

Network printers   59

    are printers that are physically attached to the file server.

User menus   **60**
        are created with the NetWare MENU utility.

Network administration procedures   **60**
        should be planned before the network is up and running.

CHAPTER 5

YOU CAN FOLLOW SEVERAL PATHS IN INSTALLING A
NetWare local area network. However, no matter how you proceed,
preparing—and using—a checklist can save you a lot of time and
headaches later.

This chapter outlines a step-by-step process that can help ensure
success as you connect the wires and begin to "turn on the lights" for
your NetWare network. This outline illustrates the sequence of
events and activities. Later chapters describe each step in detail.

PREPARING FOR THE INSTALLATION

As discussed in Part I, even before the equipment arrives, you
should begin planning for the LAN installation. Your file server will
have greater stability and longevity if it operates in a dust-free, static-
free, temperature-controlled environment. (Although a file server
does not require the strict climate control of a mainframe computer, it
nevertheless will not function well if you lock it in a hot broom closet,
for instance.) In addition, to reduce any problems associated with
electrical noise, you should make sure that a dedicated and grounded
power supply is available for the file server.

You will also need to begin running the workstation cables. Here
the best approach is to obtain assistance from a professional cable
contractor. Unless you are installing a very small local area network,
running cables through ceilings and walls can be messy and frustrating. In addition, special tools are required to properly tap the cable
ends and attach the connectors. Installing cable is not a good job for
an amateur to tackle.

AN INSTALLATION CHECKLIST

Here is a checklist to follow when installing your NetWare network. Later sections in this chapter elaborate on these steps, and later chapters discuss them in detail.

1. Prepare the hardware.

    a. Ensure that NetWare supports the file server and workstations.

    b. Run setup routines as necessary.

    c. Record printer protocols as necessary.

2. Configure and install NetWare.

    a. Configure the operating system.

    b. Format and test the hard disks.

    c. Install network interface cards.

    d. Install the operating system.

3. Create user access programs.

4. Set the directory structure and load applications.

    a. Set up basic directory structure, taking into account security, convenience, and logic.

    b. Make sure selected applications are set up for network use.

    c. Load applications.

5. Set up login scripts and user groups.

    a. Write system login scripts.

    b. Write individual-user login scripts.

    c. Set up user groups.

6. Add security features.

    a. Add login and password security.

    b. Add trustee security.

    c. Add file and directory attributes security.

7. Configure and test network printers.

8. Create menus.

    a. Use MENU to create user menus.

9. Plan network administration.

PREPARING THE HARDWARE

In preparation for installing the LAN hardware, you need to ensure that the file server and workstations are supported by NetWare and have adequate memory. If these computers are new, you should run the setup routine shipped with the machines. In addition, if any serial printers will be attached to the file server, be sure to record their communications protocols (baud rate, number of stop bits, parity, and so on). You will need this information during the configuration of NetWare.

CONFIGURING AND INSTALLING NETWARE

Preparing the file server requires four basic steps:

- Configuring the operating system
- Preparing the hard disks
- Installing the network interface cards
- Installing the operating system

All of these activities, except installing the network cards, are managed by a Novell program called NETGEN. Despite the fact that it executes some extremely sophisticated operations, this menu-driven user interface is very easy to understand and operate, even for a novice.

Configuring the operating system entails selecting the operating system options to be included in the network and defining the file server hardware to be installed. Based on these selections, a custom operating system is generated.

Preparing the file server's hard disk is accomplished using a utility called COMPSURF (comprehensive surface analysis) that is shipped with NetWare. The COMPSURF program formats and tests the file server's hard disk drives. (Note that some of the newer high-capacity disk drives do not require COMPSURF. Be sure to check with your network supplier or server manufacturer to determine the requirements for your specific hardware.)

You are now ready to configure and install the network interface cards in the file server and workstations. You can perform various diagnostic tests at this point to ensure that the network interface cards (NICs) are operating properly and that the cable connections are solid.

Finally, you install the network operating system. NETGEN takes control of this process, prompting you for information as required. When installation is complete, you start NetWare by running a NetWare program called NET$OS. Now your network is up and running, but before anyone can actually log in, the user access programs must be created.

CREATING THE USER ACCESS PROGRAMS

Before you can easily use the network, you must generate the workstation shell and create a simple batch file to allow easy access for the users.

The workstation shell is created by using the SHGEN utility. Similar to NETGEN, SHGEN is menu-driven and easy to operate. SHGEN builds a network shell that reflects the configuration of your network. When the process is finished, two files are created:

- IPX.COM
- NET3.COM (or NET4.COM if you are using DOS 4.x)

These files can now be executed with other DOS batch file commands to create a custom user interface for your network that executes the network shell and prompts the user for a login ID and password.

You can now test your network by logging on from a workstation.

SETTING THE DIRECTORY STRUCTURE AND LOADING APPLICATIONS

With your network up and running, you can start making decisions about the directory structure and where applications will be loaded on the hard disk. Unlike a standalone computer, the hard disk in a file server is accessed simultaneously by multiple users. Therefore, special considerations affect where programs and user files are stored. Because security is an issue, you will want to isolate user files by user names. In addition, you may want to facilitate the backup process by grouping together files that are frequently updated.

Loading applications on a file server generally is as straightforward as in a standalone environment. Make sure, however, that the programs you load are intended (and licensed) for a local area network. Running single-user programs on a LAN can cause problems, and these programs may perform inconsistently. In addition, such use almost always is in violation of the program's license agreement.

SETTING UP LOGIN SCRIPTS AND USER GROUPS

The next step in preparing the local area network for use is to write the login scripts and create the user groups.

Login scripts are a set of instructions that direct the workstation to perform various functions. Login scripts are frequently used to produce a greeting message, such as that shown in Figure 5.1, and to assign drive letters to specific subdirectories. NetWare allows you to create two types of login scripts: system login scripts, which

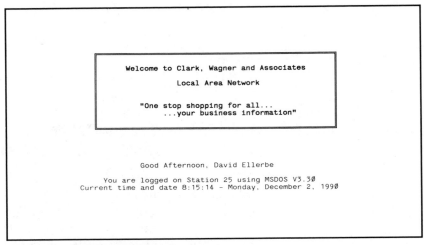

Figure 5.1: Sample greeting message

apply to everyone that accesses the network, and individual login scripts, which are specific to the user.

Creating user groups allows you to grant use rights to several users at once instead of assigning them individually. User groups can be created and modified with a NetWare utility called SYSCON. Groups can be added and changed later, but now is an excellent time to start thinking about how network users can be logically grouped for the purposes of security and convenience.

ADDING SECURITY FEATURES

NetWare allows four types of security:

- Login and password security
- Trustee security
- Directory security
- File and directory attributes security

You should implement the types of security appropriate for your local area network.

The first level of security is login security. To access the LAN, the user must enter an active user name. To add an additional layer of security, entry of a password can (and should) be required. NetWare also allows you to customize the degree of security associated with login and password security. For example, you can restrict the number of concurrent connections, limit access to specific workstations, and force users to select new passwords after a specified period of time.

Once the network has been accessed, the primary security mechanism is trustee security. Trustee security regulates a specific user's rights to use a particular directory. NetWare can limit users' rights to read files, write to files, open files, and so on. Trustee rights must be explicitly granted to an individual or a group by a system supervisor.

The next level of security is directory security. Directory security regulates users' rights to use a directory, regardless of their trustee security rights. Directory security can be used to grant or revoke rights to the use of an individual directory.

The final level of security is file and directory attributes security. This type of security determines whether particular files or directories can be altered. For example, an individual file can be flagged as read only, which means that no user, regardless of any other right the user has, can write to, rename, or delete the file. You can set similar attributes for directories and subdirectories.

Novell offers comprehensive security features. Proper planning of the security strategy is important for protecting essential and sensitive files, while at the same time ensuring that users are not unnecessarily constrained.

CONFIGURING AND TESTING NETWORK PRINTERS

The next step is to complete the configuration of the network printers. A variety of tools are available to help you define printers and establish the way print jobs are handled by the various output devices attached to the file server. Although your ability to perform rigorous testing is limited at this point because the application software has not been installed, you can make sure that the printers are at least operating. Any fine tuning can be done later.

CREATING MENUS

The final step in the installation process is to create menus to assist users in navigating through the network. The MENU utility, included with NetWare, lets you create easy-to-use custom menus for your local area network. An example of a menu created with the MENU utility is shown in Figure 5.2.

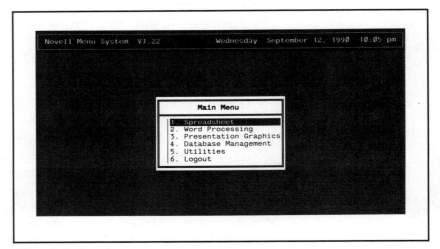

Figure 5.2: Sample menu

PLANNING
NETWORK ADMINISTRATION

All local area networks require at least some degree of ongoing maintenance. Backup of files must be made regularly, and over time, additional users will need to be added, software will need to be upgraded, new programs will need to be included, and security requirements will change. Most of these activities can be managed by a part-time system administrator. If possible, the network administrator should be involved in the installation process.

SUMMARY

This chapter provided a thumbnail sketch of the work that lies ahead in installing your NetWare network. In the next chapter, we'll get out our screwdrivers, open the computers, and start installing the hardware.

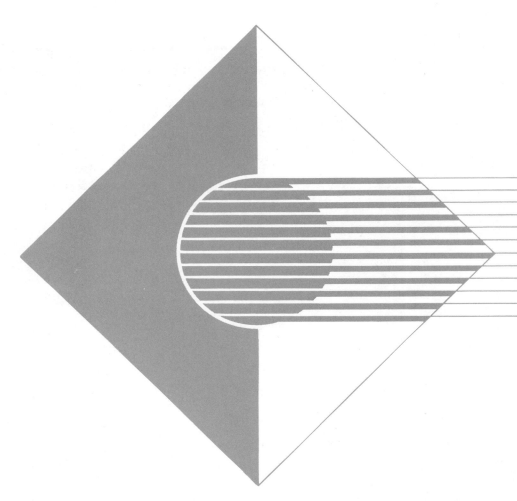

PREPARING THE HARDWARE

FAST TRACK

Site preparation should include   **65**
> protecting the file server from static electricity, heat, electrical noise, power surges, and power outages.

File server requirements include   **67**
> equipping the file server with at least 1 MB of RAM if the disk has less than 70 MB, and a minimum of 2 MB of RAM if the disk has more than 70 MB. More memory is recommended. For best results, you should use an 80386-based computer, even though NetWare will run on an 80286-based computer.

Workstation requirements include   **67**
> any 8088-, 80286-, or 80386-based computer with a minimum of 384 KB of memory. Because of the NetWare shell memory requirements, 640 KB is the practical minimum memory required to allow workstations to run most applications software.

Minimum preparation for network computers includes   **68**
> running the SETUP program that comes with the computer and checking that each computer is capable of running DOS.

Up to five network printers   **68**
> (two serial and three parallel printers) can be attached to a file server. If serial printers are used, configure them with the following parameters:
>
> - Baud rate: 9600
> - Word length: 8 bits

- Stop bits: 1 bit
- Parity: None
- XON/XOFF protocol: No

Document the cable layout   **69**

with a spreadsheet or database capable of producing updated
reports regarding what cable goes where. Be sure to keep this
report current as new workstations are added. Post the cable chart
in the wire room. Additionally, physically tag each cable with its
corresponding office location.

Attach the network printers   **69**

to the appropriate ports on the back of the file server computer.
If additional ports are needed, add them by adding an adapter
card to the file server. Be sure to have a qualified technician
help with this procedure.

CHAPTER 6

AS DISCUSSED IN THE LAST CHAPTER, THE FIRST STEP in building your local area network is preparing the hardware. You begin this process by inspecting the sites where the file server and workstations will be located, to ensure that they are suitable. Next, you check and prepare your computers and printers to make sure they meet NetWare's requirements. Finally, you cable your computers and attach your printers.

If this is your first local area network, you should not attempt to set it up alone. Because hardware installation can be complicated, you should leave this process to a reputable local network company. This chapter assumes that you have engaged the services of a network installer. It therefore provides just an overview of the steps in the installation process. This basic information will help you effectively manage the installation process and diagnose any problems that may surface later.

PREPARING THE FILE SERVER LOCATION

The environment of your file server site is extremely important to the stability of this key computer. The file server needs to be protected against static electricity and heat and against electrical noise, power surges, and power outages.

PROTECTING AGAINST STATIC ELECTRICITY AND HEAT

Particularly if your climate is conducive to static electricity, you should take precautions to protect all computer hardware from static charges. Such precautions are especially important for the file server, because its performance affects the entire network. Among the precautions you can take are regularly treating the carpet with antistatic chemicals, using protective covers for carpets, and installing the file server on a work surface that is connected to an earth ground.

Excessive heat and cold is also a potential hazard to the health and well-being of your file server. Keep the temperature in the file server room between 65° F and 80° F and be sure air can circulate freely around the cooling fan.

PROTECTING AGAINST ELECTRICAL NOISE, POWER SURGES, AND POWER OUTAGES

Electrical noise is caused by inconsistencies in the delivery of electricity to the computer. You can help protect the file server against electrical noise by installing a dedicated power line for the file server. Do not connect other devices to this power supply, however, as they may generate electrical noise themselves, thus diluting the protection offered by the dedicated source. The power source should be standard three-wire cable, with the ground wire grounded to the earth.

You should also guard against power surges and the occasional power outage. This is best accomplished by installing an uninterruptible power supply, or UPS. A UPS allows your file server to remain active for a short time even in the event of a commercial power failure. You may also want to install uninterruptible power supplies on workstations that run critical applications, to protect these workstations from loss of data during a power failure. In addition, every device on the network should have electrical power filtered with a surge protector.

PREPARING YOUR HARDWARE TO RUN NETWARE

Your next step is to check each computer that will be used on the network to ensure that it meets NetWare's requirements.

CHECKING COMPUTER REQUIREMENTS

Although NetWare supports most PC-DOS machines being marketed today, many older machines do not meet the minimum hardware and memory requirements. For both file servers and workstations, you should confirm with your NetWare dealer that the brand you choose has been tested and certified by Novell.

Novell recommends the following minimum random-access memory (RAM) for dedicated file servers running NetWare 286:

- Hard disks with less than 70 MB: 1 MB RAM
- Hard disks with more than 70 MB: 2 MB RAM

Adding additional memory beyond these minimums increases server performance. Also, even though NetWare will run on an 80286-based computer, for the best performance you should use a file server that is based on the faster 80386 processor.

For your workstations, you can select from a broad range of computers. Any of the following computers can be used as workstations, so long as they have at least 384 KB of memory:

- IBM or Compaq 80386-based computer
- IBM Personal System/2 (any model)
- Compaq Deskpro (any model)
- IBM PC AT (or compatible)
- IBM PC XT (or compatible)
- IBM PC (or compatible)

Although 384 KB is the minimum memory requirement, you should consider adding additional memory to any machine that has less than 640 KB. The memory that the NetWare shell consumes may prevent applications that operate satisfactorily on a standalone computer from running on a workstation.

Again, for maximum performance and expandability, you should select a workstation based on the 80386 processor.

PREPARING NETWORK COMPUTERS

If any of the computers, including the file server, that will be included on the network have not been configured using the manufacturer's setup routine, you should now run the SETUP program. Then test each machine to be sure it can boot from DOS.

PREPARING NETWORK PRINTERS

NetWare 286 can support up to five printers: two serial printers and three parallel printers. Printers attached to the file server can be shared by everyone on the network.

If any of the printers on your network are serial devices, you need to record the data transfer protocols. This information will be used in the next chapter when we configure the operating system. (Parallel printers do not need communications parameters to communicate with a file server.)

If possible, you should configure serial printers to the following parameters:

Baud rate	9600
Word length	8 bits
Stop bits	1 bit
Parity	None
XON/XOFF protocol	No

These are the default settings used by NetWare during configuration, and using these settings simplifies the installation procedure. If you use these communications parameters, however, make sure they do not reduce the performance of your printer. Check the printer's documentation to determine the communications parameters that optimize performance.

CABLING THE WORKSTATIONS

If there is an Achilles' heel associated with local area networking, it is cabling. Cable problems are the number-one cause of network malfunctions and are usually the most difficult kind of problem to diagnose. Therefore, make sure the cabling is installed correctly in the first place, by a reputable cable installer.

For each type of topology, specific rules govern such network limitations as the maximum number of workstations and maximum cable lengths. Even if you employ an experienced cable contractor, make sure that you understand the limitations of your network's topology. These are outlined in detail in the topology supplement that accompanies NetWare.

The best approach to establishing a network is to start small and expand in limited increments after testing. In other words, begin the installation with just two machines: the file server and a single workstation. Make sure that these computers are communicating properly. Then expand the network one machine at a time. This approach will let you more easily diagnose any problems that occur during the initial installation.

DOCUMENTING THE CABLE LAYOUT

Make sure that the physical layout of your network is well documented, especially if your network is configured so that cables branch out from a central location. Because the cables run through walls and ceilings, after they are installed you will need to perform a low voltage test to determine which cable leads to which device.

If your network is relatively large, set up an electronic spreadsheet or database application to generate a cabling chart and then keep this chart up to date. Post the cabling chart in the wire room, so that it can be easily found when troubleshooting is necessary. In addition, physically tag the cables with their corresponding office locations. (Remember that all cables coming through a conduit look alike.)

INSTALLING THE NETWORK PRINTERS

Following the instructions outlined by the printer manufacturers, attach the network printers to the file server. If you need additional printer ports, you can install them in the file server bus.

Be sure to record the printer ports (for example, LPT1 or COM1) used for each output device. You will need this information when you configure the NetWare operating system.

SUMMARY

In this chapter, you began the installation of your local area network. This chapter told how to check your site and prepare your computers and printers for installation. It also offered some tips on cabling your computers and attaching the network printers to the file server.

Now that we have the preliminaries out of the way, let's open the big red Novell box and begin to configure the network operating system.

CHAPTER 7

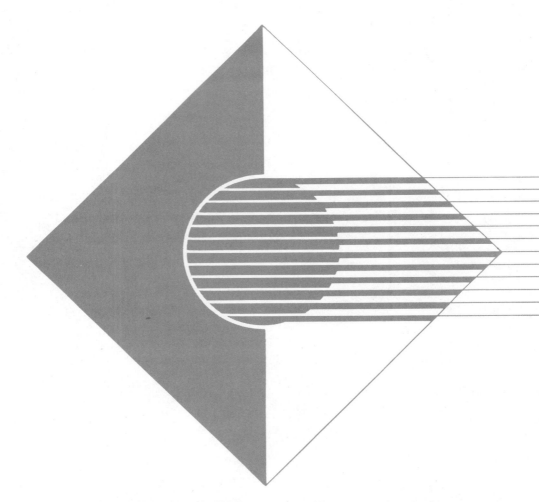

INSTALLING NETWARE

FAST TRACK

Step 1 in installing NetWare is   76
    executing the DOS DISKCOPY command for each NetWare
    disk to create a working copy of the operating system.

To start NETGEN,   77
    Place the working copy of the NETGEN disk in drive A, and at
    the DOS prompt enter the NETGEN command for your con-
    figuration method. Then choose Select Network Configuration
    from the first menu.

Select operating system options   78
    by choosing whether to use SFT NetWare 286 with TTS.

Select your LAN drivers   80
    by choosing your LAN topology from the list provided.

Select your disk drivers   81
    by choosing the appropriate disk drivers.
      1. Enter 0 (zero) as the channel number.
      2. Scroll through the options to choose the driver type that
         corresponds to the hard drive. If the file server has more
         than one hard drive, repeat the process to install drives
         on subsequent channels.
      3. Press **Esc** to return to the Available Options menu.
      4. Select Save Selections and Continue and press ←.

Identify the file server network card address   82
    at the next prompt.
      1. Enter the correct network address.

2. Enter the number of communication buffers you'll need.

3. Press **Esc** to continue. NETGEN will build your operating system and ask you to insert disks as needed.

To prepare the file server hard disk, 86

1. Boot the file server with DOS version 3.0 or higher and make sure CONFIG.SYS allows at least 10 open files.

2. Insert the NETGEN disk in drive A and enter **A:NETGEN -CS**.

3. Select Analyze Disk Surface from the options list.

4. Select an interleave factor.

5. Indicate the number of passes the utility will run.

Install the operating system 88

when COMPSURF has finished its processing. Reboot the server with DOS and run NETGEN -DS. Check to make sure the drivers list is correct. When you are satisfied that everything is correct, press **Esc** to continue.

Name the file server and supply other information 91

when prompted. Then exit NETGEN by pressing **Esc**.

Boot the file server 92

by activating the server under DOS. Insert the OSEXE-1 disk in drive A and enter **NET$OS**. After a moment, you will be prompted to insert the OSEXE-2 disk. When this disk is loaded, the server will be operating under NetWare.

CHAPTER 7

WHEN YOU FIRST OPEN THE NETWARE BOX, BE prepared to be overwhelmed by the number of manuals and disks. Network software by its nature is complex, and thus the supporting materials may seem voluminous compared to those for applications.

In this chapter, we'll put these materials to use as we walk through the installation procedure for Advanced NetWare 286. We will use a relatively simple example LAN to illustrate the process of installing NetWare on a network designed to support a small business or professional organization.

We'll begin by generating the operating system configuration. For this, we will use NETGEN, the NetWare network generation utility. Next we will install the network interface card in the file server and prepare the hard disk to accept NetWare. Then we will load the operating system, along with the other NetWare files, on the file server's hard disk. Finally, we'll breath life into our network by booting the file server.

CONFIGURING THE OPERATING SYSTEM

Configuring the Advanced NetWare 286 operating system consists of five easy-to-follow steps:

1. Prepare working copies of NetWare disks.

2. Select a configuration method.

3. Select operating system options.

4. Define and configure the file server hardware.

5. Generate the operating system and communications utilities.

PREPARING
WORKING COPIES OF NETWARE DISKS

Before you begin the configuration process, you must create working copies of the NetWare disks. Although you may be tempted to skip this step, you cannot. The second set of disks does more than simply protect the originals. The disks shipped from the factory are write-protected. Because various files will be added or modified during the configuration process, you can successfully configure your system only when using copies.

You must use the DOS DISKCOPY command—not the COPY command—to make the working copies. This command ensures that the volume names, subdirectories, and files are identical. After you make the copies, label each working disk exactly like the original.

SELECTING A CONFIGURATION METHOD

You can configure the network operating system at either of two levels: the default level or the custom level. At the default level, you rely on NETGEN to make intelligent decisions about the configuration options. At the custom level, you can customize some or all of the operating system parameters. The default level is adequate for most installations, especially those being configured for the first time. For more sophisticated installations, or where fine-tuning is required, use the custom level. The example in this chapter uses the default level.

You can also configure the NetWare operating system using standard floppy disks, a RAM disk, a hard disk, or the network drive.

When NETGEN is run, one of the first menus lists the installation alternatives. Alternatively, you can specify the installation approach as an optional parameter when the NETGEN command is entered at the DOS prompt. Once you select an installation approach (for example, the standard floppy disk method), NETGEN handles the rest of the process automatically.

The simplest approach is to execute the entire configuration operation from floppy disks. Although this approach is the slowest, it is the easiest to execute.

Using a RAM disk is similar to using floppy disks. However, in this approach the most frequently used disk is copied to a virtual disk (the RAM disk). The virtual disk is configured before the installation by setting aside part of the computer's extended memory with the VDISK DOS driver (VDISK.SYS). This copy speeds up the configuration process by reducing the number of times that disks have to be inserted into a drive. To use the virtual disk installation approach, the computer must have at least 1 MB of memory.

For a faster approach, you can configure your system using a hard disk. NETGEN copies to the hard disk the files required for linking and configuring the operating system. This reduces the amount of disk swapping required and accelerates the configuration process.

If you are configuring a new file server that is being installed on an existing network, you can use a network (file server) drive to perform the configuration. This method also eliminates the need for disk swapping and improves the efficiency of the configuration process.

The example in the next section uses the standard floppy disk approach. Especially if you are configuring multiple file servers, however, you will most likely prefer one of the other, faster approaches.

SELECTING OPERATING SYSTEM OPTIONS

Before you can run NETGEN, you must first boot DOS (version 3.0 or higher) on the computer that will process the configuration.

Next you need to set up sufficient memory buffers and ensure that the processor can handle up to 20 concurrently open files. Using a text editor, add the following statements to the CONFIG.SYS file:

```
FILES = 20
BUFFERS = 20
```

Note that the computer you use for the configuration process does not have to be the file server so long as it has at least 640 KB of memory. At this point, you are only configuring the operating system. You will load it on to the file server hard disk later.

To start the configuration process, insert the working copy of the NETGEN disk in drive A and enter the following command at the DOS prompt:

```
A:NETGEN -NDS
```

The parameters "NDS" tell the NETGEN program that this will be a *N*ew operating system using the *D*efault system configuration processed with the *S*tandard floppy disk method. (To create a custom system configuration, you would enter **C** instead of D, or **NCS**.)

The NETGEN program will start loading, and you will be prompted to insert the SUPPORT disk. Remove the NETGEN disk and replace it with the copy of the SUPPORT disk. Then press any key to continue.

At this point, the Network Generation Options menu will appear, as shown in Figure 7.1. This menu presents two options: Select Network Configuration, and Exit NETGEN.

Select the first option by highlighting it and pressing ◄─┘. NETGEN will now take over the configuration process. As additional program files are required, you will prompted to insert the appropriate disk. When this initial process is completed, the menu shown in Figure 7.2 will appear.

The first option that you need to select is Set Operating System Options. This option lets you specify whether you want to use the transaction tracking system (TTS). TTS protects against database corruption if a workstation fails during update processing. With TTS turned on, each database update is viewed as a single transaction that must either be executed successfully or aborted. In other words, if

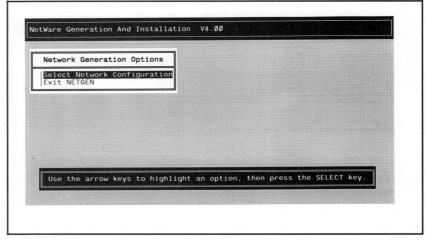

Figure 7.1: Network Generation Options menu

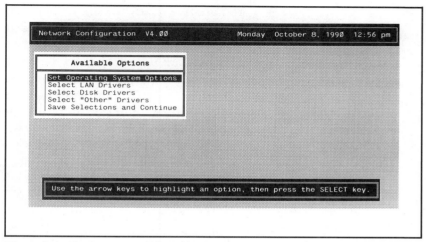

Figure 7.2: Network Configuration menu

the transaction cannot be completed in its entirety, TTS backs out of the transaction and restores the database to its most recent complete state.

For this installation, we will include TTS. Select Set Operating System Options. From the submenu that appears (see Figure 7.3) select the SFT NetWare 286 with TTS option.

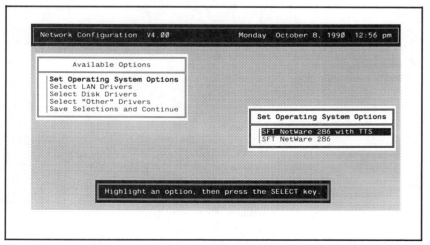

Figure 7.3: Set Operating System Options submenu (Available Options)

You are now ready to define the file server drivers, including the network and disk channel interface boards. Let's start by specifying the LAN interface board.

This network uses only one type of interface board: that for the IBM Token Ring topology. However, Advanced NetWare 286 can support up to four electrical topologies. When you install the corresponding network interface cards, the multiple networks are internally bridged together.

To select the LAN driver, choose Select LAN Drivers from the Available Options menu. The screen that appears will resemble Figure 7.4. This screen contains a window for displaying the selected LAN drivers. It also contains the LAN Driver Options submenu. For our example, choose the first option on this submenu. A second window appears with a list of all of the drivers included on the NetWare disks. You can now scroll through the list with the arrow keys and select the appropriate LAN drivers by pressing ←┘.

Occasionally, Novell releases new or updated LAN drivers. The second selection on the LAN Driver Options menu—Load and Select Item—allows you to load new drivers from a floppy disk.

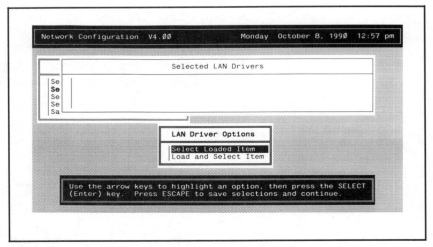

Figure 7.4: Select LAN Drivers screen

For our example, select IBM Token Ring. This topology is the first selection (for this LAN, it is the only topology available), so it is designated "LAN A," or the file server's primary LAN. If other LAN drivers were available, they would be designated "LAN B," "LAN C," and "LAN D." When you have selected the LAN drivers for your network, press the **Esc** key to return to the Available Options menu.

The next step is to select the disk drivers. This procedure is similar to that for selecting LAN drivers. Our example network will have one hard drive, although Advanced NetWare 286 can support up to five hard disk channels.

Choose Select Disk Drivers from the Available Options menu. The screen in Figure 7.5 will appear. For this example, from the Disk Driver Options submenu choose Select Loaded Item. When prompted, enter **0** (zero) as the channel number. (Zero is the channel number for the first hard drive in the system.) Then scroll through the options and choose the driver type that corresponds to the hard drive installed in the file server computer. If your file server has more than one hard drive, repeat this process to install the additional drivers. When you are finished, press **Esc** to return to the Available Options menu.

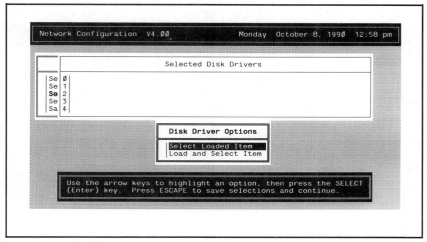

Figure 7.5: Select Disk Drivers screen

Similar to the parallel option on the LAN Driver Options menu, the Load and Select Item option on the Disk Driver Options menu lets you load new or updated disk drivers from a floppy disk.

The Select "Other" Drivers option is used to configure the operating system to communicate directly with other hardware devices. For example, the NetWare streaming tape backup unit requires a controller board installed in the file server.

For our example network, however, we are done selecting hardware options. To save the changes, highlight Save Selections and Continue on the Available Options menu and press ◄─┘.

DEFINING AND CONFIGURING THE FILE SERVER HARDWARE

NETGEN will now prompt you for the network address and the number of communication buffers, displaying the screen shown in Figure 7.6.

The network address uniquely identifies each network interface card in the file server. When a network uses multiple electrical topologies, NetWare uses the network address to manage and coordinate

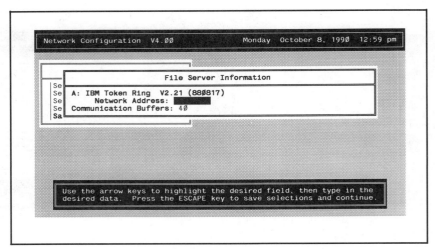

Figure 7.6: File Server Information screen

communications among the systems. The network address can consist of any positive hexadecimal number up to eight digits long, with the following constraints:

1. Each electrical topology (such as Ethernet or Token Ring) must have a unique address.

2. All stations attached to a network must have a common network address.

3. If a network contains more than one file server, these servers must share the same network address.

For our network, enter **AAAAAAAA** as the network address.

The second parameter that must be established is the number of communication buffers. Communication buffers are used by the operating system to temporarily hold packets of data as they arrive from the workstations prior to being processed by the file server. The number of buffers can range between 10 and 150. As shown in Figure 7.6, the default value is 40.

As a rule of thumb, you should start with the default value of 40 and then add one communication buffer for each workstation that is likely to be connected to the network at any one time. For example, if you anticipate that, on the average, a total of 15 workstations will have the NetWare shell loaded at any one time (though these workstations may not necessarily be logged in), then the number of buffers should be 55 (40 + 15 = 55). Let's change the number of communication buffers to 55. Type *55*. Your screen should now look like Figure 7.7. Press **Esc** to save your selections and continue.

The next screen that appears, shown in Figure 7.8, displays the configuration settings that have been automatically determined by NETGEN. Record these settings now. You must record these settings so you will know how to install the file server hardware.

GENERATING THE OPERATING SYSTEM AND COMMUNICATIONS UTILITIES

After you have reviewed and recorded the configuration settings, press **Esc** to continue. You will now be prompted to either continue

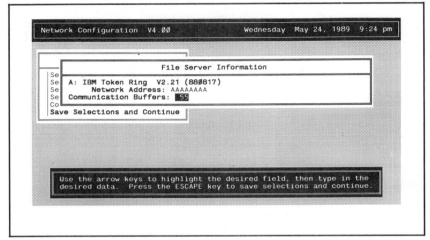

Figure 7.7: The completed File Server Information screen

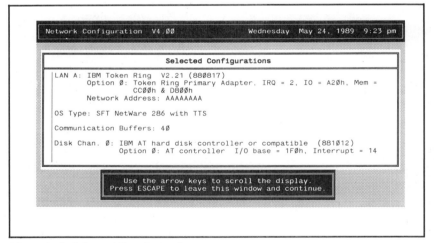

Figure 7.8: Selected Configurations screen

the network generation using the selected configurations or abandon the process. Although you can manually change the hardware configurations by electing to abandon the network generation process, this is rarely necessary when configuring a file server for a relatively simple local area network.

Now NETGEN continues building your network operating system, asking you to insert disks as program files are required. Your wrist will probably get a little tired before this part of the procedure is over because so much disk swapping is required. (Remember that the other methods of generating the operating system require significantly less disk handling.)

When the configuration process is complete, NETGEN returns you to the Network Generation Options menu. Before you can go any further with NETGEN, you must prepare the hardware, so now select Exit NETGEN and return to the DOS prompt.

INSTALLING THE NETWORK INTERFACE CARDS AND PREPARING THE HARD DISK

Now that the network operating system has been configured, the next step is to set and install the network interface cards and to test and format the hard disk with COMPSURF.

SETTING AND INSTALLING THE NETWORK INTERFACE CARDS

Before the network interface cards can be installed in the file server and workstations, their settings must correspond to the configuration of the operating system. IBM Token Ring interface cards require two settings, set by DIP switches. The first sets the ROM address, and the second sets the base input/output (I/O) address. (Other topologies require you also to set a unique station address for each NIC.)

The Selected Configurations screen (see Figure 7.8) provides the information you need. In our example, the ROM address for the file server is CC00h and D800h, and the I/O address is A20h. The topology supplement included in the NetWare package contains diagrams that illustrate the switch settings that correspond to these addresses.

The ROM address CC00h is also used for the network workstations, though if this address causes conflict with other devices, alternative ROM addresses can be used. A conflict, for example, might occur with a device such as a mouse that tries to use the same hardware settings. The topology supplement that accompanies NetWare outlines the alternative addresses that can be used by changing the DIP switch settings.

The workstation network interface cards also use the base I/O address of A20h.

To install a network interface card in a computer, unplug the computer's power cord and disconnect all of the cables from the back of the computer. Next, remove the computer's cover and carefully insert the card into any available slot in the bus. Make sure that the NIC is firmly secured with a screw. Then reposition the cover and reconnect the cables.

PREPARING THE HARD DISK

Before the network operating system can be loaded, the file server hard disk must be tested and formatted with the comprehensive surface analysis, or COMPSURF, utility. To execute the COMPSURF utility, boot the file server using DOS (version 3.0 or higher). The CONFIG.SYS file should include the statement FILES = 10. (If the DOS boot disk does not have a CONFIG.SYS file, you can create one with a text editor or the DOS COPY CON command.) Insert the NETGEN disk in drive A of the file server computer and enter the following command:

    A:NETGEN -CS

The optional parameters -CS execute the *C*ustom configuration options using the *S*tandard floppy disk method.

As before, you will be prompted to insert the SUPPORT disk. When the Netware Generation and Installation program is loaded, the Network Generation Options menu reappears. You specified C, for custom configuration, so this time the menu contains an extended list of options, shown in Figure 7.9. Select the Analyze Disk Surface option and press **Y** or ← to respond Yes to the *Continue?* prompt. NETGEN then asks you to insert the UTILEXE-1 disk. This request is followed by a message that reminds you that the COMP-SURF utility will destroy all of the data on the disk.

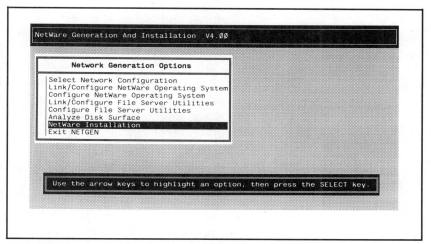

Figure 7.9: Network Generation Options menu

To display a list of the drives currently attached to the file server, press **Esc**. Select the drive that you want to test and format with COMPSURF by highlighting the drive name and pressing ←┘. NETGEN then displays options indicating whether to format the disk, the interleave factor, the media defect record, the number of passes for the sequential test, and the number of inputs and outputs for the random test.

The interleave factor helps determine the efficiency with which data can be written to a disk. For most hard disks in an IBM PC AT (or compatible computer), the optimal interleave factor is 2. For IBM PS/2 models, the best interleave factor is 1. Check the documentation or ask your disk supplier to determine the interleave factor for the other hard disks.

If this is the first time that COMPSURF has been run on the disk, you will need to create a list of disk areas that cannot reliably hold data. This media defect record helps prevent data from being lost due to any imperfections in the hard disk's surface.

The number of sequential passes indicates the number of times that the COMPSURF utility will write patterns sequentially to the disk to analyze its surface. Novell recommends that at least three passes be conducted for best results.

The number of reads and writes specification in the random test functions similarly to the sequential passes specification, except that the writes are to random locations on the disk. Novell recommends 8000 inputs and outputs in the random test.

The default settings should be adequate for our example installation, since we're using the other default parameters. The default settings include an interleave factor of 2, three passes of the sequential test, and 8000 I/O's in the random test. However, if you are using an IBM AT–type file server with an internal hard disk, you must carefully enter the list of media defects. (A bad block list is included with the documentation of the hard disk.) These disks do not contain a NetWare-compatible bad block table. Failure to manually record the media defects can (and usually will) cause problems as the file server attempts to write to disk areas that cannot reliably hold data. Press ← to accept the default parameters and enter the bad block table. You enter the media defects into a form that appears on the screen.

The COMPSURF utility will now execute automatically. It will inform you of its progress on the screen.

COMPSURF processing takes several hours to complete, so you may want to execute COMPSURF earlier in the installation process. For example, you may want to run COMPSURF the night before the network installation, so that it does not interrupt your progress.

When COMPSURF is finished, the screen displays the message *Surface Testing Finished - disk passed*. You will be asked whether you want to display or to print the bad block table. You should select the option to print the bad block table so that it can be included in your setup documentation for future reference. Then press **Esc** to leave the COMPSURF program.

When you return to the Network Generation Options menu, select Exit NETGEN. Now it's time to prepare the file server for the operating system installation.

INSTALLING THE OPERATING SYSTEM

As when you run COMPSURF, you must prepare the file server computer by booting it using DOS (version 3.0 or higher). The

CONFIG.SYS file again must contain the statement **FILES = 10**. Place the working copy of the NETGEN disk in drive A and enter the following command:

A:NETGEN -DS

This command activates the *D*efault level of NETGEN using the *S*tandard floppy disk method. We'll use the default settings for our installation.

When the Network Configuration Options menu appears, select the Network Installation option. NETGEN will analyze the file server and create a list of all of the drives that are attached to the file server. (Be prepared for more disk swapping during this process.) Figure 7.10 shows a drive list.

You should carefully inspect the information on the screen. Any incorrect information about the hard drives could prevent a successful installation or cause operating problems later. When you are satisfied that the descriptions of the file server drives are correct, press **Esc** to continue.

NETGEN now displays a confirmation menu with three options:

- Drive List Is Correct

- Reexamine Drive List

- Drive List Is Not Correct

If the list is not correct, highlight the last option and press ⏎ to return to the Network Generation Options menu. When the drive list is correct, select the first option and continue the installation.

NETGEN will now ensure that the drives have been tested and formatted with COMPSURF. If NETGEN finds an improperly formatted drive, NETGEN displays a message that states in part, *The drives listed above have not been tested by the surface analysis program COMP-SURF.* Then NETGEN terminates the installation procedure.

When the drives have been properly prepared with COMPSURF, the NETGEN program displays the Installation Options menu, as shown in Figure 7.11. Select the first option, Select Default Installation Options, to initiate automatic selection of the installation options using the default settings.

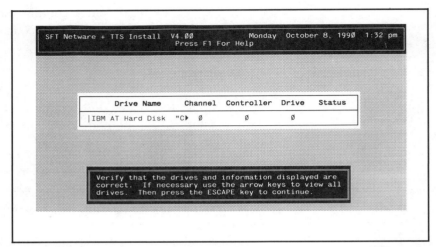

Figure 7.10: File Server Disk Verification screen

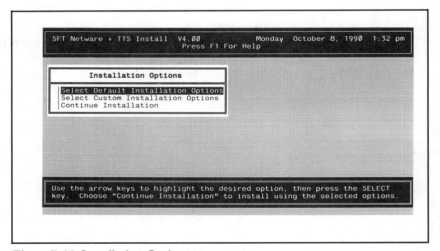

Figure 7.11: Installation Options menu

NETGEN now begins the installation by automatically setting up each drive as a single NetWare volume. A NetWare volume is either a physical hard disk or a portion of a hard disk's storage space. The first drive is always given the name "SYS." Any additional hard disks are named "VOL1," "VOL2," and so on. These drive names will be displayed on the screen, and you should record them for future reference. When you are finished, press **Esc** to continue the installation.

The next step is to name the file server. A pop-up window will appear for you to enter the name. Let's name our file server **FS1**. This file server name is short, but in fact the name can be up to 45 characters long, with the following restrictions:

- The file server name must contain at least two characters.

- The first character cannot be a period.

- Certain nonalphanumeric characters cannot be included: spaces, double quotation marks, asterisks, plus signs, commas, slashes, backslashes, bars, colons, semicolons, equal signs, less-than signs, greater-than signs, question marks, left brackets, and right brackets.

- If the network uses multiple file servers, each name must be unique.

After typing the name in the window, press ←┘.

The next screen that appears presents the configuration for the file server. It includes the following parameters:

- The file server name

- The maximum number of open files that can be opened in the file server simultaneously

- The maximum number of indexed files that can be opened in the file server simultaneously

- The transaction backout volume when TTS is turned on (that is, the volume used to temporarily store transaction information to ensure that it can be backed out in the event of a system failure)

- The maximum number of user transactions that can be active at one time (when TTS is turned on)

As before, record these system configuration parameters. When you are finished, press **Esc** to continue the installation.

The next step is to enter information concerning the printers that will be attached to the file server. The first prompt asks you if the port COM1 will be used for a network printer. This prompt will be followed by similar prompts for COM2, LPT1, and the other printer ports installed in the file server. If a serial printer is selected, NETGEN assumes that the default communications parameters outlined in Chapter 6 will be used.

When you have entered the information for all of your printers, a window displays a summary of your selections. Record the information, along with the other system configuration data, and press **Esc**.

The NETGEN program now returns you to the Installation Options menu. To complete the installation process, select Continue Installation. You will be asked if the networking software is to be installed on the file server. Press **Y** or ⏎ to respond Yes to this prompt. NETGEN then begins the final system configuration and transfer of the operating system to the file server's hard drive. Once again, since we are using the standard floppy disk method, be prepared for disk swapping as the process executes.

After all of the files have been copied onto the hard disk (volume SYS), this message appears: *System files successfully installed*. You are then returned to the Network Generation Options menu. All that remains now is booting the file server.

BOOTING THE FILE SERVER

To bring up the file server, you first need to exit NETGEN by pressing **Esc**. Next, boot the file server using DOS (version 3.0 or higher). (You do not need to reboot the file server if it has not been turned off since you ran NETGEN.) Insert the OSEXE-1 disk in drive A and enter the following command at the DOS prompt:

NET$OS

After a few seconds of processing, you will be prompted to insert the OSEXE-2 disk. The file server will now be under the NetWare operating system.

SUMMARY

In this chapter, we generated the network operating system for the file server. We began the process by selecting the configuration options. Then we installed the network interface card in the file server and prepared the hard disk by running COMPSURF. Finally, we loaded the operating system and booted the file server.

In the next chapter, we'll generate the workstation shells, create a login batch file, and for the first time actually log in to the network.

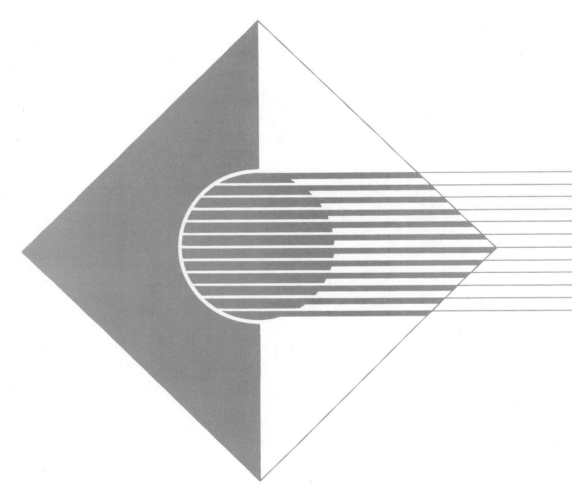

CREATING USER ACCESS PROGRAMS

Fast Track

Prepare workstation shell disks   **97**

> by using the SHGEN program to prepare the necessary programs. Be sure to have a blank formatted disk ready for storing the shell files.

Start the SHGEN program   **98**

> by booting the computer with DOS. Insert the SHGEN-12 disk into drive A and enter **SHGEN-NDS**. When the program asks for a LAN driver, select the appropriate drivers. Several program files will be created that you'll need for the master shell disk.

Prepare other files (if needed).   **101**

> For the IBM Token Ring network, you'll need files from IBM's LAN support program. For a basic installation, these files include DXMA0MOD.SYS, DXMC0MOD.SYS, and DXMT0MOD.SYS. These drivers must be referenced in the CONFIG.SYS file.

Set the long machine type   **101**

> if you are using a non-IBM computer (for instance, if you are using an IBM-compatible computer). You set the long machine type by creating a file on the workstation called SHELL.CFG. You can use any text editor to create this file. For example, enter **LONG MACHINE TYPE = COMPAQ** if you are using Compaq computers on the network. You can use the %LMACHINE variable to set a search path for the proper version of DOS.

To test logging in,   **102**

> boot a workstation on DOS, making sure the proper drivers are loaded from CONFIG.SYS. Then, with the master shell disk

in drive A, enter **IPX** and press ◄┘. Then enter **NET3** and press ◄┘. (This procedure assumes you are using a version of DOS between 3.0 and 4.0.)

To create a login batch file,   104

place all the necessary commands in a batch file named LAN-.BAT. This file can include any number of commands. It should include at least the following statements, one per line: **IPX, NETx, F:, LOGIN FS1/.**

To add special greetings to the batch process,   105

create colorful screens or courtesy messages with ANSI codes. Be sure to add **DEVICE = ANSI.SYS** to your CONFIG.SYS file. Make sure the DOS-supplied ANSI.SYS file is in the workstation boot disk root directory or is set appropriately to find the file in another directory.

A chart of ANSI color attributes is located   108

in Table 8.1.

When logging in from a hard drive,   110

place the LAN drivers and files in a subdirectory off the root directory.

To diagnose problems at the workstation level,   112

use the NetWare COMCHECK utility. This utility lets you identify and check each workstation on the network.

CHAPTER 8

NOW THAT YOUR FILE SERVER IS UP AND RUNNING, the next step is to create the user access programs necessary to log in to the network from a workstation. You'll find that the process for generating workstation shells is very similar to configuring and installing the network operating system with NETGEN.

This chapter describes how to use SHGEN, a NetWare utility program, to generate the workstation shell files. This chapter also describes how to create a boot disk so network users can easily access the file server.

GETTING READY FOR WORK

Before you can begin the actual generation of the workstation shell, you need to perform a few preliminary tasks. First, you need to prepare a master disk for the shell files. You also need to select the configuration method.

PREPARING A MASTER DISK

The SHGEN program creates six files:

- IPX.COM
- NET2.COM, NET3.COM, and NET4.COM
- NETBIOS.EXE
- INT2F.COM

IPX.COM and NETx.COM are the primary shell files that allow the workstation to communicate with the network. You need NET-BIOS.EXE and IN2F.COM to run programs written for IBM-type networks.

When these files are created with SHGEN, you will need a blank disk to store them on. So before you get started, make sure that you have a formatted disk handy. If you don't have one on hand, use the DOS FORMAT command to prepare a disk. Set this disk aside until you need it later.

SELECTING A CONFIGURATION METHOD

As with NETGEN, you can employ several approaches when generating the shell files.

SHGEN has three program levels: default level, intermediate level, and custom level. The default level is adequate (and recommended) for workstations that use the default settings on the network interface card. If the hardware configuration settings require modification, or if unusual LAN drivers are required, then you need to use the intermediate or custom level. For our example network, we will use the default settings on the Token Ring interface cards, so we will use the default level to configure our workstation shell.

There are also three methods of running SHGEN: the standard floppy disk method, the hard disk method, and the network drive method. The advantages to each of these approaches are the same as those for the three methods of running NETGEN (see Chapter 7). For simplicity, we'll create our network shell files using the standard floppy disk method.

GENERATING
THE WORKSTATION SHELL FILES

To start SHGEN, boot any computer with at least 640 KB of memory using DOS (version 3.0 or higher). Then insert the working copy of the SHGEN-1 disk into drive A. Make sure that drive A is the default drive and enter the following command at the DOS prompt:

SHGEN -NDS

This command executes the SHGEN program to create *N*ew shell files using the *D*efault shell configuration processed with the *S*tandard floppy disk method.

When SHGEN is loaded, it displays the screen for selecting the LAN driver, as shown in Figure 8.1. Highlight the appropriate driver and press ◄┘. For our example network, select the IBM Token Ring driver.

SHGEN will now display a screen, similar to Figure 8.2, to confirm the LAN driver selection. If the information is correct, press ◄┘ to continue. At this point, you will be prompted to do some disk swapping as SHGEN generates the shell files. (Remember to use the working disks you created.) When the process is finished, this message appears on the screen:

> A valid shell has been placed on SHGEN-2
> <Press ESCAPE to Continue>

Press **Esc**. This exits SHGEN. The shell files are now configured.

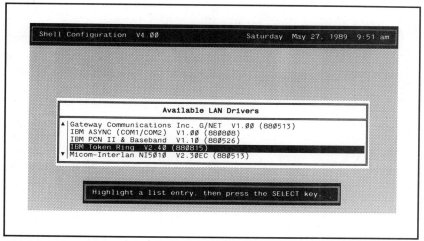

Figure 8.1: SHGEN LAN driver selection screen

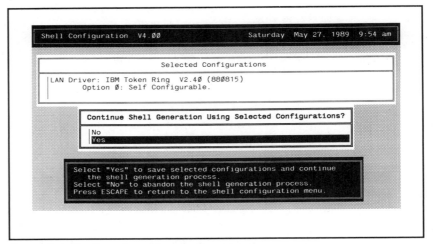

Figure 8.2: Shell configuration confirmation screen

CREATING A MASTER SHELL DISK

Before you can actually log in to the network, you must create a master shell disk. This disk will contain the shell files and any additional drivers required by the network interface card.

With the SHGEN-2 disk in the disk drive, enter the DOS command **DIR**. A directory listing similar to the following will appear:

```
Volume in drive A is SHGEN-2
Directory of  A:\

NETBIOS    EXE    13882    12-08-88      3:22p
INT2F      COM      640     7-28-88     11:48a
NET3       COM    41375    11-23-88      4:25p
NET4       COM    41764    11-23-88      4:24p
NIMLOAD    BIN     5376     6-03-88     12:58a
IPX        OBJ    17046    11-23-88      4:26p
NET2       COM    37967    11-23-88      4:25p
IPX        COM    30597     5-27-89      9:58a
       8 File(s)    168960 bytes free
```

You need to copy the shell files to a master shell disk. The master disk should be formatted as a bootable disk (that is, formatted with the /S parameter). Use the DOS COPY command to copy the NETx.COM, IPX.COM, NETBIOS.EXE, and INT2F.COM files. The version of DOS that the workstations will run determines which NETx.COM file is required. For example, workstations using DOS 3.x will need NET3.COM.

Depending on the electrical topology of your network, you may need additional configuration files or drivers to activate the network interface card and initiate communications on the network. (The topology supplements included with the NetWare package detail these requirements.)

The IBM Token Ring network that we are installing uses a program named DXMAID on the LAN Support Program disk (this disk accompanys the IBM Token Ring NIC) to create the supplemental files. Run this program. When you finish, four files will be generated:

DXMA0MOD.SYS

CONFIG.SYS

DXMC0MOD.SYS

DXMT0MOD.SYS

Our workstation shell will use only the DXMA0MOD.SYS, DXMC0MOD.SYS, and CONFIG.SYS files, so copy these three files to the master shell disk. The DXMT0MOD.SYS file is IBM's NetBIOS emulator program. It can optionally be used in lieu of the Novell NetBIOS emulator, NETBIOS.COM.

If workstations other than IBM computers will be connected to your network, you will also need to create a shell configuration file (SHELL.CFG). You use the shell configuration file to set a variety of options for IPX.COM, NETx.COM, and NETBIOS.COM. The option that we'll include in the SHELL.CFG file is the long machine name. This option lets us use the %LMACHINE variable to set a search path for the proper version of DOS, as you'll see in Chapters 9 and 10.

The default long machine type is IBM_PC, so you will need a SHELL.CFG file on the boot disk for each non-IBM workstation. You can use a text editor or the DOS COPY CON command to create the file. For example, if Compaq computers will be connected to the network, enter the following at the DOS prompt:

```
COPY CON SHELL.CFG
LONG MACHINE TYPE = COMPAQ
^Z (press the [F6] function key)
```

The machine-type name can consist of up to 15 characters, and it must be unique for each type of workstation.

Your master shell disk should now contain the following files:

COMMAND.COM

NETx.COM

IPX.COM

CONFIG.SYS

NETBIOS.COM

INT2F.COM

DXMA0MOD.SYS

DXMC0MOD.SYS

SHELL.CFG

(A SHELL.CFG file should exist for each non-IBM workstation.

The master shell disk is now complete. You are ready to log in to the file server for the first time.

LOGGING IN FOR THE FIRST TIME

To log in to the file server, first make certain that the file server is running. Then boot a workstation with a copy of the master shell disk. At the DOS prompt, enter the following commands:

```
IPX
NETx
```

These commands will load IPX and NETx.

Your screen should now look similar to Figure 8.3. The screen information indicates that you are now connected to the file server named FS1.

Your next step is to change the default drive to the first network drive. If you are running DOS version 3.0 or higher, the first network drive usually is drive F. You then enter the following login command:

LOGIN FS1/SUPERVISOR

This command logs you in to the network with the user name SUPERVISOR. The screen displays the default login script shown in Figure 8.4.

You can use the network drive much like any personal computer drive. For example, you can execute internal DOS commands such as DIR, and you can change the default directory with the CD command. In addition, as you'll see in later chapters, NetWare supplements DOS with its own commands. For example, if you type **WHOAMI**, the screen displays the following message:

> You are user SUPERVISOR attached to server FS1 connection 1.
> Server FS1 is running SFT NetWare 286 TTS V2.15.
> Login Time: Saturday May 27, 1990 1:17 pm

```
A>ipx
Novell IPX/SPX V2.12 Rev. C
(C) Copyright 1985, 1988 Novell Inc.  All Rights Reserved.

LAN Option: IBM Token Ring
Hardware Configuration: Self Configurable.

A>net3
NetWare V2.12 rev. A - Workstation Shell for PC DOS V3.x
(C) Copyright 1983, 1988 Novell, Inc.  All Rights Reserved.

Attached to server FS1
Saturday, May 27, 1989    1:17:05 pm

A>
```

Figure 8.3: IPX and NETx information screen

```
A>F:

F>LOGIN FS1/SUPERVISOR

Good afternoon, SUPERVISOR.

Drive A     maps to a local disk.
Drive B     maps to a local disk.
Drive C     maps to a local disk.
Drive D     maps to a local disk.
Drive E     maps to a local disk.
Drive F  := FS1/SYS:SYSTEM
Drive G  := FS1/SYS:LOGIN
Drive Y  := FS1/SYS:PUBLIC
         -----
SEARCH1  := Z:. [FS1/SYS:PUBLIC]

F>
```

Figure 8.4: Default login script

Let's log off the network. Enter **LOGOFF** at the DOS prompt. Now we will begin creating a custom login program for the network users.

CREATING A CUSTOM LOGIN PROGRAM

The users of the network could log in as you just did by executing IPX and NET and then entering the LOGIN command. However, with very little effort you can automate the login process and make logging in easier for network users.

You could simply enter the login commands in a batch file with the following statements:

```
IPX
NETx
F:
LOGIN FS1/
```

You could then name this batch file **LAN.BAT**.

You can create an even friendlier procedure by including courtesy screens that are displayed as the batch file executes.

GENERATING MESSAGE SCREENS

By using the DOS ANSI.SYS device driver, you can easily create custom message screens. ANSI.SYS manages the screen display. With this driver, you can display and erase characters, move the cursor, and select colors. To use this device driver, you must copy the ANSI.SYS file from the DOS disk to the master shell disk. Then add the following statement to the CONFIG.SYS file:

DEVICE = ANSI.SYS

Using a set of ANSI code sequences created with a text editor, you now can manipulate the cursor position and screen colors when displaying files with the TYPE command. For example, the following ANSI sequence, named TEST.SCN, displays the window shown in Figure 8.5 when **TYPE TEST.SCN** is entered at the DOS prompt:

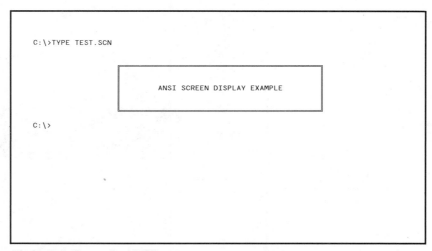

Figure 8.5: Example ANSI screen

In this code sequence, [ESC] represents the Escape character that is created by pressing the **Alt** key and typing **027** on the number pad. (Your text editor must be capable of producing the Escape character.) The ANSI codes in this simple example designate the cursor position in terms of rows and columns. The graphics characters that make up the window are created with the following key sequences:

[Alt] 201

[Alt] 205

[Alt] 187

[Alt] 200

[Alt] 188

Let's now add a courtesy message that will be displayed as IPX and NETx are loading. The following ANSI code sequence, named WAIT.SCN, creates the window shown in Figure 8.6:

```
[ESC][Ø2J

[ESC][Ø5;19f[ESC][37;44m
[ESC][Ø6;19f
[ESC][Ø7;19f    Loading Files for Connection to the LAN
[ESC][Ø8;19f
[ESC][Ø9;19f            [ESC][5;33m **** PLEASE WAIT **** [ESC][Ø;37;44m
[ESC][1Ø;19f
[ESC][11;19f
[ESC][Øm[ESC][15;19f→
```

Figure 8.6: Please Wait courtesy message

To create the message shown in Figure 8.6, the ANSI device driver interprets the codes in the following fashion. The first code, [ESC][027J, clears the screen. The ANSI sequence following the first cursor position [ESC][37;44m, changes the screen colors to white on blue. The code immediately before the message *Please Wait*, [ESC][5;33m, causes the characters to blink and changes their color to yellow. The next code, [ESC]0;37;44m, turns the blink attribute off and sets the screen colors back to white on blue. The last codes, [ESC][0m[ESC][15;19F, restore the screen colors to white on black and position the cursor at screen location 15,19.

Let's create a similar courtesy message, named LOGIN.SCN, that prompts the network user to enter his or her login ID and password. Using a similar code sequence, you can create the screen shown in Figure 8.7:

```
[ESC][Ø2J

[ESC][Ø5;19f[ESC][37;44m┌───────────────────────────────────────────────────────┐
[ESC][Ø6;19f
[ESC][Ø7;19f             Please Enter Your Login ID
[ESC][Ø8;19f
[ESC][Ø9;19f            and Password at the Prompt
[ESC][1Ø;19f
[ESC][11;19f└───────────────────────────────────────────────────────┘
[ESC][Øm[ESC][15;19f→
```

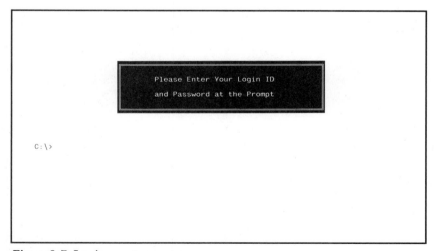

Figure 8.7: Login courtesy message

Table 8.1: ANSI Color Commands

COLOR	FOREGROUND	BACKGROUND
Black	30	40
Red	31	41
Green	32	42
Yellow	33	43
Blue	34	44
Magenta	35	45
Cyan	36	46
White	37	47
ATTRIBUTE		
Reset to white on black	0	
Bright	1	
Blink	5	

ANSI commands provide an easy way to add a little zip to the otherwise dull execution of a batch file. To help you further customize your login screen, Table 8.1 lists the ANSI color commands. In addition, many good ANSI editors are available to make the creation of these screens a little less painful. Many editors are even available in the public domain in the form of shareware programs.

WRITING THE LOGIN BATCH FILE

Copy the files for the courtesy messages WAIT.SCN and LOGIN.SCN to the master boot disk. You are now ready to write the login batch file.

The objective of the boot disk is to directly connect the workstation to the network, so we'll use AUTOEXEC.BAT as the batch file to control the login process. Using this file will automate the login procedure to the extent that all the user has to do is turn on the workstation and enter a login ID and password.

Using a text editor, create a file named AUTOEXEC.BAT on the master boot disk. Enter the following commands:

```
:File Server FS1 Boot Diskette
:IBM Token Ring/IBM Workstation
:Created by: CAG
:Date:  May 31, 1990
ECHO OFF
CLS
PROMPT $P$G
TYPE WAIT.SCN
IPX
NET3
TYPE LOGIN.SCN
F:
LOGIN FS1/
```

The first four lines of this program are simply comments that describe the batch file. They have no effect on the file's execution. The CLS command clears the screen. PROMPT PG sets the DOS prompt to display the current directory and a greater-than sign (C:\NETWARE>). The next command, ECHO OFF, turns off the display of the remaining commands as they are executed.

The first ANSI message appears on the screen when the TYPE WAIT.SCN command is executed. This message remains on the screen as IPX and NETx are loaded. Then the screen is cleared, and the login message appears, followed by the prompt asking the user to enter a login name, as shown in Figure 8.8.

Your login program is complete. Make a working copy of your master boot disk and store the original for safekeeping. Create the additional boot disks you need from the working copy. Make certain as you duplicate the disks that they are formatted with the correct version of DOS, and that the correct long machine type is included in the SHELL.CFG files for any non-IBM workstations.

Figure 8.8: Login courtesy message and login prompt

BOOTING FROM A HARD DISK

At least some of your workstations may have a hard disk installed. You can set up these computers to boot directly from their internal drives. You can use the same shell files as in the previous section by copying them to the hard disk. For housekeeping purposes, and to guard against accidentally erasing the files, you should set up a LAN subdirectory for storing all of the network files.

To create a LAN subdirectory, type **MD LAN** at the DOS prompt. (Make sure that you are at the root directory.) Now copy the files from the master boot disk to the LAN subdirectory. You won't need the copies of COMMAND.COM, ANSI.SYS, and CONFIG.SYS in the LAN subdirectory, so you can delete them.

Next, rename AUTOEXEC.BAT as **LAN.BAT**. This renaming allows you either to access the LAN directly when the machine boots or to access it by typing **LAN** at the DOS prompt. To ensure that the batch file executes from the LAN subdirectory, modify LAN.BAT to include the change directory (CD) command as follows:

```
:File Server FS1 Boot Diskette
:IBM Token Ring/IBM Workstation
:Created by:  CAG
```

```
:Date:  May 31, 1990
CD\LAN
ECHO OFF
CLS
PROMPT $P$G
TYPE WAIT.SCN
IPX
NET3
TYPE LOGIN.SCN
F:
LOGIN FS1/
```

If the root directory contains a CONFIG.SYS file, you must modify this file so that the device drivers can be found. You can use a text editor to modify (or create) the CONFIG.SYS file.

Add the following statements to CONFIG.SYS for the IBM Token Ring network that we are installing:

```
DEVICE = C:\LAN\DXMA0MOD.SYS
DEVICE = C:\LAN\DXMC0MOD.SYS
DEVICE = C:\DOS\ANSI.SYS
```

The last statement assumes that ANSI.SYS is stored in a subdirectory named DOS located directly under the root directory.

You also need to modify, or add, the PATH command in the existing AUTOEXEC.BAT file. The PATH command tells DOS where to look for command files if if cannot find them in the current directory. LAN.BAT is located in the LAN subdirectory, so the PATH command should resemble the following:

```
PATH C:\LOTUS;C:\DOS;C:\LAN
```

In this example, the disk operating system will look for executable files (those with .COM, .EXE, and .BAT extensions) in the current directory and in the LOTUS, DOS, and LAN subdirectories.

With these modifications made, you have two options for configuring the connection to the network. You can either establish the connection via the AUTOEXEC.BAT file, or you can permit the user to enter a command when access is needed. If you want to automatically load the workstation shell, add **LAN** as the last command in AUTOEXEC.BAT. Otherwise, the user can simply enter the command **LAN** to establish the network connection.

DIAGNOSING PROBLEMS

In this local area network installation, we were lucky. Everything went just as planned. Unfortunately, in the real world things don't always go quite so smoothly. Occasionally, network interface cards will not function, or cabling will cause problems. To help you diagnose these types of difficulties, you can use the NetWare communication check utility, COMCHECK. This program tests whether the network stations are communicating properly across the cabling system.

To run COMCHECK, boot the computer with a disk that contains all the workstation shell files. Then load IPX. If IPX does not load properly, then one of the following problems is likely the culprit:

- Faulty or mismatched configuration of the workstation shells
- Missing device drivers (for example, DXMC0MOD.SYS for an IBM Token Ring network)
- Defective network interface card

Once IPX executes, place the working copy of the NetWare DIAGNOSTICS disk into drive A and enter this command:

COMCHECK

When COMCHECK loads, you will be prompted to enter a unique identifier for the workstation you are testing. For example, you can type **STATION 1** or the office number where the workstation is located.

If the station is cabled properly, a screen similar to Figure 8.9 will appear. The information on the screen includes the network address of the cabling system, the physical station (node) address of the workstation in hexadecimal notation, the unique identifier that you entered, and the date and time that the test was initiated. The asterisk indicates the workstation that is currently being viewed. As

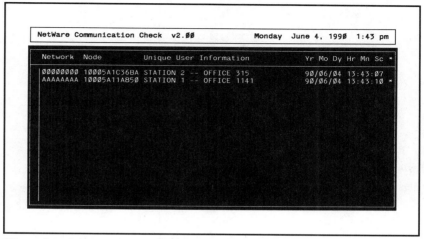

```
NetWare Communication Check   v2.ØØ                Monday   June 4, 199Ø   1:43 pm

Network   Node           Unique User Information        Yr Mo Dy Hr Mn Sc ▪
ØØØØØØØØ 10005A1C36BA STATION 2 -- OFFICE 315        90/06/04 13:43:07
AAAAAAAA 10005A11A850 STATION 1 -- OFFICE 1141       90/06/04 13:43:10 ▪
```

Figure 8.9: COMCHECK diagnostics screen

COMCHECK is executed at additional stations, information about them also will appear on the screen.

If any problems occur, COMCHECK does not display the workstation information on the diagnostics screen. In this case, you should investigate the physical connections between the computer and the rest of the network. If everything appears to be correct, then the problem is most likely a duplicate or illegal station address setting.

SUMMARY

This chapter completes the initial installation process for your local area network. You have learned how to generate the workstation shell, create a master boot disk, and automate the login process with a batch file that includes custom message screens. You also used the COMCHECK utility to troubleshoot potential cabling problems.

Now that the network is operational and users can log in, you can turn to the chapters in the next part for guidance through the process of creating the user environment.

PART III

CREATING
THE USER ENVIRONMENT

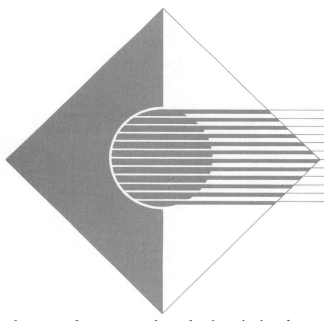

Before the users of your network can begin enjoying the services of the LAN, you must create the user environment. This includes setting up the directory structure, loading programs, adding users, establishing security, and creating menus. These tasks are the subject of this part of the book.

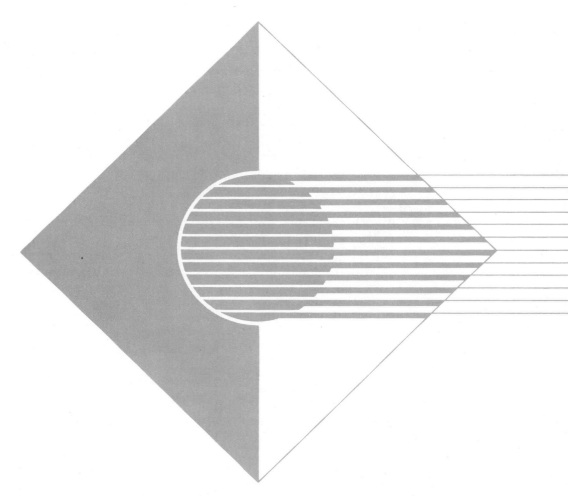

LAYING THE FOUNDATIONS FOR THE USER ENVIRONMENT

FAST TRACK

NetWare directory structures   **119**
  are similar to DOS structures except they include a file server
  and volume. For example, a fully qualified file location in
  NetWare would look like this:

  FS1/SYS:DATA/WORDS/GILLETT.TXT

  Compare this to the fully qualified file location in DOS:

  C:\DATA\WORDS\GILLETT.TXT.

The basic NetWare installation creates four directories: **121**
  SYS:SYSTEM, SYS:PUBLIC, SYS:LOGIN, and SYS-
  :MAIL. You must create new directories and sudirectories. To
  do so, you can either use the DOS command MD *directory name*
  or the NetWare FILER utility.

Networks use drive maps to   **122**
  easily locate directories. Maps can locate local drives, network
  drives, or search drives.

DOS reserves a certain number of local drives unless   **123**
  you place the LASTDRIVE command in the CONFIG.SYS
  file.

To map network drives,   **124**
  assign a drive letter to a specific directory or subdirectory.

To map search drives,   **124**
  assign a drive letter and search drive designation to a specific
  directory or subdirectory that you want set in the search path.

NetWare sets default drive maps if   **124**

no other maps are specified in the system or user login scripts.

Custom drive maps can be set   **125**

by creating login scripts or by executing MAP commands from the DOS prompt. For example, to include the SYS:UTIL directory in the search path, enter **MAP S2: = SYS:/UTIL** at the DOS prompt.

A good basic directory structure should   **126**

consider simplicity, security, and a logical grouping of files. Our example network adds the following directories from the root directory of the SYS volume: PROGRAMS, UTIL, DOS, PRIVATE, COMMON, GROUPS, DEFAULT. You add directories with the DOS Make Directory (MD) command or by using the NetWare FILER utility.

Add subdirectories next.   **129**

Add one subdirectory for each application program under the PROGRAMS directory, one subdirectory for each DOS version under the DOS directory, and one subdirectory for each user under the PRIVATE directory. (Note: You may want to wait to add the PRIVATE subdiretories until after the initial user login names are created.)

Loading DOS onto the network requires   **130**

a little extra work now, but saves confusion later. This step requires you to make subdirectories for each version of DOS that the network will support.

CHAPTER 9

THIS CHAPTER REVIEWS THE BASICS OF NETWARE directory structures and the concept of drive maps. With this foundation in mind, we then develop a directory structure for our network that allows us to manage multiple versions of DOS.

USING DIRECTORIES AND SUBDIRECTORIES

As a personal computer user, you are probably familiar with directories and subdirectories. A directory system lets you easily maintain a multilevel file structure. A multilevel file structure helps you manage large numbers of files by logically grouping them into subdirectories.

For example, your hard disk may contain application programs such as Lotus 1-2-3 and WordPerfect as well as data. Rather than mixing all of the files together on the disk, you can group them into directories and subdirectories, as shown in Figure 9.1. In this figure, the full directory name for the file named GILLETT.TXT in the WORDS subdirectory is

    C:\DATA\WORDS\GILLETT.TXT

USING NETWARE DIRECTORIES

Like DOS, NetWare also lets you set up directory structures for managing files. However, since the network environment is more complex, the directory structure hierarchy has an additional level. Figure 9.2 illustrates how the directory structure shown in Figure 9.1 might be represented on a file server hard disk.

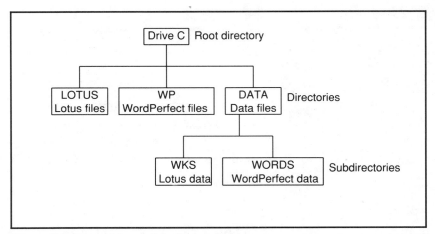

Figure 9.1: Typical hard disk directory structure

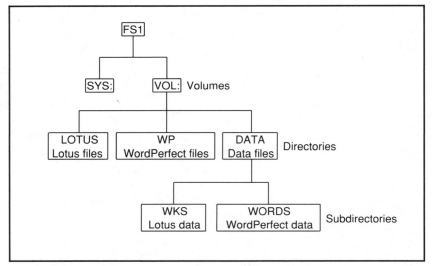

Figure 9.2: Typical file server disk directory structure

As the figure shows, the file server hard disk is divided into volumes, then into directories, and finally into subdirectories. (Our file server has only one volume: SYS.) The full directory name for the GILLETT.TXT file in the WORDS subdirectory is now

FS1/SYS1:DATA/WORDS/GILLETT.TXT

USING SYSTEM DIRECTORIES

When you configured and installed the NetWare operating system, NETGEN automatically created four directories:

SYS:SYSTEM

SYS:PUBLIC

SYS:LOGIN

SYS:MAIL

The SYSTEM directory contains various NetWare files that are usually restricted to use by the network manager. The files stored in PUBLIC are mostly utility programs intended for general use. The LOGIN directory contains the programs required for logging in to the network. The MAIL directory is used to store files used by the electronic mail system and other NetWare programs.

To observe this directory structure, log in to the network as **SUPERVISOR**. Then enter **CD** to return to the top level of the SYS volume, type **DIR**, and press ◄──┘. The directory listing will then appear as follows:

```
Volume in drive F is SYS
Directory of  F:\

SYSTEM       <DIR>
LOGIN        <DIR>
MAIL         <DIR>
PUBLIC       <DIR>
      4 File(s)  35471360 bytes free
```

CREATING DIRECTORIES

You create new directories and subdirectories on a file server hard disk the same way as on an internal drive in a standalone microcomputer. For example, to create a directory named PROGRAMS, simply enter the following command:

```
MD PROGRAMS
```

Now enter **DIR** to see the directory structure. The screen will look similar to the following:

```
Volume in drive F is SYS
Directory of  F:\

SYSTEM        <DIR>
LOGIN         <DIR>
MAIL          <DIR>
PUBLIC        <DIR>

PROGRAMS      <DIR>      6-10-90      12:14p
        4 File(s)  35471360 bytes free
```

Notice that the directory that you just created contains a date and time stamp, whereas system directories do not. System directories are protected by NetWare and cannot be modified or deleted.

You can also create and modify directories using FILER, the NetWare file maintenance utility. To execute the FILER utility, enter **FILER** at the DOS prompt. A window will appear with a list of topics. Use the ↓ key to move the light bar to Subdirectory Information. Then press ←┘. A list of the current subdirectories will appear in a pop-up window. To add a new subdirectory named UTIL, press the **Ins** key. Then simply type **UTIL** in the box that appears, as shown in Figure 9.3.

USING DRIVE MAPS

Drive maps provide NetWare with a road map for finding files within the directory structure. Sometimes referred to as drive pointers, drive maps point to a specific network location and so allow information to be located easily. There are three types of drive maps:

1. Local drive maps

2. Network drive maps

3. Search drive maps

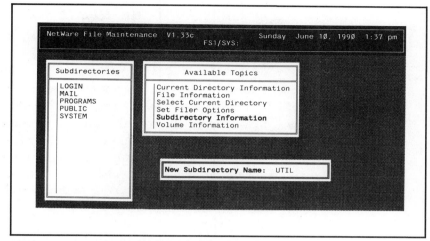

Figure 9.3: NetWare file maintenance utility screen

USING LOCAL DRIVE MAPS

Local drive maps point to disk drives installed in the local workstation. For example, drive A is usually a floppy disk drive, and drive C is usually a locally attached hard disk. Local drive maps let you access and store information on storage media at the workstation rather than on the file server hard disk.

The disk operating system always reserves a certain number of drive letters for local storage devices. However, you can change the number of local drives by adding the DOS LASTDRIVE command to the CONFIG.SYS file. For example, if you enter the following command in the CONFIG.SYS file, DOS will assign only two drive letters for local use:

LASTDRIVE = B

Changing the number of drives is useful when you want to increase the number of drive letters available for network drives.

The first network drive is always named using the first drive letter that has not been reserved for local use.

USING NETWORK DRIVE MAPS

Network drive maps are similar to local drive maps except that they point to a location on the file server's hard disk. In addition, network drive maps can point to a specific subdirectory on the drive. For example, using the directory structure illustrated in Figure 9.2, you can map a drive to go directly to the WORDS subdirectory. This map lets you change the current drive simply by entering the drive letter rather than typing the entire directory path.

It is important to remember that network drive maps are logical, not physical, features. That is, a separate physical drive does not exist for the location NetWare points to, unlike with local drive maps. In addition, network drive maps usually are different for different users. Therefore, if you store a file on drive G, another user may be unable to find it without knowing the full directory name.

USING SEARCH DRIVE MAPS

Search drive maps also assign a drive letter to a specific network location, similar to network drive maps, but search drive maps also allow the operating system to automatically search the mapped directory for a requested file. Search drive maps are similar to DOS paths. When you execute a command at the DOS prompt, the NetWare operating system looks for the corresponding file within the current subdirectory. If the system cannot find the file, it then searches any directories that are mapped as search drives. Search drive maps apply not only to executable files (that is, those with .COM, .EXE, and .BAT extensions), but also to data files accessed by executable files.

For example, in most network configurations the DOS subdirectory is mapped as a search drive. This mapping allows users to execute DOS commands from any place in the network without changing to the DOS subdirectory.

USING NETWARE DEFAULT DRIVE MAPS

NetWare automatically assigns default drive maps. To view the default maps, enter **MAP** at the DOS prompt. Unless you have changed the default maps, information similar to the following will appear:

```
Drive  A:  maps to a local disk.
Drive  B:  maps to a local disk.
Drive  C:  maps to a local disk.
Drive  F: = FS1/SYS:SYSTEM
Drive  G: = FS1/SYS:LOGIN
Drive  Y: = FS1/SYS:PUBLIC
          -----
SEARCH1: = Z:. [FS1/SYS:PUBLIC]
```

This information tells you that drives A, B, and C are mapped as local drives. Drive F is a network drive that points to the SYSTEM subdirectory on volume SYS. Similarly, drives G and Y are network drives that point to the LOGIN and PUBLIC subdirectories. Finally, drive Z is a search drive that allows files in the PUBLIC directory to be located from anywhere on the network.

ADDING OR CHANGING DRIVE MAPS

As you'll see in the next chapter, drive maps usually are set by login scripts. (The login scripts contain a set of instructions that direct workstations to perform specific actions during the login process.) However, you can also modify drive maps from the DOS prompt.

For example, suppose that you want to map drive R as a network drive pointing to the PROGRAMS directory. The following command performs this function:

```
MAP R: = SYS:/PROGRAMS
```

Similarly, the following command adds a second search drive that points to the UTIL directory:

```
MAP S2: = SYS:/UTIL
```

To make sure that the remap occurred, you can again enter **MAP** at the DOS prompt. The map information should reflect the changes, as follows:

```
Drive  A:    maps to a local disk.
Drive  B:    maps to a local disk.
Drive  C:    maps to a local disk.
Drive  F:    = FS1/SYS:SYSTEM
Drive  G:    = FS1/SYS:LOGIN
Drive  R:    = FS1/SYS:PROGRAMS
Drive  Y:    = FS1/SYS:PUBLIC
             -----

SEARCH1:  = Z:. [FS1/SYS:PUBLIC]
SEARCH2:  = X:. [FS1/SYS:UTIL]
```

There are now two search maps, so the operating system will search for files first in the current drive and then in each of the search drives in order. You may want to use two search drives if you have two files with the same name: one located in PUBLIC and the other in UTIL. With only one search drive, the search will end when the file in PUBLIC is found; the second file, in UTIL, will not be located.

DEVELOPING A DIRECTORY STRUCTURE

Obviously, an unlimited number of directory structures can be employed in a local area network. Our task for our example system is relatively simple because we have only one file server and one volume. Nevertheless, we must plan the directory structure carefully.

When planning the directory layout, you should consider three important issues. The first issue to consider is the simplicity of the structure. You do not want the directory structure to be so complicated that users (and administrators) cannot find program and data files. Second, you must consider security, because many of NetWare's security provisions relate to directories and subdirectories. Finally, you need to consider logic: Files should be logically grouped to enhance the efficiency of the network.

CREATING THE DIRECTORIES

In our example network, we'll add the following seven directories to the four created by NetWare:

PROGRAMS

UTIL

DOS

PRIVATE

COMMON

GROUPS

DEFAULT

To create these directories, enter the DOS MAKE DIRECTORY command (MD) followed by the directory name and press ←⌐. For example, to make the PROGRAMS directory, enter the following command:

MD PROGRAMS

The PROGRAMS directory will contain various subdirectories that hold the application programs, such as Lotus 1-2-3 and Word-Perfect. The UTIL directory will provide a storage location for various utility programs, such as text editors. The DOS directory will contain subdirectories for each version of the disk operating system from which a workstation on the network can be booted. (The next section discusses DOS subdirectories in detail.) The PRIVATE directory will be used to store the individual data files for each LAN user. Subdirectories will be used to partition the data by user. The COMMON directory will provide a temporary storage location for files so they can be accessed by other users. The GROUPS directory will contain subdirectories that are shared by individuals in the same work groups. The DEFAULTS directory will contain a subdirectory for each user. This subdirectory will store any files that are specific to the individual.

Figure 9.4 illustrates the directory structure for the network hard disk. This approach meets the criteria established earlier for the

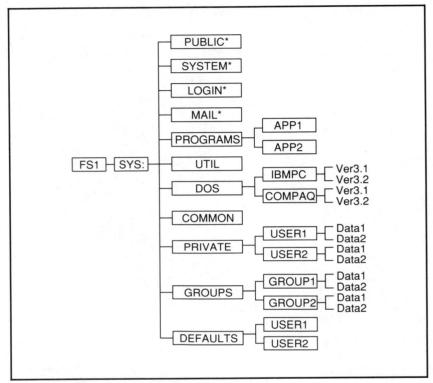

Figure 9.4: A directory structure

directory layout. First, it is simple. The SYS volume contains only seven directories (excluding the NetWare system directories), and the names clearly reflect the directory contents. Second, the directory structure facilitates effective security by allowing security rights to be assigned to individuals and groups. For example, access to data files in the PRIVATE directory can be restricted to individual LAN users. Third, the data files are logically grouped in the seven directories. Software applications are separated from data files, and each user's data is segregated.

By using the DOS MAKE DIRECTORY (MD) command or the FILER utility, you can create these directories on the network's hard disk. When you are finished, executing the DOS DIR command will produce a screen similar to the following:

```
Volume in drive F is SYS
Directory of  F:\

SYSTEM        <DIR>
LOGIN         <DIR>
MAIL          <DIR>
PUBLIC        <DIR>
DOS           <DIR>       6-24-90        12:21p
UTIL          <DIR>       6-24-90        1:37p
COMMON        <DIR>       6-24-90        12:21p
PRIVATE       <DIR>       6-24-90        12:21p
GROUPS        <DIR>       6-24-90        12:21p
PROGRAMS      <DIR>       6-24-90        12:14p
DEFAULTS      <DIR>       6-24-90        12:14p

        11 File(s)  35459072 bytes free
```

CREATING THE SUBDIRECTORIES

You also need to create the necessary subdirectories within each directory. The PROGRAMS directory should contain a subdirectory for each application that will be loaded on the network. In the DOS directory, you will need a subdirectory for each machine type (IBM, Compaq, or whatever computers are attached to the network) and another level of subdirectory for each version of the operating system that each machine type uses (for example, V3.1, V3.2).

The PRIVATE directory will contain a subdirectory for each user. The user login names are good names for these subdirectories. Each PRIVATE subdirectory should also contain subdirectories for the various types of data files. For our example LAN, let's use WORDS for word processing files, WKS for spreadsheet files, and PIC for graphics files.

For the GROUPS directory, we can use an approach similar to that for the PRIVATE directory, except instead of subdirectories for each user, we will create a subdirectory for each work group. In our example, we will create a subdirectory named ACCTNG for the accounting department and a subdirectory named MRKTNG for the marketing department. Within each of these subdirectories, we will also create the WORDS, WKS, and PIC subdirectories to store the various types of files.

The DEFAULTS directory also needs a subdirectory for each user. You'll see in later chapters how certain files can be stored in the DEFAULT subdirectories to customize the network for each user.

VIEWING THE DIRECTORY STRUCTURE

When you have completed creating the directories and subdirectories, you can use a NetWare command to view the directory structure. From the root directory of volume SYS (drive F), enter the following command to list all of the directories and subdirectories for our example LAN:

```
LISTDIR /S
```

The /S parameter specifies that you want to view all levels of subdirectories.

Your screen should look like Figure 9.5. The indentions indicate subdirectory nesting levels.

LOADING FILES INTO DIRECTORIES

Now that we've created our directories, we can begin to load files into them. In this chapter, we will load files into the DOS and PROGRAMS directories. The other directories will be reserved for files created by the users of the network.

LOADING DOS FILES

Our example network will have two types of workstations attached to it: IBM and Compaq workstations. Therefore, we created two DOS

```
The sub-directory structure of FS1/SYS:
    SYSTEM
        040015
    LOGIN
    MAIL
        1
        20007
    PUBLIC
    DOS
        IBM_PC
            VER_3.1
            VER_3.2
        COMPAQ
            VER_3.1
            VER_3.2
    UTIL
    COMMON
    PRIVATE
        GILLETT
            WKS
            PIC
            WORDS
        CURRID
            WORDS
            PIC
            WKS
        KRUEGER
            WORDS
            PIC
            WKS
        JORDEN
            WORDS
            PIC
            WKS
        CLARK
            WORDS
            PIC
            WKS
    GROUPS
        ACCTNG
            WORDS
            PIC
            WKS
        MRKTNG
            WORDS
            PIC
            WKS
    DEFAULTS
        GILLETT
        CURRID
        KRUEGER
        JORDEN
        CLARK
    PROGRAMS
53 sub-directories found
```

Figure 9.5: LISTDIR listing of subdirectory structure

subdirectories, named IBM_PC and COMPAQ. In addition, the network will allow multiple versions of DOS to boot the workstations.

The use of multiple versions of DOS does not create a problem in the NetWare environment, but it does require a little management.

We discussed the LONG MACHINE TYPE variable in Chapter 8. As you'll see in the next chapter, we'll use the LONG MACHINE TYPE variable in the user login script to direct NetWare to the appropriate version of DOS on the file server.

To prepare the file server, you must copy the DOS files from the original DOS disks to the corresponding subdirectories. For example, to copy the Compaq DOS (version 3.1) files, place the first DOS disk in drive A and enter the following commands:

```
CD\DOS\COMPAQ\V3.1
NCOPY A:\*.*
FLAG *.* SRO
```

The first command simply changes the default directory to the appropriate DOS subdirectory. NCOPY (NetWare's version of the DOS COPY command) copies all of the files from drive A to the DOS subdirectory. The FLAG command flags all of the files as shareable/read only (SRO) so that multiple users can read the files, but cannot modify or delete them. Continue the copy process until all of the DOS files have been copied to the file server.

LOADING APPLICATIONS AND DATA

The next step is to load the software applications and any data needed on the file server. In general, the installation procedure for network software is similar to that for applications on standalone computers. The only difference is where the files are loaded on the hard disk. For example, when you load Lotus 1-2-3, the files are copied to the PROGRAMS\LOTUS subdirectory. Make sure, however, that you are installing a network version of the software. Not only is it usually illegal to run single-user versions of a software package on a network, but such versions frequently will not perform as intended when multiple users attempt to access the same files.

When loading network software, you will generally use the FLAG command to flag the files as shareable/read only (SRO). Some software, however, needs to write to files during application execution. Thus, some files must be flagged shareable/read-write (SRW). To load applications properly, carefully follow the installation documentation. Otherwise, problems may occur later, and diagnosing software anomalies that result from incorrect file flags can be time consuming and frustrating.

Multiple-version software is usually licensed either to a site or to a particular number of simultaneous users. With site-licensed software, an unlimited number of simultaneous users can run the application at the licensed site. Software licensed for a maximum number of simultaneous users may come with a sophisticated counter that monitors the number of active users and blocks access when the maximum number is reached. Alternatively, the software manufacturer may rely on the honor system to restrict the number of users.

With the application software installed, you can execute an application by changing the default directory to the program subdirectory and entering the appropriate command. In the next chapter, we'll create batch files that automatically remap drives to simplify the process of running application programs.

SUMMARY

This chapter discussed the basics of network directories and drive maps. In addition, we created the directory structure for our example file server hard disk and loaded the application software. The next chapter continues this network preparation by showing you how to write login scripts and batch files to manage LAN operations.

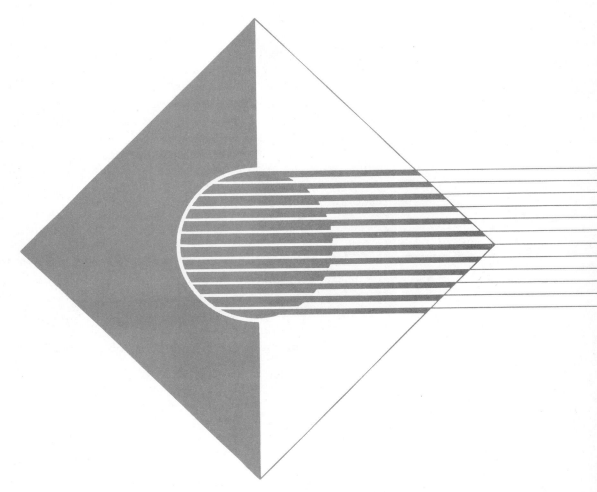

ADDING USERS AND GROUPS

*F*AST *T*RACK

You can set up three categories of users: **137**
  network supervisors, network operators, and regular network
  users. Because of the broad range of power given to supervisors, you should limit the number of users with supervisor
  rights. Network operators can be defined as regular network
  users who have been granted additional privileges to use some
  of the special network utilities.

Network groups can be defined by   **138**
  function or project. For example, a functional group could be
  all users who are members of the accounting department.
  A project group could be all users who are working on a specific
  project.

To add, change, or delete a user,   **138**
  use the SYSCON utility. (Make sure you are logged on to the
  network as a supervisor or as a user with supervisor rights.)

  1. Select User Information from the SYSCON menu.
  2. Press **Ins** to add a new user.
  3. Enter the name of the user (we recommend limiting the
     user name to eight characters so that user names later
     can be used as subdirectory names).
  4. Follow the menu to add other information. Recommended
     information is Change Password (to use an initial
     password) and Full Name.

To add a group,   **142**

use SYSCON.

1. From the SYSCON Available Topics menu, choose Group Information and press **Ins**.

2. Enter the name of the new group (for example, **ACCTNG**) and press ←⏎.

3. Highlight ACCTNG and press ←⏎ to display the Group Information menu.

4. Fill in the group's full name and assign group members. To add new group members, highlight Members and select from the user list.

To display online help for any of the NetWare utilities,   **144**

press **F1**. Help is context sensitive. To leave the help function, press **Esc**.

CHAPTER *10*

OUR NEXT MAJOR TASK IN PREPARING OUR LOCAL
area network is adding users and groups to the system. This chapter
describes how the NetWare system configuration utility, SYSCON,
manages the addition, modification, and deletion of users and
groups. The chapter begins with a discussion of the various types of
network users. It also discusses how groups can be used to facilitate
data sharing and network security. Next, the chapter presents the
mechanics of adding users and groups. The chapter ends with a discussion of security considerations.

DEFINING NETWORK USERS

NetWare recognizes three levels of users: network supervisors, network operators, and regular network users.

The highest level of user is the network supervisor. Network supervisors have access to all NetWare utilities (such as SYSCON) and all subdirectories on the network's hard disk. NetWare automatically creates a
SUPERVISOR user when the operating system is installed. In addition, other users can be granted supervisor rights.

Because of the broad authority granted to supervisors, you will want
to limit the number of people with supervisor privileges. You may also
want to set up different user names for supervisors to use when they are
performing supervisor activities. For example, you might want to give
Ken Krueger the user name of KRUEGER for regular network work
and the supervisor name of SKRUEGER for supervisor activities. Such
a naming system can help prevent problems arising from a supervisor's
ability to modify and delete files.

The second level of user is the network operator. These individuals
are regular network users who have been granted additional privileges
to use one or more of the NetWare utilities. For example, you might

grant a network maintenance technician access to FCONSOLE, the file server console utility, to check the efficiency of the file server.

The third type of user is the regular network user. Most of the people who use your local area network will fall into this classification. The regular network user typically has access only to his or her own data files and to application programs such as Lotus 1-2-3 and WordPerfect.

DEFINING NETWORK GROUPS

Network users can also be grouped to permit them to share data. By granting group privileges to a subdirectory, for example, the members of a group can access shared files that are not available to other network users. In addition, the NetWare SEND command (discussed in Chapter 16) can direct messages to all members of a group. Most network electronic-mail applications also permit you to route mail to all members of a network group.

Groups are usually defined in either of two ways: by function or by project. A functional group, such as the ACCTNG group that we will add to this network, includes all of the individuals that perform a particular task. A project group is composed of individuals working on a particular project. Project groups often cross functional boundaries.

ADDING, CHANGING, AND DELETING USERS

Three steps are necessary to add users to the network. First, you must physically update the network's bindery with the name of the new user. (The bindery is the database maintained by the network's operating system to keep track of users, groups, servers, and so on.) Second, you must modify the account restrictions as necessary and set the initial password for the user. Third, you need to enter the full name of the user.

As already mentioned, the NetWare utility for creating and modifying users and groups is SYSCON. To access the SYSCON utility, type **SYSCON** at the DOS prompt. The screen that appears will look similar to Figure 10.1.

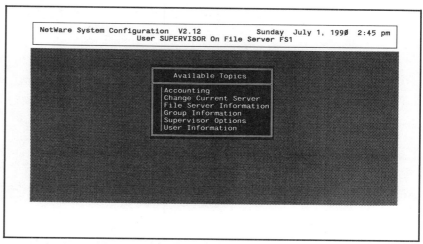

```
NetWare System Configuration  V2.12          Sunday  July 1, 1990  2:45 pm
                          User SUPERVISOR On File Server FS1



                            ┌─────────────────────┐
                            │   Available Topics   │
                            ├─────────────────────┤
                            │ Accounting           │
                            │ Change Current Server │
                            │ File Server Information │
                            │ Group Information    │
                            │ Supervisor Options   │
                            │ User Information     │
                            └─────────────────────┘
```

Figure 10.1: SYSCON screen

To add a new user to our network, select the User Information option on the Available Topics menu by highlighting it and pressing ←⏎. A window will then appear displaying a list of the current users.

Since we have not added any additional users, the two default users created automatically by NETGEN—SUPERVISOR and GUEST—are all that are listed. The user SUPERVISOR is granted access to all directories on the network; these privileges cannot be modified or revoked, and the user SUPERVISOR cannot be renamed or deleted. The user GUEST is granted no explicit access privileges. However, since the user GUEST is a member of the group EVERYONE, any privileges granted to this group also apply to GUEST. The user GUEST can be modified and even deleted from the network.

Let's add a user. Press the **Ins** key while the User Names window is displayed. A small window will appear with a prompt for the new user name. Enter the name of the user you are adding (for example, **CURRID**), as shown in Figure 10.2. The user name can be any unique combination of alphanumeric characters up to 47 characters long. (However, we'll limit our user names to eight characters. This restriction will allow us to use user names as subdirectory names in the PRIVATE directory. You will see the importance of this approach when we create the login scripts in the next chapter.) When you are finished, press ←⏎. The new user will be added to the User Names list.

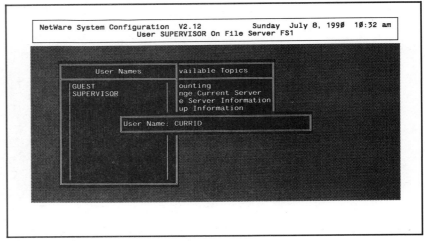

Figure 10.2: Adding a new user name

To change the default properties associated with the new user, highlight the name and press ←⏎. The User Information menu will appear. This menu lists eleven options, as follows:

Account Balance	When the NetWare accounting functions are used, allows the supervisor to set up the amount of a given service for a user
Account Restrictions	Manages the password and login restrictions for each user
Change Password	Assigns the user's password
Full Name	Permits the entry of the user's full name (for example, Cheryl C. Currid)
Groups Belonged To	Allows the supervisor to add and delete group membership for a user
Login Script	Permits the supervisor to customize the set of instructions that are executed when the user logs in

Other Information	Displays miscellaneous information about the user (such as the time that the user last logged in and the amount of disk space in use)
Security Equivalences	Used by the supervisor when establishing network security
Station Restrictions	Allows the supervisor to limit the locations from which an individual user can log in
Time Restrictions	Allows the supervisor to limit the times that a user can log in
Trustee Assignments	Used by the supervisor when establishing network security

All of these instructions are initially set so that they do not apply. If you want them to apply, you must explicitly set them.

On our LAN, we want to require the use of passwords, so select the Account Restrictions option. A window appears. Move the cursor to the line that reads *Require Password* and press the **Y** key to select Yes. Passwords are now required to access the network.

Set the options as shown in Figure 10.3. You can change any of these restrictions at any time simply by moving the cursor to the corresponding field and entering a new value. For example, you can increase the number of days between required changes of the password or increase the minimum password length for added security. When you are finished modifying the account restrictions, press **Esc**. The User Information menu will reappear.

We are now ready to add the initial password for the new user. To accomplish this, select the Change Password option and enter the password for the user. Typically, you will want to enter something easy to remember, such as **12345**.

The initial password automatically expires when the user first logs in, so its security is not an important issue. However, when users are prompted to change their password, you should encourage them to select one that is difficult for someone else to guess. The use of a spouse's name, for example, is generally not a good choice.

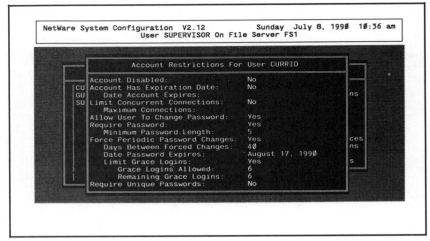

Figure 10.3: Account Restrictions window

The final step in adding a new user is to enter his or her full name. Select the Full Name option from the User Information menu and enter the user's full name (for example, **Cheryl C. Currid**).

The supervisor can change any of the user attributes in the same way that we just selected the initial properties. Now is a good time to change the account restriction for user SUPERVISOR so that a password is required and to set an initial password. To execute these actions, you again use the Account Restrictions and Change Password options on the User Information menu.

Occasionally, you will need to delete a user from the network. The process for deleting users is similar to that for adding users. Let's delete the user GUEST. Press **Esc** to return to the User Name window. Then highlight GUEST and press **Del**. As a safety precaution, NetWare prompts you to make sure that you indeed want to delete the user.

CREATING GROUPS

The process for creating groups is similar to that for adding new users. This process also has three basic steps. First, you define the group by adding it to the network's bindery. Second, you enter the full name of the group. Third, you add the users (or members) to the group.

From the SYSCON Available Topics menu, select the Group Information option. A list of the groups presently defined appears. In our example LAN, the only group listed at this point is EVERYONE.

Like the users SUPERVISOR and GUEST, the group EVERYONE is created automatically when NetWare is installed. When new users are added, they are automatically included in the group EVERYONE. As you'll see in Chapter 12, the group EVERYONE allows the supervisor to establish certain security parameters that apply to all network users. You can, however, delete selected users from the EVERYONE group.

To add a new group, press **Ins**. You will now be prompted to enter the name of the group that is being added. Like user names, group names can be any unique alphanumeric combination up to 47 characters long. Let's enter ACCTNG as our first group name. Type **ACCTNG** and press ←.

Now highlight ACCTNG and press ←. The Group Information menu will appear. This menu offers four options, as follows:

Full Name	Permits the entry of the group's full name (for example, Accounting_Department)
Other Information	Displays miscellaneous information about the group (such as console privileges and the internal group ID)
Trustee Assignments	Used by the supervisor when establishing network security

Select the Full Name option and enter **Accounting_Department** as the full name of the group. To see the group's current members, choose the Member List option. This displays a list of the users included in the group. Since we have not added any members, the list will be empty.

To add group members, press **Ins**. This displays a second window that lists all users who are not included in the group. You can now scroll through the list and select members one at a time by highlighting the user's name and pressing ◀—. (Pressing the first letter of the name you are searching for takes you directly to the first entry that begins with that letter.)

If you are adding several users, you can accelerate the entry process by marking the user name. Highlight the appropriate names and press the **F5** key. When a user name is marked, it will appear as a highlighted entry on the screen. To unmark a user name, highlight the name and press **F5** again. When all of the users that you want to add to the group are marked, press ◀—. They will be added to the group.

Our LAN has three users who need to be included in the ACCTNG group: Currid, Jorden, and Krueger. Figure 10.4 shows the screen after they have been added to the ACCTNG group.

As with users, you can alter groups by changing the attributes from the Group Information menu. Likewise, you can delete a group by highlighting its name and pressing **Del**.

GETTING ONLINE HELP

Any time that you are using one of NetWare's menu utilities (such as SYSCON), you can obtain online help by pressing **F1**. When you

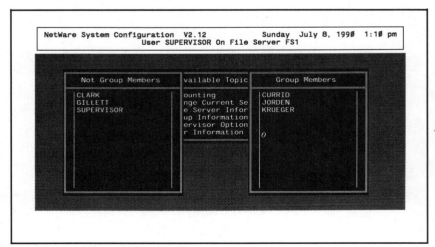

Figure 10.4: Group Members screen

have finished reviewing a help message, press **Esc** to remove it from the screen.

The help messages that appear are context sensitive; that is, they display information about the NetWare function that you are currently using. In addition to describing the function conceptually, the help screens also contain detailed information about the operation being performed. NetWare's online help can be especially useful to a network supervisor who is working with the LAN in a location away from the reference manuals.

SECURITY CONSIDERATIONS

Your group and directory structures provide the foundation for your network's security. As explained further in Chapter 12, two important elements of the NetWare security scheme are trustee security and directory security.

Through trustee security, you can assign directory and file access rights and privileges to individuals and groups. Therefore, the definition of your groups and directories plays an important role in maintaining the security of the network's data (and in simplifying the life of the network administrator). If, for example, you want to limit access to certain files to managers, then you can establish a MANAGEMENT group to which all managers belong. You can then assign trustee rights to the group instead of to each individual manager.

SUMMARY

In this chapter, we added users and groups to our NetWare local area network. The chapter discussed the different types of network users and the role of user groups and presented the mechanics of adding, changing, and deleting users and groups using NetWare's SYSCON utility. In the next chapter, you will learn how to write login scripts to perform various functions as the users log in to the network.

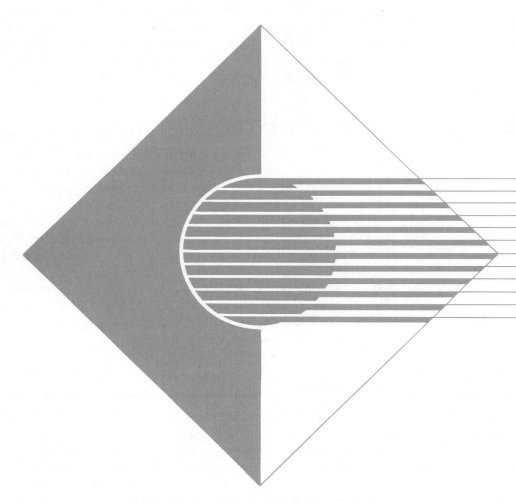

CREATING LOGIN SCRIPTS AND BATCH FILES

FAST TRACK

NetWare uses two types of login scripts: **149**
the system login script and user login scripts. NetWare always
creates the system login script first. Then it executes the user
login scripts (if any).

To begin creating the system login script,   **151**
Log in to the network with supervisor rights and enter **SYSCON**
at the DOS prompt. From the Available Topics menu, select
System Login Script. Enter the text of the login script.

To set up drive maps in the system login script,   **152**
use the MAP command to set up the proper search drives. We
recommend that you always search the SYS:PUBLIC drive
first, then SYS:DEFAULTS, then SYS:UTIL, and finally
SYS:PROGRAMS.

To set up a search drive for DOS,   **154**
map the next search drive. Enter **MAP S5: = FS1/SYS:DOS**
%MACHINE\%OS\%OS_VERSION. This command permits
DOS to be searched from the network.

To set up other (nonsearch) drives,   **154**
use the MAP command to map drive F to **FS1/SYS:LOGIN**.
Map drive G to **FS1/SYS:**. Map drive H to **FS1/SYS:/PRIVATE/**
%LOGIN_NAME. Map drive I to **FS1/SYS:\COMMON**. Map
drive J to **J: = H:.**

In setting up environmental parameters,   **155**
we recommend that you first set the command processor to
the network drive to look for COMMAND.COM. Enter

COMSPEC +S5:COMMAND.COM. Set up one environment variable: **SET USER + "%LOGIN_NAME**. Set the DOS prompt to show the current logged on subdirectory by entering **SET PROMPT PG**. Specify the starting drive as **DRIVE H:**.

To set up a welcome message,   156

use the WRITE statement. You may wish to verify the date, time, user's name, and station number.

To create a user login script   159

1. From the SYSCON Available Topics menu, choose User Information.
2. Select the Login Script option.

The user login script can contain all the system login script commands. Because it is executed after the system login script, the user login script can modify any of the maps or environmental parameters set in the system login script.

To copy a user login script to another user,   161

use SYSCON. Choose User Information from the Available Topics menu. Then select the user that you want to receive the login script. If the user doesn't have a login script, you can type the name of the user you want to copy the script from at the next prompt.

To map drives in batch files,   164

include the MAP command in the batch file. This method always positions the users exactly where you want them before they execute a program.

CHAPTER *11*

UP TO THIS POINT, WHEN YOU LOGGED IN TO THE file server, the NetWare default login script set up the drive maps. Usually, however, you will want to create your own login scripts to customize the operating environment for your LAN users.

In this chapter, we'll explore the use of login scripts to assign drive maps, establish various system parameters, and display a friendly user interface. Then we'll write program batch files that dynamically modify the drive maps as they are executed. We'll begin with a general discussion of the types of login scripts and then work through the actual process of writing commands.

TYPES OF LOGIN SCRIPTS

A login script is nothing more than a small computer program containing instructions that execute as a user logs in to the network. The system login script provides a uniform set of commands for all users on the network. Only the supervisor can create or modify system login scripts. In addition, each user can have a personal login script that executes after the system login script. Both the supervisor and network user can create and modify personal login scripts.

As you write the login scripts for your network, the best strategy is to place as many commands as possible in the system login script. This helps maintain consistency across the network and makes maintenance easier because only one login script has to be modified when changes are necessary.

LOGIN SCRIPT COMMANDS

NetWare recognizes 18 login script commands and also allows you to run some external programs during the execution of the login script. Table 1.1 lists the NetWare login script commands and their functions.

Table 11.1: NetWare Login Scripts

COMMAND	FUNCTION
ATTACH	Connects the user to another file server
BREAK	Permits the user to abort login script execution by pressing **Ctrl-Break** or **Ctrl-C**
COMSPEC	Specifies the location of the correct version of the command processor (COMMAND.COM)
[F]DISPLAY	If DISPLAY is specified, displays the contents of a specified file; if FDISPLAY is specified, filters out any special characters in the document and displays only the text
DOS BREAK	Permits the user to abort the execution of any program or DOS command after logging in
DOS SET	Sets a variable in the DOS environment to a specified value
DOS VERIFY	Verifies that data copied to a local drive has been replicated without errors
DRIVE	Specifies a drive other than the first network drive as the default drive
EXIT	Terminates login script execution
FIRE PHASERS	Emits a noise that can be used to alert the user to an error or to some other condition
IF...THEN	Permits the conditional processing of login script commands
INCLUDE	Allows the inclusion of subscripts that contain login script commands not included in the current login script
MACHINE NAME	Sets the machine name of the workstation to a specified name

Table 11.1: NetWare Login Scripts (continued)

COMMAND	FUNCTION
MAP	Used with a variety of parameters to manage and display drive maps
PAUSE	Creates a pause in login script execution
PCCOMPATIBLE	Tells the operating system that the workstation is an IBM-compatible computer
REMARK	Allows the insertion of explanatory text into the login script
WRITE	Displays custom messages on the screen during login script processing

In addition to these commands, the # symbol can be used to execute a program (such as a menu program) that is external to the login script.

CREATING THE SYSTEM LOGIN SCRIPT

Writing a NetWare login script is similar to creating any other computer program. To help ensure that the script performs as you want, your first step is to outline the desired functions. We want the system login script to perform three basic functions for all users:

- Set up the drive maps
- Define the environmental parameters
- Display a welcome message

To begin writing the system login script, log in to the network as user **SUPERVISOR** (remember that only the supervisor can create or modify the system login script). Then enter **SYSCON** at the DOS prompt to bring up the NetWare system configuration utility. Choose the Supervisor Options selection from the Available Topics menu and then choose the System Login Script option from the submenu.

Your workstation will display a blank screen that operates like a text editor or simple word processor. You can enter text and move around the screen with the arrow keys. You can use the **Ins** key to insert a line at the position of the cursor, and you can use the **Del** and **Backspace** keys to erase characters.

Let's begin creating the system login script by typing a header to identify the script, as shown here.

```
* * * * * * * * * * * * *FS1 Login Script
* * * * * * * * * * * * * * * *Created 7/22/90 by Craig Gillett
```

Your screen should look like Figure 11.1. The asterisk (*) can be used in lieu of the REMARK command to insert explanatory text into the login script. Lines preceded by an asterisk are ignored when the login script is processed.

SETTING UP THE DRIVE MAPS

Your next step in the development of the system login script is to define the drive maps. You'll need search drive maps so that NetWare can find programs in different subdirectories and store data files in other mapped drives.

For our example network, we'll define search drives for the following subdirectories:

PUBLIC

DEFAULTS

PROGRAMS

UTIL

In addition, we'll use identifier variables to map a drive to the subdirectory that contains the proper version of the disk operating system for each workstation.

We'll start by adding a comment line that explains the purpose of the commands, as shown here.

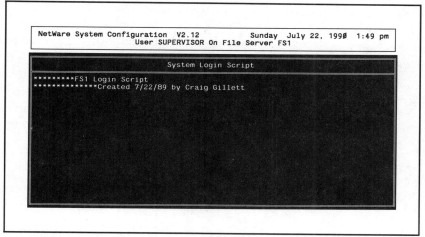

```
NetWare System Configuration  V2.12              Sunday  July 22, 1990  1:49 pm
                       User SUPERVISOR On File Server FS1

                              System Login Script
*********FS1 Login Script
**************Created 7/22/89 by Craig Gillett
```

Figure 11.1: System login script text editor


```
* * * * * * * * * * * * * * * * * * * * * * * * * * * * * * * * * * * * *
* Set up drive maps
* * * * * * * * * * * * * * * * * * * * * * * * * * * * * * * * * * * * *
```

Next, we'll turn off the login script and error messages screen display with the following commands:

```
SET DISPLAY OFF
MAP ERRORS OFF
```

If the login script does not execute correctly, you can remove these commands (or use REMARK to keep them from executing) so that you can use the screen display and error messages to facilitate debugging.

We'll use the MAP command to establish the search drive maps for the PUBLIC, DEFAULTS, PROGRAMS, and UTIL subdirectories. Enter these lines of code:

```
MAP S1: = FS1/SYS:PUBLIC
MAP S2: = FS1/SYS:DEFAULTS
MAP S3: = FS1/SYS:UTIL
MAP S4: = FS1/SYS:PROGRAMS
```

The final search drive map will be for the DOS subdirectory that corresponds to the version of the disk operating system used to boot the individual workstation. We can build intelligence into this command by using identifier variables. These variables contain text values, stored by NetWare, that describe various system parameters such as the user's full name, the operating system, and the workstation number. When used in a login script command, identifier variables must be preceded by a percentage sign (%) and typed in uppercase letters.

Recall from Chapter 9 that the DOS subdirectory has three components:

- Machine type (for example, IBM_PC)
- Operating system (for example, MS_DOS)
- Version number (for example, V3.2)

Each component has an identifier variable that can be used to define the DOS subdirectory search drive map. Enter the following code:

MAP S5: = FS1/SYS:DOS\\%MACHINE\\%OS\\%OS_VERSION

The remaining drives that we'll map in the system login script will not be searchable. To access the files stored in these drives, the user (or program) will have to change subdirectories by typing the drive letter followed by a colon (for example, **F:**) and pressing ←┘.

Let's map one drive to the LOGIN subdirectory, one drive to the root directory of volume SYS, two drives to the user's home subdirectory, and one drive to the COMMON subdirectory. As you can see here, the identifier variable for the user's login name is used to map the drive to the home directory.

```
MAP F: = FS1/SYS:LOGIN
MAP G: = FS1/SYS:
MAP H: = FS1/SYS:\PRIVATE\LOGIN_NAME
MAP I: = FS1/SYS:\COMMON
MAP J: = H:
```

When using the LOGIN_NAME identifier variable to map the home subdirectory, make sure that login names are no longer than eight characters (the maximum number of characters allowed for a subdirectory name).

DEFINING THE ENVIRONMENTAL PARAMETERS

Your next task is to define the various environmental parameters that will be used by the network and any application programs. Again, we'll begin by entering a few lines of explanatory text to document the login script, as shown here.

```
* * * * * * * * * * * * * * * * * * * * * * * * * * * * * * * * * * * * * * * *
* Specify the operating system directory, set DOS
*   environment variable for login name, set prompt
*   designator, change to home directory
* * * * * * * * * * * * * * * * * * * * * * * * * * * * * * * * * * * * * * * *
```

The most important parameter is the location of the appropriate version of the command processor so that NetWare can find this processor when reloading is required. We have already mapped a search drive to the subdirectory corresponding to the version of DOS being run on the workstation. Now we can enter the COMSPEC command to prepare NetWare to reload the proper COMMAND-.COM, as follows:

```
COMSPEC = S5:COMMAND.COM
```

Some programs require the use of DOS environmental variables. These can be set at the DOS command line, or you can integrate them into a login script. For our example, let's set the variable USER to the value of the login name. Enter the following command:

```
SET USER = "%LOGIN_NAME"
```

Note that the syntax requires the use of quotation marks around the variable value.

Later in this chapter, we'll also use the DOS environment variable to help control the batch files used to access application programs.

You can also use the SET command to modify the command-line prompt. For our example, enter the following command to display the current subdirectory and a greater-than sign (for example, *Z:\PUBLIC>*):

> SET PROMPT PG

The final environmental condition that we'll include in the system login script is a command to change the current subdirectory to the user's home directory. You accomplish this with the DRIVE command, as follows:

> DRIVE H:

DISPLAYING A WELCOME MESSAGE

The final module of the system login script creates a custom welcome message. Here, we'll use the DISPLAY command to display a color ANSI screen (as described in Chapter 8). We'll also use several WRITE statements to customize the screen.

As always, we'll begin by adding internal documentation, as shown here.

> ```
> * * * * * * * * * * * * * * * * * * * * * * * * * * * * * * * * * * * * * * * * * * * * * * *
> * Display welcome screen (LOGIN.SCN) and message
> * * * * * * * * * * * * * * * * * * * * * * * * * * * * * * * * * * * * * * * * * * * * * * *
> ```

The DISPLAY command simply displays the contents of a specified file. If the file contains ANSI codes (and ANSI.SYS is installed as a device driver), the colors and other screen attributes will be displayed.

Create an ANSI screen named LOGIN.SCN (using the techniques described in Chapter 8) and copy it to the UTIL subdirectory. Then the following command will display the welcome message when the login script is executed:

> DISPLAY FS1/SYS:UTIL\LOGIN.SCN

You can further customize the login message by using the WRITE command. This command allows you to display both text strings and identifier variables on the screen. The syntax for the WRITE command is straightforward. Both text and identifiers must be surrounded by quotation marks. Having a semicolon at the end of the line displays the next combination of text strings and identifiers on the same line.

Enter the following command lines to insert three blank lines and then display a custom greeting that contains the user's full name and other system variables:

```
WRITE " "
WRITE " "
WRITE " "
WRITE "    Good %GREETING_TIME, %FULL_NAME."
WRITE "    You are logged on station: %STATION using %OS";
WRITE " %OS_VERSION"
WRITE "    Current time and date: %HOUR:%MINUTE %AM_PM – ";
WRITE "%MONTH_NAME %DAY, %YEAR"
WRITE " "
```

Finally, to keep the message from scrolling by, enter **PAUSE** in the final line of the login script. Figure 11.2 contains a complete listing of the system login script.

To save the login script, press **Esc**. Then follow the prompts to exit SYSCON.

TESTING THE SYSTEM LOGIN SCRIPT

To test the system login script, log in as user SUPERVISOR. Since the command MAP DISPLAY OFF is included at the beginning of the script, nothing will appear on the screen as the script executes, until the DISPLAY statement is reached. Then a welcome screen similar to Figure 11.3 will appear.

Because the last line contains a PAUSE command, the script will stop executing until a key is pressed. Then the default login script will execute, because we have not yet written a user login script for the system supervisor. The current drive maps will be displayed, as shown here.

```
Drive  A:  maps to a local disk.
Drive  B:  maps to a local disk.
Drive  C:  maps to a local disk.
```

```
**********FS1 System Login Script
***************Created 7/22/90 by Craig Gillett

***************************************************************************
* Set up drive mappings
***************************************************************************

MAP DISPLAY OFF
MAP ERRORS OFF

MAP S1:=FS1/SYS:PUBLIC
MAP S2:=FS1/SYS:DEFAULTS
MAP S3:=FS1/SYS:UTIL
MAP S4:=FS1/SYS:PROGRAMS
MAP S5:=FS1/SYS:DOS\%MACHINE\%OS\%OS_VERSION
MAP F:=FS1/SYS:LOGIN
MAP G:=FS1/SYS:
MAP H:=FS1/SYS:PRIVATE\%LOGIN_NAME
MAP I:=FS1/SYS:COMMON
MAP J:=H:

***************************************************************************
* Specify the operating system directory, set DOS environment variable for
*  login name, set prompt designator, change to home directory
***************************************************************************

COMSPEC=S5:COMMAND.COM
SET USER = "%LOGIN_NAME"
SET PROMPT = "$P$G"
DRIVE H:

***************************************************************************
* Display welcome screen (LOGIN.SCN) and message
***************************************************************************

DISPLAY FS1/SYS:UTIL\LOGIN.SCN

WRITE " "
WRITE " "
WRITE " "
WRITE "                     Good %GREETING_TIME, %FULL_NAME."
WRITE " "
WRITE " %OS_VERSION"
WRITE "           You are logged on station:  %STATION using %OS";
WRITE " %OS_VERSION"
WRITE "               Current time and date:  %HOUR:%MINUTE %AM_PM -- ";
WRITE "%MONTH_NAME %DAY, %YEAR"
WRITE " "
PAUSE
```

Figure 11.2: System login script

Drive F: = FS1/SYS:LOGIN
Drive G: = FS1/SYS:
Drive I: = FS1/SYS:COMMON

SEARCH1: = Z:. [FS1/SYS:PUBLIC]
SEARCH2: = Y:. [FS1/SYS:DEFAULTS]
SEARCH3: = X:. [FS1/SYS:UTIL]
SEARCH4: = W:. [FS1/SYS:PROGRAMS]
SEARCH5: = V:. [FS1/SYS:DOS/IBM_PC/MSDOS/V3.30]

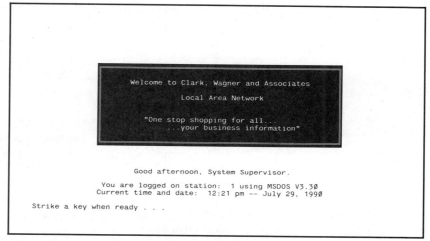

```
          Welcome to Clark, Wagner and Associates
                     Local Area Network

               "One stop shopping for all...
                    ...your business information"
```

```
              Good afternoon, System Supervisor.
          You are logged on station:  1 using MSDOS V3.3Ø
          Current time and date:  12:21 pm -- July 29, 199Ø

   Strike a key when ready . . .
```

Figure 11.3: Welcome screen

Note that drives H and J, which should be mapped to the supervisor's home directory, are absent from the drive maps. These drives are not listed because user name SUPERVISOR exceeds eight characters (the maximum length of a DOS subdirectory name). Therefore, an error occurred when the system reached the following command in the system login script:

MAP H: = FS1/SYS:PRIVATE\\%LOGIN_NAME

To avoid such a problem, in Chapter 10 we established the strategy of limiting login names to no more than eight characters. We cannot change the login name of the system supervisor (SUPERVISOR), so we'll have to correct the problem in the supervisor's user login script.

CREATING A USER LOGIN SCRIPT

To create an individual login script, access the SYSCON utility and choose the User Information option from the Available Topics menu. Then select the user (in this case, SUPERVISOR) from the list of login names and select the Login Script option from the User

Information menu. The screen that appears is similar to the editor for creating the system login script, and it works in the same way.

Let's begin by correcting the map to the home directory for the system supervisor. You can accomplish this by explicitly mapping drive H to the SYS:\PRIVATE\SUPER subdirectory. Enter the following command lines:

```
**************************************************
* Correct map for user Supervisor (required because
*    login name exceeds eight character subdirectory name
*    limit)
**************************************************

MAP H: = FS1/SYS:PRIVATE\SUPER
MAP M: = H:
DRIVE H:
```

We also need to explicitly change the DOS USER environment variable. Let's use the SET command to set the USER variable to SUPER. Enter

```
SET USER = "SUPER"
```

In addition to correcting problems, you can also add other commands to the login script that are unique to the user (or to groups of users). For example, you can include a birthday surprise that checks the current date and compares it to the user's birth date. Once a year for each user, when the dates match, "phasers" fire, and a special birthday greeting is displayed.

Suppose that the supervisor's birthday is December 2. Enter the following code to fire the phasers and display an ANSI screen named BDAY.SCN on her special day. (To create the custom ANSI screen, see Chapter 8.)

```
**************************************************
* Check date and if user's birthday, fire phasers and
*    display birthday message (requires correct birth date
*    in each users' login script)
**************************************************
```

```
IF MONTH = "12" AND DAY = "02" THEN BEGIN
    FIRE PHASERS 5 TIMES
    DISPLAY FS1/SYS:UTIL\BDAY.SCN
    FIRE PHASERS 6 TIMES
PAUSE
END
```

Of course, there are myriad uses for this type of logic. For example, you could use a WRITE command to display a text file named NEWS.TXT when certain conditions are met. Or once a month you could display a message reminding your staff that their status reports are due.

The last command that we'll include in the user login script executes the NetWare menu application (menus are discussed in Chapter 13). Because this is an external program, you must precede the command by a number sign (#). The code, including internal documentation, is shown here.

```
* * * * * * * * * * * * * * * * * * * * * * * * * * * * * * * * * * * * * * *
* Execute menu program
* * * * * * * * * * * * * * * * * * * * * * * * * * * * * * * * * * * * * * *
```

```
#MENU MAIN
```

Figure 11.4 contains a complete listing of the user login script for the system supervisor.

To save your work, press **Esc**. Then follow the prompts to exit SYSCON.

COPYING USER LOGIN SCRIPTS

Now you can create the individual login scripts for each user. Fortunately, you won't have to "reinvent the wheel" for each LAN user. Using SYSCON, you can copy an existing login script to another user and then make any changes necessary.

To copy a user login script, enter **SYSCON** and choose the User Information option from the Available Topics menu. Next, select the

```
*************************************************************
* Correct mapping for user Supervisor (required because
*    login name exceeds eight character subdirectory name
*    limit)
*************************************************************
MAP H:=FS1/SYS:PRIVATE\SUPER
MAP M: = H:
DRIVE H:

SET USER = "SUPER"

*************************************************************
* Check date and if user's birthday, fire phasers and
*    display birthday message (requires correct birth date
*    in each users' login script
*************************************************************

IF MONTH = "12" AND DAY = "02" THEN BEGIN
    FIRE PHASERS 5 TIMES
    DISPLAY FIS1/SYS:UTIL\BDAY.SCN
    FIRE PHASERS 6 TIMES
PAUSE
END


*************************************************************
* Execute menu program
*************************************************************

#MENU MAIN
```

Figure 11.4: User login script

user that you want to receive the login script. For this example, select Clark. Then choose the Login Script option from the User Information menu. As shown in Figure 11.5, user Clark does not currently have a login script, so SYSCON prompts you for the user from which to read an existing script. Let's use the script we created for the system supervisor as a model. Enter **SUPERVISOR** and press ←.

The next display will be the login script editor that contains the commands from the supervisor's script. You can edit these as necessary to customize the login process for the user. In this case, we need to remove the first module that contains the code for correcting the map to the supervisor's home directory. You can mark these lines of code by pressing the Mark key (**F5**) and moving the cursor to highlight the commands to be deleted. To eliminate the commands, press **Del**.

We also need to change the birth date in the second module. User Clark's birthday is July 22, so replace the month and day in the IF statement with **07** and **22**. The modified login script will appear in the editor as shown in Figure 11.6.

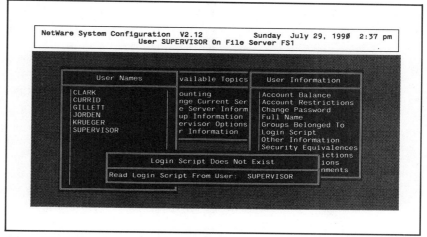

Figure 11.5: Copying a user login script

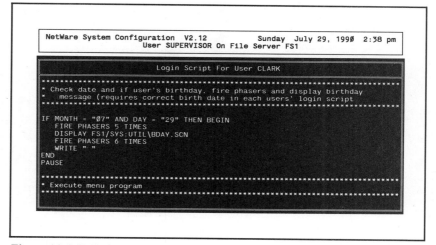

Figure 11.6: Editing a user login script

Save the login script by pressing **Esc** and responding Yes to the prompt asking if you want to save it. This login script can now be copied to other users by the same process. Remember: Unless you want to use the default login script, every user must have a user login script.

WRITING PROGRAM BATCH FILES WITH DYNAMIC DRIVE MAPPING

Accessing an application program, such as WordPerfect, requires three steps. First, the drive maps must be changed so that the system can find the application files and store the data files in the correct subdirectory. Second, the program must be executed. Third, the original drive maps must be restored.

To ensure that programs execute from the correct subdirectory, we'll explicitly remap the drives rather than use the DOS change directory command. As your network grows and you add volumes and perhaps even additional file servers, ensuring that programs execute from the right place becomes increasingly important. Few problems frustrate a user more than not being able to find data files because they were inadvertently saved to the wrong location.

PREPARING THE BATCH FILE

To simplify the application access process for the user, we can write a single batch file that allows the user to execute all steps by making a single menu bar selection.

For this example, we'll execute WordPerfect, which is located in the FS1/SYS:\PROGRAMS\WP subdirectory, and we will set up FS1/SYS:\PRIVATE\SUPER\WORDS as the default directory.

Recall that drive W is currently mapped to FS1/SYS:\PROGRAMS as a search drive. The first step is to change the drive map to FS1/SYS:\PROGRAMS\WP so that NetWare can find the WordPerfect program files. You accomplish this with a MAP command such as this:

```
MAP W: = FS1/SYS:\PROGRAMS\WP
```

When you enter the MAP command, NetWare displays the following prompt:

```
Drive W: is used by the following search map:
SEARCH3:
Do you want to change it? (Y/N)  Y
```

The default response is Yes, so the user could simply press ⏎ to confirm the map change. However, we want to automate the confirmation so that the user need not respond to the prompt. To do this, we will "pipe in" a response to the prompt. We will always want to answer the prompt with a *Y*, for Yes, so we can create a small file that automatically enters **Y** when NetWare asks for confirmation.

To create the file, change to drive W, which is a search drive mapped to the UTIL subdirectory. Then use a DOS COPY CON command to create a file named Y.CMD that contains the single character *Y*, as follows:

```
COPY CON Y.CMD
Y
[F6]
```

When we actually write the batch file a little later, we will enter the MAP command as follows:

```
MAP W: = FS1/SYS:\PROGRAMS\WP < Y.CMD
```

The less-than sign will pipe in the file named Y.CMD, which contains the character *Y*. This file will answer the prompt, and the batch file will proceed to the next command.

Since drive W was originally set up as a search drive, it retains the search attribute. Therefore, NetWare will be able to locate files within the subdirectory, even if a request is executed from another area on the drive.

Our next step is to write a MAP to change the drive H map so that the document files created in WordPerfect can be stored in the user's PRIVATE subdirectory. When we change the map of drive H, the home directory, we need to include the user's login name. The system login script included a SET command that created a DOS environmental variable named USER. The value of USER is the user's login name. We can use this variable in batch files as a parameter for the MAP command. The following command will change the drive H map to the appropriate subdirectory:

```
MAP H: = FS1/SYS:\PRIVATE\%USER\WORDS
```

As before, when the command is entered, NetWare will ask for a confirmation of the request to change the map. Again we always want to respond Yes, so we'll include the %CMD file here, too, entering the command

```
MAP H: = FS1/SYS:\PRIVATE\%USER%\WORDS < Y.CMD
```

The percent signs surrounding *USER* tell the operating system to replace %USER% with the value of the DOS environmental variable named USER (the user's login name) when executing the command.

WRITING THE BATCH FILE

We are now ready to write the batch file to execute WordPerfect. As with other batch files, we'll store them in the UTIL subdirectory, which has a search drive (W) mapped to it. Storing all batch files in UTIL ensures that we will be able to find them when we need them.

Using a text editor, let's first add commands to the batch file that will turn the display off and clear the screen. We'll also add several comment lines that provide information about the batch file. Enter the following:

```
ECHO OFF
CLS
:FILE NAME        : WP1.BAT
:DESCRIPTION      : WORDPERFECT BATCH FILE
:CREATED          : CAG 06/19/90
:LAST UPDATE      :
```

The next command lines of the batch file remap drives W and H. Enter

```
MAP W: = FS1/SYS:\PROGRAMS\WP < Y.CMD
MAP H: = FS1/SYS:\PRIVATE\%USER%\WORDS < Y.CMD
```

To execute WordPerfect, we need to change the default drive to H so that the document files will be stored in the correct location. Then we need to enter **WP** to execute the program. To perform these functions, enter

```
H:
WP
```

Finally, when the user is finished working in WordPerfect, restore the original drive maps and make sure the default directory is changed to drive H. Enter these commands:

```
MAP W: = FS1/SYS:\PROGRAMS
MAP H: = FS1/SYS:\PRIVATE\%USER%
H:
```

Save the batch file with the name **WP1.BAT**. Be careful not to name a program batch file with the same name as the program's executable file (for instance, as WP). If you do, the operating system will attempt to execute the first of the files that it encounters, which may not be the file you want.

To test the batch file, enter **WP1**. The batch file is in a search directory, so you do not need to change directories to execute it. After exiting the program, type **MAP** to make sure that the drive maps have been properly restored.

SUMMARY

In this chapter, we created both system and user login scripts. In addition to customizing the login process, we used login script commands to define various environmental parameters and to set up the initial drive maps. Once the environment was established, we wrote a sample batch file that dynamically remaps drives before an application program is executed.

If you attempt to run the batch file as any user other than SUPERVISOR, you'll find that it does not function correctly. The reason is that NetWare's security requires the explicit granting of security rights. Therefore, for example, user Clark does not have access to the subdirectory where the WordPerfect files are located. In the next chapter, we'll define and implement a security strategy for the network.

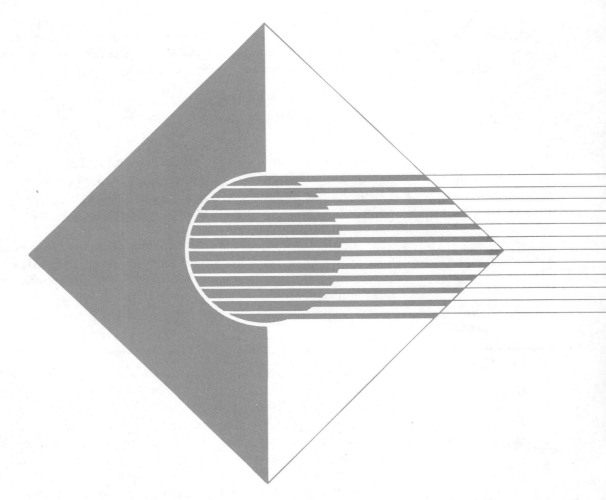

ESTABLISHING NETWORK SECURITY

Fast Track

To limit concurrent connections for a user   **174**

1. Log on to the LAN as a supervisor and execute SYSCON from the DOS prompt.
2. Choose User Information from the Available Topics menu.
3. Select a user and press ↵.
4. Choose the Account Restrictions option and use the ↓ key to move to the line that says *Limit Concurrent Connections: No*. Then change the response to Yes.
5. On the next line, indicate the maximum number of connections for the user.

To implement intruder detection and lockout,   **175**

choose Supervisors Options from the Available Topics Menu. Then select Intruder Detection/Lockout and type **Y** for Yes.

To restrict a user's LAN access times,   **176**

choose User Information from the Available Topics menu. Next, select a user and press ↵. Then select Time Restriction and use the arrow keys to move about the time matrix. To remove times, use the **Del** key. To add times, insert an asterisk (*) next to the time.

To set default time restrictions for new users,   **177**

choose Supervisors Options from the Available Topics menu. Select Default Time Restrictions and make the necessary changes.

To add trustee security   **177**

1. Choose User Information from the Available Topics menu.

2. Select a user and press ↵.

3. Choose Trustee Assignments.

4. To add additional subdirectories, press **Ins**.

To add trustee security to a group,   **180**
choose Group Information from the Available Topics menu.
Select a group and press ↵. Then choose Trustee Assignments.

To grant rights through security equivalences,   **181**
you can use the SYSCON utility to assign rights granted to one
user to another group or user. Use the User Information option
to assign rights to users and the Group Information option to
assign rights to groups.

To remove rights,   **183**
go to the trustee assignments window for a user or group and
highlight the subdirectory you want to remove. Then press **Del**.

To add directory security,   **184**
you can adjust the maximum rights mask. Restrictions entered
on this way take precedence over trustee rights. You can modify
the maximum rights mask for a directory with the FILER utility. Make sure you are logged on as a supervisor.

To determine effective rights,   **185**
enter **RIGHTS** at the DOS prompt.

To add file and directory attributes,   **187**
set the attributes as shown in Table 12.2.

CHAPTER *12*

AS WITH ANY MULTIUSER COMPUTER SYSTEM, whether a mainframe, minicomputer, or personal computer network, security is critical to maintaining the integrity of data stored on your NetWare local area network. In this chapter, we'll develop and implement a security strategy for our LAN using the four levels of file server security available through NetWare, outlined in Chapter 5. These security levels are

- Login and password security
- Trustee security
- Directory security
- File and directory attributes security

DEVELOPING A NETWORK SECURITY STRATEGY

Effective network security requires planning and attention to details. If the strategy is not well thought out, security loopholes can cause problems. For example, you want users to be able to read the disk operating system files; however, you don't want them to be able to delete them. Also, you will want to ensure that unauthorized users cannot access files that contain sensitive information.

From a broad perspective, there are two types of network security: (1) user restrictions and (2) directory and file restrictions. User restrictions limit access to certain types of network functions, whereas directory and file restrictions limit access to specific data. In the strategy we develop for our example network, we'll incorporate both types of security.

USER RESTRICTIONS

The first level of network security is password protection. In Chapter 10, we modified the account restrictions for each user to require users to enter a password to access the LAN.

Let's further tighten security with other user restrictions. To prevent an individual user from logging in to the network from several workstations, we will limit the number of concurrent connections. We also will have the network monitor the number of wrong passwords entered by a user, and if they exceed two, lock the user out of the system for 24 hours.

We will also restrict the times of day that a user can access the network. We will allow user Clark to use the network only from 8:00 a.m. to 5:00 p.m. Monday through Friday.

DIRECTORY AND FILE RESTRICTIONS

In addition to global security restrictions, we will also limit the rights that users have when they access (or attempt to access) specific directories and files.

Eight types of rights can be applied to the files and subdirectories within a directory. These are listed in Table 12.1.

Obviously, we will want to assign different rights to the various network subdirectories. For our example system, we'll change rights to the seven subdirectories that we created. However, we'll keep the default rights granted by NetWare for the system subdirectories: PUBLIC, SYSTEM, LOGIN, and MAIL.

The purpose of the COMMON subdirectory is to provide an area for sharing files. Therefore, we'll grant everyone all rights to this subdirectory.

The DOS, UTIL, and PROGRAM subdirectories contain the operating system, utilities, and application programs. For these subdirectories, we'll grant to everyone all rights except parental and delete rights. This will keep users from modifying the underlying directory structure or accidentally removing a program file. We'll also want to ensure that multiple users can access the files stored in these subdirectories, so we'll set the file attributes to shareable and read only.

Table 12.1: Directory and File Rights1

RIGHT	FUNCTION
Read	Permits the user to read (or see) the contents of a file
Write	Permits the user to modify an existing file
Open	Permits the user to open an existing file
Create	Permits the user to create a new file or subdirectory
Delete	Permits the user to delete a file
Parental	Permits the user to create, rename, or delete subdirectories within the directory (the user must also have create, modify, and delete rights)
Search	Permits the user to list the files in the directory
Modify	Permits the user to change the attributes of files in the directory

The PRIVATE and DEFAULTS subdirectories contain user data files and default configuration options. These subdirectories are intended for use by specific individuals, so we'll grant all rights to their corresponding users.

Finally, we'll set restrictions for the ACCTNG subdirectory of the GROUPS directory. We'll grant all members of the ACCTNG group all rights, except delete rights, to the ACCTNG subdirectory.

In addition, since user Currid will serve as the LAN administrator, we'll grant her supervisor equivalence rights. These rights allow her to perform any necessary maintenance functions on the network, such as adding users and assigning security rights.

ADDING PASSWORD AND LOGIN SECURITY

Let's begin implementing our network security strategy by activating the global security restrictions. As discussed, these include limiting the number of concurrent sessions, locking out potential intruders, and restricting the times of day that a user can access the LAN.

Only a network supervisor can effect these types of security restrictions, so log in to the LAN as user **SUPERVISOR** and type **SYSCON** at the DOS prompt to execute the system configuration utility.

LIMITING CONCURRENT SESSIONS

The NetWare system default setting does not limit the number of simultaneous logins. However, allowing users to log in to the network from several workstations is generally not good practice, so let's limit the number of concurrent sessions that a user can have.

At the SYSCON Available Topics menu, select the User Information option to display a list of users. From this list, you can select a user by highlighting the name and pressing ←┘. Let's start by limiting the number of concurrent sessions for user Clark.

Selecting a user's name from the User List displays the Account Restrictions screen as shown in Figure 12.1. Press ↓ to move the cursor to the line that reads

Limit Concurrent Connections: No

Then change the response to Yes.

In the next field, which indicates the maximum number of connections, enter **2** to limit user Clark to two simultaneous sessions.

To save these changes, press **Esc**. The window displaying the account restrictions for user Clark will disappear. You can now select another user and change the number of concurrent sessions allowed in the same fashion.

From now on, if user Clark attempts to log in to the network from more than two workstations at the same time, an error message will appear, indicating that the maximum number of concurrent logins has been reached, and access will be denied.

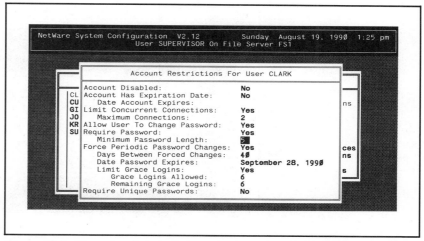

```
╔══════════════════════════════════════════════════════════════════════╗
║ NetWare System Configuration  V2.12        Sunday  August 19, 1990  1:25 pm ║
║                 User SUPERVISOR On File Server FS1                     ║
╚══════════════════════════════════════════════════════════════════════╝

              ┌────────── Account Restrictions For User CLARK ──────────┐
              │ Account Disabled:                    No                  │
          CL  │ Account Has Expiration Date:         No                  │ ns
          CU  │   Date Account Expires:                                  │
          GI  │ Limit Concurrent Connections:        Yes                 │
          JO  │   Maximum Connections:               2                   │
          KR  │ Allow User To Change Password:       Yes                 │
          SU  │ Require Password:                    Yes                 │
              │   Minimum Password Length:           5                   │
              │ Force Periodic Password Changes:     Yes                 │ ces
              │   Days Between Forced Changes:       40                  │ ns
              │   Date Password Expires:             September 28, 1990  │
              │   Limit Grace Logins:                Yes                 │ s
              │     Grace Logins Allowed:            6                   │
              │     Remaining Grace Logins:          6                   │
              │ Require Unique Passwords:            No                  │
              └─────────────────────────────────────────────────────────┘
```

Figure 12.1: Changing the maximum number of simultaneous connections

IMPLEMENTING INTRUDER DETECTION AND LOCKOUT

To increase the security of user passwords, you can have NetWare monitor the number of incorrect attempts to enter a password to access the network. After a specified number of failed attempts, you can have NetWare lock out the user for a specified period of time. This strategy stops potential intruders to the network from, for example, logging in as user SUPERVISOR and then entering passwords in the hope of guessing the correct one.

In the NetWare default configuration, the intruder detection and lockout feature is turned off. To activate this security measure, choose Supervisor Options from SYSCON's Available Topics menu. Choosing this option displays the Intruder Detection/Lockout screen shown in Figure 12.2. To toggle on this security function, change the Detect Intruders option to Yes by typing **Y** and pressing ←. On this same screen, you can also specify the number of incorrect password entries allowed within a given time period and the amount of time that must elapse before the login name is reactivated.

Change your screen to match Figure 12.2. Then press **Esc** to return to the Available Topics menu. Note that unlike the restriction

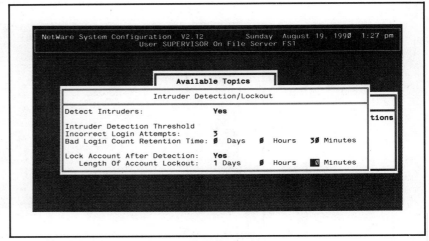

Figure 12.2: Intruder Detection/Lockout screen

on the number of concurrent sessions, which can be set differently for each login name, the intruder detection and lockout feature applies to all users.

RESTRICTING LAN ACCESS TIMES

Now limit the times of day that user Clark can access the network. The NetWare default configuration allows all users 24-hour access to the network, seven days a week.

To limit the number of hours during which a user can log in to the LAN, select the User Information option from SYSCON's Available Topics menu. From the list of user names, choose the user you want to restrict and select Time Restrictions from the User Information menu.

The screen that appears contains a matrix with the days of the week along the vertical axis, and times, in half-hour increments, along the horizontal axis. An asterisk at the intersection of a day and time indicates that the user can access the network during the corresponding period.

You can move around the Time Restriction matrix with the arrow keys. To add time periods, insert an asterisk. To delete time periods, press **Del**. Figure 12.3 shows the login times we want available for

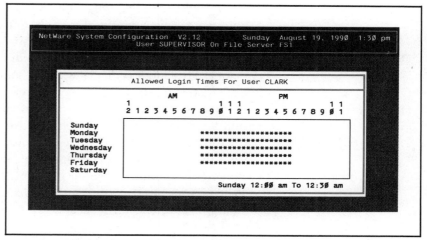

Figure 12.3: Changing user login times

user Clark. Clark will be allowed to work on the network from 8:00 a.m. to 5:00 p.m. Monday through Friday. Enter these changes and then press **Esc** twice to save them and to return to the Available Topics menu.

The login time restrictions we just entered apply only to a specific user. However, you can easily apply similar restrictions to all users. To accomplish this, choose Supervisor Options from the Available Topics menu and then select the Default Time Restrictions option. The screen that appears resembles the user Time Restriction matrix and works in the same fashion.

Restricting access to the network during specific time periods may be necessary for maintenance purposes. For example, you might want to eliminate all active connections and block logins during the time that you back up the file server's hard disk.

ADDING TRUSTEE SECURITY

Trustee security is the second level of NetWare security. You use trustee security to assign privileges to users (and groups) for work within directories. As listed in Table 12.1 at the beginning of the chapter, eight trustee rights can be granted to users: read, write, open, create, delete, parental, search, and modify.

When a new user is added to the network, the only right automatically granted is access to a special subdirectory of the SYS:\MAIL directory. This subdirectory is used by some electronic mail applications. Rights to all other subdirectories must be assigned by a supervisor.

Rights can be granted either to individual users or to all users within a group. In addition, you can assign rights directly or indirectly through the use of security equivalences. The security equivalence feature allows the supervisor to grant a user or group the same trustee rights as another user or group.

When a user has trustee rights to a directory, the user also has the same rights to any lower-level subdirectories unless these are explicitly restricted.

GRANTING TRUSTEE RIGHTS TO INDIVIDUALS

Let's begin the implementation of our network's trustee security features by granting all rights to each user for their DEFAULTS and PRIVATE subdirectories. Only a supervisor can assign trustee rights, so log in as user **SUPERVISOR** and enter **SYSCON**. At the Available Topics menu, select the User Information option and choose the user, in this case, Clark, from the list of user names. Then choose Trustee Assignments from the User Information menu.

The screen that appears contains a list of the trustee rights currently granted to user Clark. We have not previously assigned any rights to Clark, so the only listing is the user's MAIL subdirectory.

To add additional trustee rights, press **Ins**. A window will appear with a prompt that reads

Directory In Which Trustee Should be Added:

If you know the fully qualified name of the directory, enter it directly into the field.

Alternatively, you can press **Ins** again to display a list of file servers. First, select a file server by highlighting the entry and pressing ⏎. (Our example network has only one file server: FS1.) A list of the various volumes will then appear in the window. Choose the appropriate volume, in this case, 545, in the same fashion. Finally, a list of the directories on the root directory of the selected volume will appear. For our example, choose DEFAULTS from this list and then choose CLARK.

When you are finished, press **Esc**. The subdirectory name will appear in the window, as shown in Figure 12.4. To add this subdirectory to the list of trustee rights for user Clark, press ◄─┘.

When a new subdirectory is added to the list of trustee assignments for a user (or group), the default rights are read, open, and search. However, we want to grant all eight rights to each user for their DEFAULTS and PRIVATE subdirectories, so you need to add the additional privileges.

To modify rights, highlight the desired subdirectory from the list of trustee assignments and press ◄─┘. This displays a window that lists the trustee rights currently granted. To display a similar window that lists the remaining rights, press **Ins**. You select additional rights by highlighting them and pressing ◄─┘. (A quicker method is to mark the entries with the **F5** key and then press ◄─┘.)

Use either selection method to add the remaining rights in the Trustee Rights Granted window, as shown in Figure 12.5. Then press **Esc** to add these rights to the user's trustee assignments.

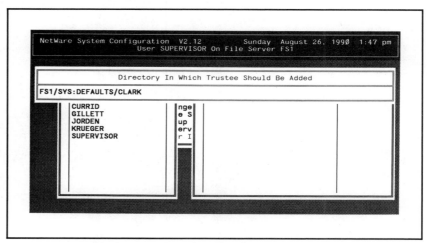

Figure 12.4: Selecting a directory for assigning trustee rights

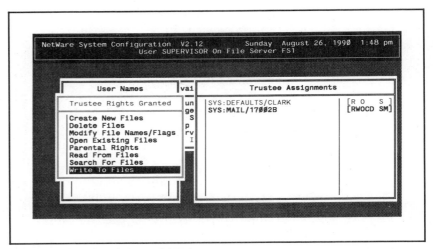

Figure 12.5: Adding trustee rights

You can now follow the same procedures to grant all rights to the SYS:PRIVATE/CLARK subdirectory. When these privileges have been granted, your screen will look like Figure 12.6. As the Trustee Assignments window shows, all eight rights have been granted to the user's DEFAULTS and PRIVATE subdirectories, along with the default rights associated with the MAIL subdirectory.

Press **Esc** to save the trustee assignments and return to the list of user names. You can now use the same process to modify the trustee assignments for the other users so they can fully use their DEFAULTS and PRIVATE subdirectories.

GRANTING TRUSTEE RIGHTS TO GROUPS

Granting trustee rights to groups is similar to granting rights to individual users. In fact, the only difference is that instead of selecting User Information from SYSCON's Available Topics menu, you choose Group Information.

When you select the Group Information option in our example system, two groups are listed: EVERYONE and ACCTNG. The group EVERYONE is automatically created by NetWare and includes all users.

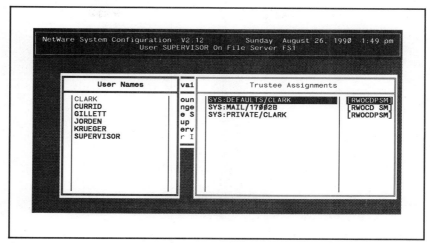

```
NetWare System Configuration   V2.12        Sunday  August 26, 1990  1:49 pm
                         User SUPERVISOR On File Server FS1
```

User Names	val	Trustee Assignments	
CLARK	oun	SYS:DEFAULTS/CLARK	[RWOCDPSM]
CURRID	nge	SYS:MAIL/17002B	[RWOCD SM]
GILLETT	e S	SYS:PRIVATE/CLARK	[RWOCDPSM]
JORDEN	up		
KRUEGER	erv		
SUPERVISOR	r I		

Figure 12.6: Trustee assignments for user Clark

Let's start by granting additional rights to the EVERYONE group. Select EVERYONE by highlighting the entry and pressing ←. This displays the current trustee assignments for the group. When NetWare is installed, the group EVERYONE is granted write and create rights to the SYS:MAIL directory, and read, open, and write privileges to the SYS:PUBLIC directory.

Supplement the default trustee assignments by adding all rights except delete and parental to the DOS, UTIL, COMMON, and PROGRAMS directories. When you are finished, your screen will look similar to Figure 12.7. Press **Esc** three times to return to the Available Topics menu.

We also want to add trustee rights for the ACCNTG group so that this group can effectively use the SYS:DEFAULTS\ACCNTG subdirectory. Following the same procedure, add the trustee assignments shown in Figure 12.8.

GRANTING RIGHTS THROUGH SECURITY EQUIVALENCES

Another way to grant trustee rights is by using the security equivalence feature. This feature allows you to assign the rights granted to

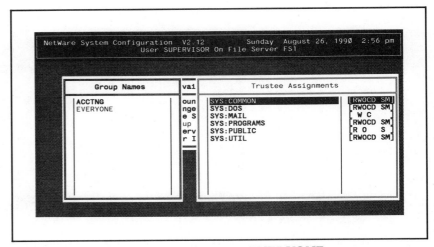

Figure 12.7: Trustee assignments for group EVERYONE

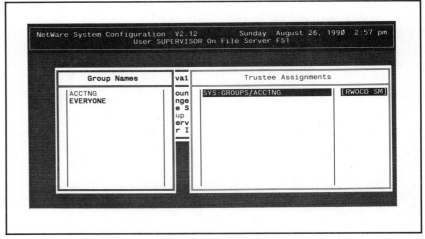

Figure 12.8: Trustee assignments for group ACCNTG

one user (or group) to another user or group. For example, user
Currid will be the LAN administrator for our network, so she will
need all of the trustee assignments held by user SUPERVISOR,
including all rights to all directories.

To assign supervisor rights to user Currid, choose the User Information option from the Available Topics menu, select Currid from the list of users, and then choose the Security Equivalences selection from the User Information menu. The window that appears will show Currid's current security equivalences. She has two: group ACCTNG and group EVERYONE.

To add additional security equivalences, press **Ins** to display a window that lists all other users and groups, as shown in Figure 12.9. To select the SUPERVISOR security equivalence, simply highlight this name and press ←┘. Then press **Esc** three times to return to the Available Topics menu. The next time that Currid logs in to the network, she will have the same rights as user SUPERVISOR.

DELETING TRUSTEE RIGHTS

Occasionally you will need to delete trustee rights granted to a user or group. You can delete rights either by eliminating the entire subdirectory from the user's (or group's) list of trustee assignments or by removing specific privileges from the subdirectory's list of trustee rights.

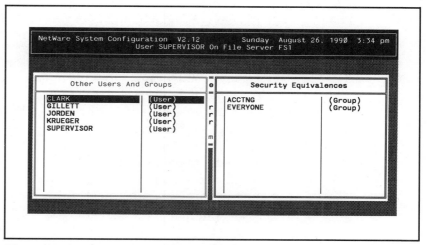

Figure 12.9: Assigning security equivalences

To remove the rights associated with an entire subdirectory, access the Trustee Assignments window for the user or group (see Figure 12.6 to refresh your memory), highlight the subdirectory that you want to remove, and press **Del**.

Likewise, deleting individual rights is similar to adding them. First, select the subdirectory that you want to modify by highlighting it in the Trustee Assignments window for the user or group and pressing ←. Next, select the right you want to delete from the Trustee Rights Granted window (see Figure 12.5) and press **Del** to remove it. If you are revoking several rights at once, you can mark each with the **F5** key and then eliminate them by pressing **Del**.

ADDING DIRECTORY SECURITY

The third level of NetWare security is directory security. This type of security is at a lower level in the NetWare scheme because it takes precedence over trustee rights. By modifying the maximum rights mask (described in the next section) associated with a subdirectory, you can prevent network users from exercising some of their trustee rights.

USING THE MAXIMUM RIGHTS MASK

The maximum rights mask, automatically created with each subdirectory, controls the rights that all trustees can exercise when working in the subdirectory. The maximum rights mask initially contains the same eight privileges that can be assigned as trustee rights to a user (that is, read, write, open, create, delete, parental, search, and modify). By deleting rights from the maximum rights mask, trustee rights can be overridden. For example, if the create right is removed from the maximum rights mask for the FS1/SYS:PROGRAMS subdirectory, no one can create a file in the PROGRAMS subdirectory, regardless of the user's trustee rights. The maximum rights mask always takes precedence over trustee rights. Once a right has been removed from the maximum rights mask, only a system supervisor can perform the deleted function.

For example, we assigned to the group EVERYONE all trustee rights to the UTIL subdirectory except delete and parental. Suppose that, to ensure compliance with license agreements, you implement a policy permitting only the system supervisor to install new utilities on the network. You accomplish this either by deleting the create trustee right or by removing the create right from the directory's maximum rights mask.

Although both approaches have the same effect, there are differences between removing the right from the trustee privileges and removing the right from the maximum rights mask. First, as already mentioned, the maximum rights mask takes precedence over any trustee rights. Thus, a deletion from the maximum rights negates any trustee rights granted, whereas the converse is not true. The second difference is that when a right is deleted from the maximum rights mask for a directory, the restriction applies only to the specific subdirectory. Directory rights do not extend downward as they do for trustee rights.

You can modify the maximum rights mask for a directory with the NetWare FILER utility. Let's use FILER to remove the create right from the UTIL directory's maximum rights mask.

Log in to the network as user **SUPERVISOR** and enter **FILER** at the DOS prompt. FILER's Available Topics menu will appear. Select the Subdirectory Information option and, when the list of sub-directories appears, choose UTIL. Next, from the Subdirectory Information menu, select the Maximum Rights option. A window will list the eight rights associated with the UTIL subdirectory. Move the cursor to the Create New Files entry and press **Del**. This key-stroke displays a window, shown in Figure 12.10, that prompts you to confirm that the create new files right is to be removed. Press ⏎ to delete the right from the list. (If you do not want to remove the right, highlight No and press ⏎.) Then press **Esc** four times to back out of FILER. Now the create right is deleted from the maximum rights mask of the UTIL subdirectory.

DETERMINING EFFECTIVE RIGHTS

The rights effective for any particular subdirectory are determined by the combination of the user's trustee rights and directory rights. For example, user Krueger's effective rights for the UTIL subdirectory are read, write, open, search, and modify. The delete and parental rights are excluded because the trustee privileges for the group EVERYONE did not include these rights. Although the group's trustee rights do include create, this right was removed from the

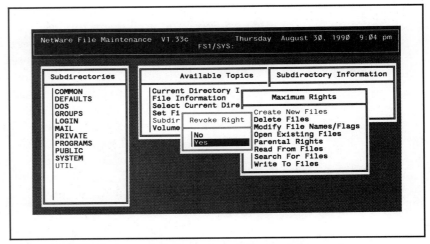

Figure 12.10: Deleting a right from the maximum rights mask

maximum rights mask for the UTIL subdirectory, and the maximum rights mask takes precedence over trustee rights.

NetWare includes a utility for checking the effective rights associated with a subdirectory. For example, if you log in as user Krueger, change to the UTIL (drive W) directory, and enter the command **RIGHTS** at the DOS prompt, the following message will appear on the screen:

```
Your Effective Rights are [RWO  SM]
     You may  Read from Files          (R)
     You may  Write to Files           (W)
     You may  Open existing Files      (O)
     You may  Search the Directory     (S)
     You may  Modify File Status Flags (M)
```

ADDING FILE AND DIRECTORY ATTRIBUTES SECURITY

The fourth level of NetWare security is file and directory attributes security. File and directory attributes take precedence over even a directory's effective rights.

SETTING FILE ATTRIBUTES

Table 12.2 lists the principal file attributes related to network security.

Table 12.2: Principal File Security Attributes

ATTRIBUTE	FUNCTION
Shareable	With adequate effective rights, more than one user can read the file at the same time.
Nonshareable	With adequate effective rights, only one user at a time can read the file.
Read-write	With adequate effective rights, a user can read, write, rename, or delete the file.
Read only	With adequate effective rights, a user can read the file.

When new files are created in the NetWare environment, the default file attributes are set to nonshareable and read-write. These attributes allow only one user to access and manipulate the file (assuming that user has adequate effective rights). You will want to modify the attributes of some files, such as batch files, to permit multiple users to read them, but not to change or delete them.

Using the FILER utility, let's change the attributes of the Word-Perfect batch file (WP1.BAT) to shareable and read only. Log in to the network as user **SUPERVISOR** and change to the UTIL (drive W) directory. Enter **FILER**, and from the Available Topics menu that appears, select File Information. From the list of file names, choose WP1.BAT. Then from the File Information menu, select Attributes. A list of the attributes currently assigned to the file will appear. Next, press **Ins**. Select the Read Only and Shareable attributes from the list.

When you have finished, your screen will look like Figure 12.11, indicating that the additional attributes have been added to the file. Press **Esc** four times to exit FILER and save the revised file attributes.

A quicker way of modifying file attributes is to enter NetWare's FLAG command at the DOS prompt. This command allows you to change the attributes of several files at the same time without using FILER.

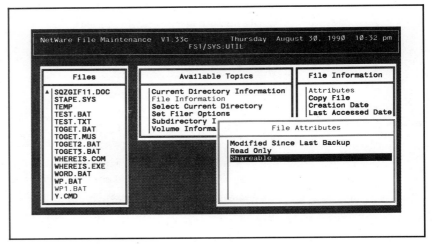

Figure 12.11: Changing file attributes

Let's use the FLAG command to change the file attributes of the DOS files to shareable and read only. Log in as user **SUPERVISOR** and change to one of the DOS subdirectories (such as FS1/SYS:DOS-\IBM_PC\MSDOS\V3.30). At the DOS prompt, enter the following command to flag all of the files as shareable and read only:

FLAG *.* SRO

As the command executes, the file names will scroll past the screen, indicating that their attributes have been changed.

You can modify the attributes of specific files by entering their names in lieu of the wildcard indicators (*.*).

The FLAG command qualifiers can be used to change the following file attribute combinations:

FILE ATTRIBUTES	*QUALIFIERS*
Shareable and read only	SRO
Shareable and read-write	SRW
Nonshareable and read only	NSRO
Nonshareable and read-write	NSRW

You can also use the FLAG command to check the attributes assigned to a file. For example, entering the statement **FLAG COMMAND.COM** in the DOS subdirectory returns the following response:

COMMAND.COM   Shareable   ReadOnly

SETTING DIRECTORY ATTRIBUTES

You assign attributes to directories in essentially the same way you assign attributes to files. Table 12.3 lists the directory attributes typically associated with security.

Table 12.3: Principal Directory Security Attributes

ATTRIBUTE	FUNCTION
Hidden	Eliminates the directory from view during a directory listing, but does not prevent users from accessing the directory
Private	Permits users to see the directory during a directory listing, but not the directory contents

When you use FILER, the process for modifying a directory attribute is identical to that for changing a file attribute, except that instead of choosing the File Information option from the Available Topics menu, you select Current Directory Information.

You can also modify directory attributes from the DOS prompt with the FLAGDIR command (which is similar to the FLAG command for modifying file attributes). For example, to hide the UTIL directory, enter the following command from the root directory:

FLAGDIR UTIL H

The UTIL subdirectory will no longer be listed in directory searches.

Other qualifiers that you can use with the FLAGDIR command include N (normal) and P (private).

SUMMARY

This chapter presented the fundamentals of NetWare security. The four levels of security permit an installation to implement a customized strategy that helps ensure the integrity and safety of the data stored on the file server's hard disk. With NetWare, you can provide either rigorous or loose security for all or part of the network's information resources.

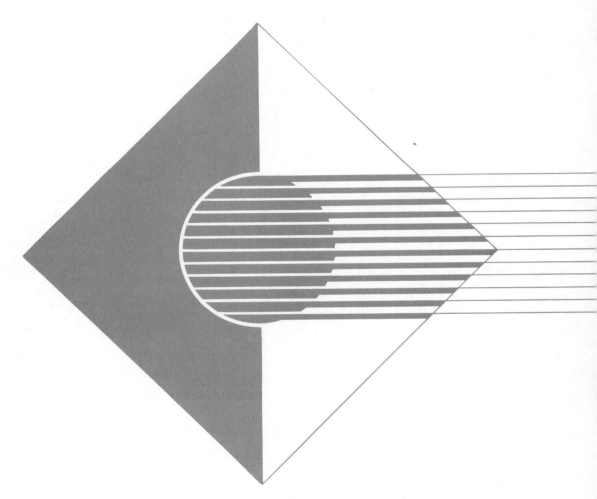

DEFINING PRINTER OPTIONS

FAST TRACK

To change or create custom printer functions,   **197**

    use the NetWare PRINTDEF utility. You can change the default print orientation, pitch, and type font size.

To import printer definitions,   **197**

1. Log on as supervisor and enter **PRINTDEF** from the DOS prompt. You will be prompted for the directory in which to store printer definition files.
2. Press ⏎ to accept the default location: SYS:PUBLIC.
3. Select the printer definition file from the list to import the file for the printer you want to use.

To edit Printer device options,   **198**

    use the NetWare PRINTDEF utility. Simply highlight the printer name and press ⏎ to display the Edit Device Options menu. Select Device Mode to add or change the device options for the mode.

To define special forms,   **200**

    use the NetWare PRINTDEF utility. Special forms, such as letterhead or mailing labels, usually require some special handling or setup. To add a new form for mailing labels,

1. Select Forms from the PRINTDEF options menu.
2. Press **Ins** and enter **Labels** as the form name.
3. Enter **66** as the form length and **35** as the form width.
4. Press **Esc** when you are finished to exit from PRINTDEF.

To set up special print jobs,   **202**

use the NetWare PRINTCON utility.

1. Enter **PRINTCON** at the DOS prompt and select Edit Print Job Configuration.

2. To add a new configuration, press **Ins** and enter the name of the configuration you want to set up.

3. Press ⏎ to confirm the name and review the options for the report. Use the arrow keys to move about the options. Overtype any entry that you wish to change.

4. Press **Esc** when your changes are complete.

To copy printer configurations to users' files,   **203**

use the NetWare PRINTCON utility. Use the PRINTCON copy feature to copy to other users' files.

To add a print queue operator,   **205**

use the NetWare PCONSOLE utility.

1. Log on as supervisor and execute PCONSOLE from DOS.

2. From the Available Topics menu, select Print Queue Information.

3. Highlight the print queue for which you want to add an operator and press ⏎.

4. Select Queue Operators to display a list of current operators. Press **Ins** to add another operator.

5. Press **Esc** to exit PCONSOLE.

CHAPTER *13*

ONE MAJOR BENEFIT OF A LOCAL AREA NETWORK is the capability to share expensive peripheral devices such as laser printers and plotters. NetWare lets you take full advantage of this capability by allowing you to customize the printer options for your LAN.

This chapter reviews the concepts associated with printing in a network environment and then explores the major options available to meet your printing needs. We'll begin by looking at how the network uses queues to manage printing tasks. Then we'll evaluate the default printer configuration created when the NetWare operating system was generated and learn to modify it using the PRINTDEF and PRINTCON printer utilities. Finally, we'll look at how the PCONSOLE utility can be used to manage print queues.

This chapter focuses on configuring the printer options. The process of actually producing printed output is discussed in Part IV.

USING PRINT QUEUES AND SERVERS

When you print from a standalone computer with a printer attached, the print job is routed directly from the computer to the print device. In a network environment, you can still send print requests to a locally attached printer (if one exists), or you can route them to a network printer. Print jobs sent to a network printer must be coordinated with print requests originating at other workstations. This is the role of print queues and servers.

When a user initiates a print job on a LAN, the job is not sent directly to the network printer, but rather to a print queue on the file server. Here the job is stored until the printer is available to print the request. A print server monitors the availability of the printer and sends print requests to the printer in an orderly fashion. This process of queing and sending printer transmissions is sometimes referred to as printer mapping.

NetWare automatically sets up print queues and servers when the operating system is configured. In addition, third-party vendors market add-on products that expand printer options by adding to the network print servers that are not directly managed by the file server. These products allow you to set up satellite printing locations that are not physically attached to the file server.

USING THE NETWARE PRINTER DEFAULT SETTINGS VERSUS CUSTOMIZATION

The default printer configuration created during the NETGEN process is usually adequate for a small network such as ours. The default settings include the following:

- One print queue is assigned to each network printer.
- The group EVERYONE is assigned to each print queue.
- The user SUPERVISOR is assigned to each print queue as the operator.
- The default printer definitions are used.
- One copy of each print job is printed.
- Each print job includes a banner page that lists the name of the user that initiated the print request.

When we configured the NetWare operating system in Chapter 7, we included a single Hewlett-Packard LaserJet Series II printer as the network printer. When a network has only one printer, this printer is automatically named PRINTER0, and its corresponding queue is PRINTQ_0.

The group EVERYONE is assigned to the print queue, so every user on the network can send print requests to the network printer on a first come, first served basis. The user SUPERVISOR is the print queue operator, so he or she can exercise special privileges, such as changing the queue position of print requests and suspending, or even deleting, print jobs.

As your network expands, you may need to modify the default settings. For example, you may want to assign additional print queue operators and change a printer's default parameters. The NetWare tools available to perform these functions are PRINTDEF, PRINT-CON, and PCONSOLE.

USING THE PRINTER DEFINITION (PRINTDEF) UTILITY

The PRINTDEF (printer definition) utility allows the system supervisor to manage a database of printer parameters that control the network printer. These parameters control such printer functions as page orientation, type pitch, and type font size.

The printer parameters can then be combined to change the printer output. For example, the default settings for the LaserJet Series II printer are 10 characters per inch (cpi) and portrait (vertical) orientation. To change the output to compressed print and landscape (horizontal) orientation, you set up a print mode that contains the appropriate command sequences.

PRINTDEF also lets you specify the printing of different types of forms on the printer, such as letterhead, address labels, and checks.

To make the process of printer definition easier, NetWare includes print device definitions for 30 printers, including the LaserJet Series II. You can copy these directly to the PRINTDEF database rather than manually entering the printer codes.

IMPORTING PRINT DEVICE DEFINITIONS

NetWare includes print device definitions for the most common printers used with local area networks, so we'll begin by copying the existing definitions into our PRINTDEF database. Log in to the network as user **SUPERVISOR** and enter **PRINTDEF**.

At the PRINTDEF Options menu, select Print Devices. Then choose Import Print Device from the Print Device Options menu. A window will appear with a prompt for the directory where the printer definition files are stored. We have not moved the printer definitions, so press ◄─┘ to accept the default location, FS1/SYS:PUBLIC.

The screen now displays a list of available files, as shown in Figure 13.1. Highlight HPLASER.PDF and press ◄─┘ to select the definition file for the LaserJet printer.

The file will now be imported into our file server's PRINTDEF database. To confirm that the importation occurred, select the Edit Print Devices option from the Print Device Options menu. The screen will display the listing *Hewlett Packard Laser Jet I/II*.

EDITING DEVICE OPTIONS

With Hewlett Packard Laser Jet I/II highlighted, press ◄─┘ to display the Edit Device Options menu. This menu has two options: Device Modes and Device Functions. If you select the Device Modes option, a screen similar to Figure 13.2 appears. This screen lists the modes currently available for the LaserJet printer. As you can see, you can currently print with condensed print, on letterhead, sideways on the page, and so on.

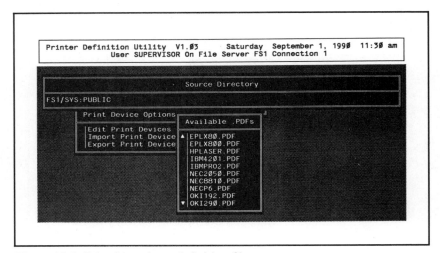

Figure 13.1: Selecting printer definition files

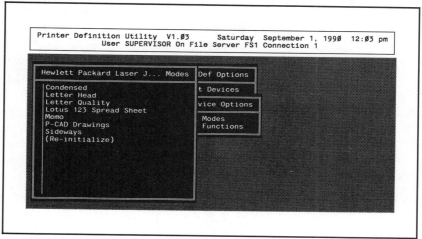

Figure 13.2: Default LaserJet device modes

Each mode is composed of one or more device functions. Press **Esc** and then select the Device Functions option from the Device Options menu to display a list of the underlying functions available, as shown in Figure 13.3. You can add additional functions to the list by pressing **Ins** and entering the name of the function and its corresponding code (or Escape sequence).

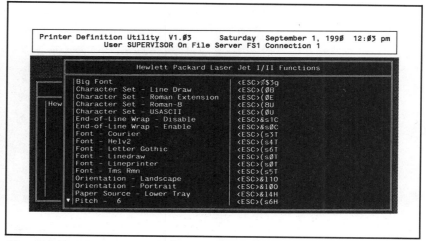

Figure 13.3: Default LaserJet device functions

Let's add a new mode to the available selections. Press **Esc** to return to the Device Options menu and then select Device Modes. Press **Ins** to display a window for entering the name of the new mode. We'll configure a mode that prints horizontally on the page in compressed print. Enter **Landscape 6 Point 14 Pitch**.

To add functions to this mode, press **Ins**. A list of the available functions appears in a window. Let's start by selecting Orientation - Landscape. Then select Point - 6 and Pitch - 14. When you are finished, your screen will look similar to Figure 13.4.

Press **Esc** five times to save the printer mode and return to the PrintDef Options menu.

DEFINING FORMS

PRINTDEF also allows you to define different types of forms that will be used by the printer. For example, mailing labels usually are small and narrow. PRINTDEF lets you define the characteristics of a form to ensure that the printer prints on it properly.

Let's define a form for printing a sheet of mailing labels that is 3.5 inches wide by 11 inches long. First, select Forms from the PrintDef

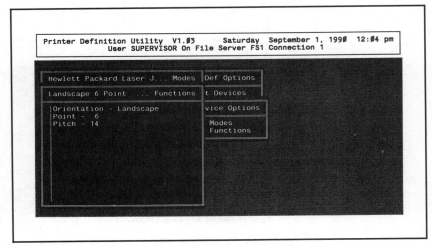

Figure 13.4: Adding a new printer mode

Options menu to display a list of the forms currently defined. We have not created any form definitions, so the list will be blank.

To add a new form, press **Ins**. The Forms Definition Form will appear on the screen with boxes for four entries: Name Labels, Numbers, Length, and Width. For this example, enter **Labels** as the form name. For the form number, enter **0**. (The file server recognizes forms by either their names or their numbers.) The form length is measured by the number of lines on the page. Enter **66** for the length. The width is measured as the number of characters per line. Enter **35** for the width. Figure 13.5 illustrates the Forms Definition Form with the values that we just entered.

Now also create forms for printing on regular (8.5 inch by 11 inch) paper using both portrait and landscape orientations so that these definitions can be transmitted to the printer when necessary.

When you are finished, press **Esc** and follow the prompts to exit the PRINTDEF utility and save the print device and form definitions. Later in this chapter, you'll see how to use these definitions to control printing on the network printer.

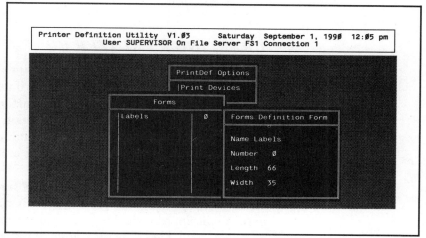

Figure 13.5: Creating a form

USING THE PRINTER CONFIGURATION (PRINTCON) UTILITY

The PRINTCON (printer configuration) utility can be used by the system supervisor and users to regulate the way the printer handles print jobs. Supervisors can set up configurations that can be used by everyone, and individual users can create custom configurations using the modes and forms created by the supervisor as well as other print options.

Some of the configuration options that PRINTCON lets you set are the following:

- The number of copies to be printed
- The type of form to be used
- The tab size
- Whether to print a banner
- If a banner is printed, the banner contents
- The file server and queue to be used
- The printer mode

CREATING A PRINTER CONFIGURATION

Let's use PRINTCON to create a printer definition that will print two copies of a report on the network printer using the mode that we created earlier with PRINTDEF. To start, enter **PRINTCON** on the command line. From the Available Options menu, select Edit Print Job Configuration. This displays a window with the existing print job configurations. This window will be empty, because we have not yet defined any printer configurations.

Let's add a new configuration. Press **Ins** and enter **Daily_Report** as the name of the print job configuration. When you press ←┘, a screen will appear with fields for the various configuration options that are available. You can move about this entry form with the arrow keys and type new values over any of the existing values. In addition, pressing ↵ when the cursor is positioned over the File Contents, Form Name, File Server, Print Queue, Device, or Mode field displays a list of all of the available options for that field.

Let's edit the print job configuration default values to match Figure 13.6. Change the number of copies to **2**, the form name to **Landscape**, the device to **Hewlett Packard Laser Jet I/II**, and the mode to **Landscape 6 Point 14 Pitch**. We'll leave the rest of the default values alone for now.

When you are finished making changes, press **Esc** to save the new printer configuration.

COPYING PRINTER CONFIGURATIONS

The system supervisor can copy print job configurations from one user to another. This capability is especially useful for helping novice users. As user SUPERVISOR, you can create general configurations and then copy them for use by other network users.

To copy print job configurations, make sure that you are logged in as user **SUPERVISOR**. Then access the printer configuration utility by typing **PRINTCON** on the command line. At the Available Topics menu, select the Supervisor - Copy Print Job Configurations option.

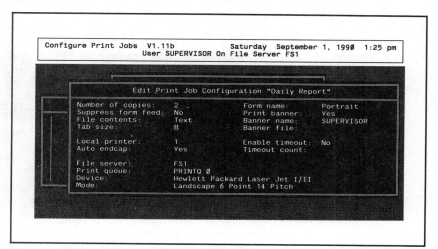

Figure 13.6: Creating a print job configuration

When you are prompted for the source user, enter **SUPERVISOR** and press ←. The next window, shown in Figure 13.7, prompts you for the target user. Enter **CLARK** to copy the supervisor's print job configurations to user Clark.

When you are finished, press **Esc** and follow the prompts to exit PRINTCON.

SELECTING THE DEFAULT PRINT JOB CONFIGURATION

When user Clark logs in to the network, the print job configurations created by the supervisor will be available. If more than one configuration is available, Clark can select one of the configurations as the default setting when print requests are sent to the printer.

To select the default configuration, enter **PRINTCON** and choose the Default Print Job Configuration option from the Available Topics menu. This displays a list of the print job configurations that are currently defined, as shown in Figure 13.8. To select the default configuration, highlight the entry and press ←.

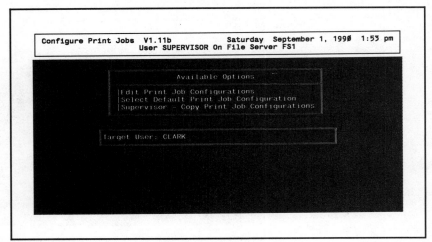

Figure 13.7: Copying print job configurations

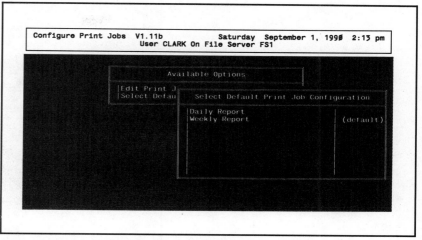

Figure 13.8: Selecting a default print job configuration

USING THE PRINTER CONSOLE (PCONSOLE) UTILITY

The third printer utility is PCONSOLE (printer console). The system supervisor can use PCONSOLE to assign queue users and operators. In addition, as you'll see in Part IV, PCONSOLE can also be used by network users to submit print requests to a print queue.

The group EVERYONE was automatically designated as a user of the print queue, so we do not need to add any users. However, let's assume that Clark needs priority access to the printer, so we'll designate him as a queue operator. Then Clark will be able to change the order of print requests in the queue when necessary.

Make sure that you are logged in as user **SUPERVISOR** and enter **PCONSOLE** on the command line. From the Available Topics menu, select Print Queue Information. The screen will display a list of the print queues. We have only one printer defined, so only one queue name, PRINTQ_0, appears. Press ◄━┘ to display the Print Queue Information menu. Now you can select queue operators to produce a list of the users designated as operators for queue PRINTQ_0.

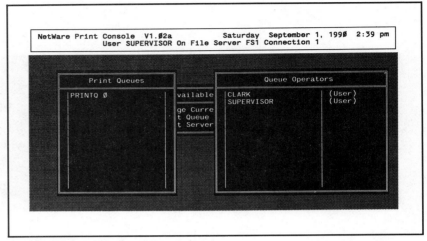

Figure 13.9: Adding a queue operator

To add user Clark as a queue operator, press **Ins** and select Clark's name from the list that appears in the window, as shown in Figure 13.9. Then exit PCONSOLE by pressing **Esc**.

SUMMARY

The stage is almost set for the first users to log in to the network. With the work accomplished in this chapter, we have completed the behind-the-scenes activities necessary to ensure that the LAN printer handles print jobs properly.

Obviously, sharing a printer among several users on a network introduces a higher degree of complexity than in the standalone world. But with the flexibility and tools provided by NetWare—including the three printer utilities: PRINTDEF, PRINTCON, and PCONSOLE—you can make this complexity a benefit to the user.

CHAPTER 14

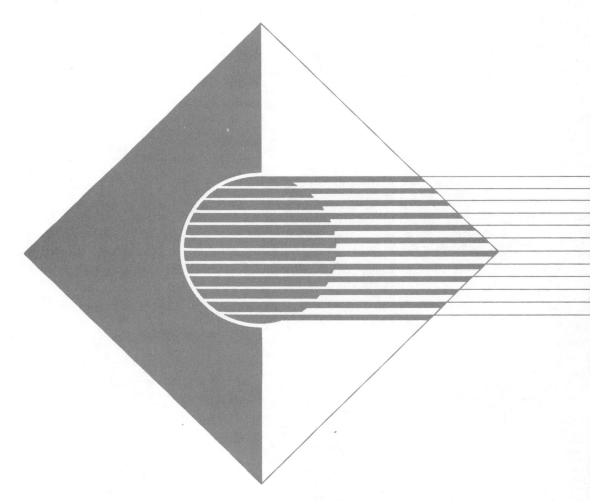

CREATING USER MENUS

FAST TRACK

The minimum network menu should contain   **211**
> menus for applications programs, network utilities, special programs that the user may require, and a facility to log out of the network.

The program files needed to use the NetWare menu utility   **212**
> are located in the SYS:PUBLIC directory. They can be searched without modifying drive maps. We recommend that you do not place the menu definition files in the SYS:PUBLIC directory. This strategy keeps the SYS:PUBLIC directory from becoming cluttered with nonoperating-system files.

To create a menu definition file,   **214**
> use any text editor that is capable of printing a plain ASCII file.

To format a menu file,   **214**
> begin each new menu with a percent sign (%). Menu options can call other menus by using a percent sign. A common programming convention is adding an ellipsis (...) after menu options that lead to other menus. This convention tells the user which menus have submenus.

To create submenus,   **214**
> add options beneath the menu heading. Place the application name or identifier on the first line and follow this with indented instructions. Each menu option can call a batch file or an executable program or can execute other DOS command-line instructions.

To change a menu instruction,

you can edit the menu file. Using batch files as menu options makes maintenance and the use of multiple menus on the network easier.

CHAPTER *14* _____

FROM THE USER'S PERSPECTIVE, ONE OF THE MOST important parts of the network is the menus. Because of their size and number of applications, networks can be difficult for many users to use. With their search drives and many, multilayered subdirectories, networks can confuse even the most ambitious users.

Clear, easy-to-use menus can make many of these network complexities transparent to the user and can be the difference between a network that is successful and one that is not. Thus, developing network menus that are flexible and logically designed is an important task.

This chapter discusses the options available for creating user menus. We will create some sample menus for our example network by using the NetWare menu program. You should, however, also look at other commercially available menu-creation utilities, especially if you are creating menus for a large system, because many of these packages offer functions beyond the scope of the NetWare menu utility.

PLANNING THE MENUS

You should plan the basic functions of your menus before you begin writing them. Over time you will find that the number of applications on your network will grow. Each time you add an application, you will need to add a menu option in a logical place. Well-designed and well-thought-out menus will make network support a lot easier, because users will learn to anticipate menu setup and procedures and thus make fewer help calls.

You should first plan the types of menus you want to create. At the least, you should create menus to help network users launch and access programs and utilities. Depending on network users' needs and sophistication, you may also wish to include menus of DOS utility functions, such as file copying and deletion functions. You might also create menus to help users perform such functions as displaying text messages and connecting to other networks or communications services.

Your next step should be to divide menus by major function or application category. For example, for our sample network, we will divide our menus into four groups:

- Applications Programs
- Network Utilities
- Special Programs
- Logout of Network

Each of these groups will become a selection on our main menu.

Under each major area, plan to nest (or layer) your menus in logical sequences. For example, under the first option, Applications Programs, list the major applications on the network: your spreadsheet, word processor, file managers, and so on.

Thus, the menu selection Applications Programs will pass the user to another menu from which the user can select the actual application to use.

Figure 14.1 shows a diagram of a sample menu plan.

Once the basic menu architecture is planned, you can begin actually building and programming the menus.

USING THE NETWARE MENU UTILITY

As mentioned, this chapter illustrates network menu creation using the NetWare menu utility. This utility comes with the operating system and is loaded onto the file server when the system is initially generated.

The files necessary for the utility are located in the SYS:PUBLIC directory. The menu utility requires the following files:

MENUPARZ.HLP

MENU.EXE

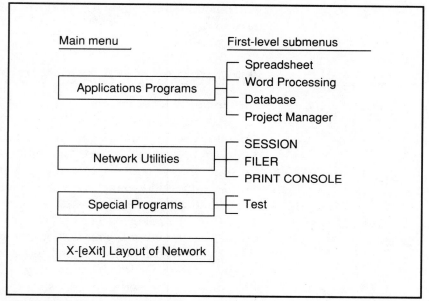

Figure 14.1: Sample menu plan

MENUPARZ.EXE

SYS$MSG.DAT

SYS$ERR.DAT

IBM$RUN.OVL

SYS$HLP.DAT

When we installed NetWare and configured our login scripts, we included the SYS:PUBLIC directory in our search path. Thus, even if we store the actual menus in another directory, the necessary files for the menus will be readily available to them. We want to store the menu files in another directory because the menu files, although a part of NetWare, are more easily maintained in a directory other than a NetWare directory.

We will place our menus in the SYS:UTIL directory. Because the system searches this directory after it searches our DEFAULTS\-USER directory, we can include generic menu files for all LAN users. However, by placing a menu file for specific users earlier in the search path, we can easily supersede these files with files for individual users.

CREATING THE MENUS

To use the NetWare menu program, you must first create a menu file. This file can be created with any text editor or word processing program that can send output to a plain ASCII file. If you are in doubt about your program's suitability, try typing the file to the screen. If you see readable text, then everything is okay. If your text includes some odd-looking characters, then formatting characters are embedded in the text. Try using another text editor or check the manual for the editor or word processor to see if the program provides a way to output the file without these characters.

Our main menu selections will mostly call submenus. The first step in using the menu program is to group the menu and submenu selections. For the NetWare menus, you will begin each menu with a percent sign (%).

Type the following lines to create the main menu. Note that each main menu selection begins with a percent sign (%).

```
%Main Menu,5,20,0
Applications Programs...
    %Applications
Network Utilities...
    %Network Utilities
Special Programs...
    %Special
X-[eXit] Logout of Network
    !logout
```

When you finish entering the code, name the menu file **MAIN.MNU**.

Now create the submenus for each main menu selection. The submenus will appear as pop-up windows. Enter the following:

```
%Applications
Spreadsheet
    lotusnet.bat
```

```
Word Processing
   wp.bat
Database
   rb.bat
Project Manager
   proj.bat
%Network Utilities
Session
   session.exe
Filer
   filer.exe
Print Console
   printcon.exe
%Special
Test
```

This simple file creates a set of nested menus, with the first submenu for each main menu option displayed when the user selects an option.

To execute the menus from DOS, enter **MENU MAIN**. This brings up the main menu, shown in Figure 14.2.

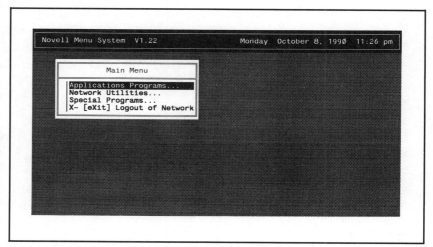

Figure 14.2: The main menu

Note that the menu we created here calls batch files to bring up applications. All of the batch files are located in the search path, in the SYS:UTIL subdirectory.

For example, using our menu to bring up the word processing program, we select WP.BAT. We could have typed the actual map instructions to execute the word processing software directly in the menu instruction file. We chose not to do so, however, because changing the batch file is easier than changing the menus. To change a menu, all users first must be logged out of the menu system. Also, some network users may elect to use other menu systems, and those menus can access the same batch files to launch programs. Thus, our scheme provides a flexible network that allows users a choice of menu systems to access the same software.

As you test the options, note that NetWare's menu program places the options in alphabetical order—not in the order in which you entered them. Keep this feature in mind as you name options.

To exit the menu and return to DOS, press **Esc** and respond Yes to the prompt.

SUMMARY

The importance of good menus cannot be overstated. Menus are what the user sees. To the user, the menus *are* the network.

In this chapter, we created a sample menu. This sample menu is meant to be a base, not a complete menu system. You should modify this base as necessary and add to it the options that your network users need.

Now we have completed the installation and configuration of our LAN, and we are ready to open our network to users.

PART IV

TAKING THE NETWORK FOR A TEST DRIVE

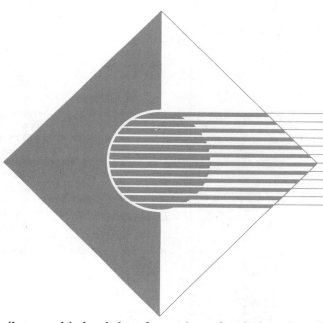

Up until now, this book has focused on the design, installation, and configuration of a NetWare local area network. In the next two chapters, we'll look at how the network actually works.

CHAPTER *15*

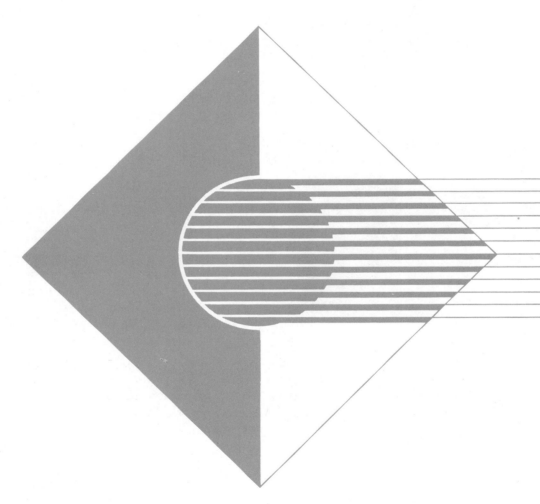

LOGGING IN AND
PRINTING FROM THE NETWORK

FAST TRACK

Three ways to prepare the network for users are to   **221**

    1. Recruit test pilots.

    2. Sponsor high-level training.

    3. Ensure adequate start-up support.

Network test pilots should be   **221**

eager volunteers. You should provide them with minimal training, a login name, and a password. Often these users will uncover network problems missed by the network installation team.

High-level training should include   **222**

just enough instruction for users to be comfortable with the network. Train users to log in. Explain the network security system. Tell users how to share some files and how to keep others in their PRIVATE subdirectories.

Start-up support should include   **222**

ample staff to answer questions and deal with the inevitable installation bugs. Also, staff should walk the halls to ensure that the system is operating as it should be.

Make boot disks   **223**

for each workstation that doesn't have a hard disk. Color-coded disks are helpful to distinguish the LAN boot disk. For hard-disk computers, create and place the LAN access files in a C:\LAN directory. Modify the AUTOEXEC.BAT file if you want workstations to boot directly to the LAN.

Provide users with instructions about   **223**

logging in and using passwords. The initial password will expire the first time a user logs in, so be sure to explain how to change passwords.

Using a local printer to print from the network   **225**

generally presents no difficulty with most software packages.

To print a plain ASCII file from PCONSOLE,   **225**

select the Print Queue Information option from the Available Topics menu and select the queue. Then choose the Current Print Job Entries option and press **Ins** to select the directory and file entries from a pop-up window.

To change the order of print jobs,   **227**

use PCONSOLE if you are a supervisor or designated console operator. To change the order of entries, or delete entries, in the print queue, choose the Current Print Job Entries option from the Available Topics Menu. Then highlight the entry. Press **Del** to delete a job. To change a parameter press ↩ and select options from the menu that follows.

Use the NPRINT command to   **228**

print from the command line and name the file you want to print. You can also direct the file to a print queue and change the banner.

CHAPTER *15*

THE ATTENTION THAT WE GAVE TO THE CREATION
of user access programs and menus will pay big dividends when the
first users begin logging in to the network. If we did our job right, the
transition from using a standalone computer to working on a network should be easy. In fact, using the computer may even be easier,
and more resources will likely be available to the individual user.

This chapter discusses how to prepare users for the "grand opening" of the network. It also discusses how users log on to the network
for the first time and print using a network printer.

PREPARING FOR NETWORK USE

Before your network is opened for everyday use, you should help
prepare the users. Their acceptance, to a large extent, will determine
the success of your efforts. Three activities that can help prepare network users are

- Recruiting a few test pilots
- Sponsoring high-level network training
- Ensuring adequate start-up support

In addition, you should prepare yourself for initial user login.

RECRUITING TEST PILOTS

Before you let the first users loose on your network, a useful practice is to allow a few eager test pilots to try out the LAN.

As soon as you feel confident that the network has adequate security and is stable enough to support a few users, provide a login name
and password to two or three volunteers. Then give these test pilots a

minimal amount of tutoring and let them begin using (or at least exploring) the network. Such users often can uncover problems missed by even the most exhaustive testing.

HIGH-LEVEL NETWORK TRAINING

Particularly if your users are already using standalone personal computers, they won't require a great deal of training to begin using the network. Learning to enter a login name and password is about all that is required to get started. The menus and prompts that you created will take over from there.

Of greater importance is helping ease the transition to the LAN and developing a sense of trust. Time should be spent acquainting users with the concept and components of a local area network. Demonstrating the benefits of file sharing, regular backup processing, electronic mail, and a greater variety of software will help motivate users to use the new system.

In addition, reassuring users that the system and data are secure is important. Explain how the network security protects the files stored in their PRIVATE subdirectory. A major benefit of the local area network—maintaining data integrity—will be lost if users continue to save data on floppy disks instead of on the network drive.

START-UP SUPPORT

Regardless of how much attention you paid to the technical details of your LAN and how much time you spent preparing the users, anticipate and plan for problems on the first day. Logging in to the LAN and accessing programs with the menus will be straightforward for most users, but unexpected problems likely will occur. The inability to access files, for example, because of incorrect group definitions or the failure to assign trustee rights can be frustrating to the novice user.

Make certain that a support staff is available and ready to assist users with any start-up difficulties. If the support staff is limited, ask the test pilots to help out. Also, walk the halls and see how things are going. Some users may be having problems and not even realize it.

PREPARING FOR THE NETWORK USERS

Before you open the network, you need to create boot disks, prepared from the master boot disk, for each workstation without a hard disk. Using colored disks, such as yellow or red, can help users quickly identify the boot disks.

For workstations with hard disks, you need to copy the network access programs into a LAN subdirectory. You will also need to modify the AUTOEXEC.BAT file if you want the workstation to automatically load the network shell and access the LAN.

You should also prepare a short set of instructions that outlines the procedure for logging in to the network. Include a reminder that the LAN password will need to be changed by each user after the user logs in for the first time, and include a telephone number to call for help.

LOGGING IN FOR THE FIRST TIME

When the users boot their computers with LAN access programs, the network shell will load, and they will be prompted to enter their login name and password, as shown in Figure 15.1. For security reasons, the password will not appear on the screen.

The initial password was set by the supervisor, and it will automatically expire when the user logs in. A prompt will then appear asking the user if the password should be changed on file server FS1. If the user responds Yes, the user will be prompted to enter a new password and to validate this entry by typing it a second time. Finally, the user will be asked if the passwords on all attached file servers should be synchronized. If the user is attached to more than one file server, password synchronization will change all of the passwords at the same time.

If the user fails to change the password when the prompt appears, the user will be locked out of the system after the specified number of grace logins. Recall from Chapter 12 that our example network allows the user six grace logins.

```
                     Please Enter Your Login ID

                     and Password at the Prompt



   Enter your login name:  KRUEGER
   Enter your password:

   Password has expired.
   Would you like to change your password on server FS1? (Y/N) Y


   Enter your new password:
   Retype your new password:
   Password on server FS1 synchronized.

   Would you like to synchronize your passwords on all attached servers? (Y/N) Y
```

Figure 15.1: Logging in for the first time

Once the user has changed the password, the welcome screen will appear, as shown in Figure 15.2. The user can now press any key to continue. Then the main menu will be executed automatically from the user login script. The user can now begin using all of the resources available on the LAN.

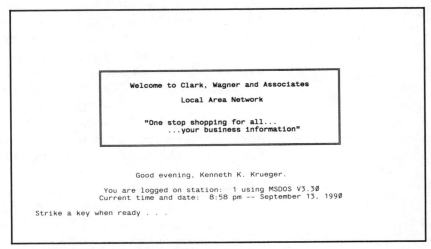

```
         Welcome to Clark, Wagner and Associates

                    Local Area Network

            "One stop shopping for all...
                      ...your business information"
```

```
            Good evening, Kenneth K. Krueger.

        You are logged on station:  1 using MSDOS V3.30
        Current time and date:  8:58 pm -- September 13, 1990

   Strike a key when ready . . .
```

Figure 15.2: Network welcome screen

PRINTING FROM THE NETWORK

Sooner or later, all users need to print a document. If a printer is directly attached to the user's workstation, printing on the network and printing with a standalone personal computer is essentially the same. However, printing on a network printer does present a few differences.

PRINTING FROM APPLICATIONS

The network versions of most common application programs support printing on a NetWare LAN. When the software is installed, the printer options simply need to be set to recognize the print queue and the printer.

Some software, however, does not support LAN printing. When this problem is encountered, the user can use the NetWare CAPTURE and ENDCAP commands to route the print stream to the network printer.

The CAPTURE command intercepts print streams destined for a parallel port on the workstation (for example, LPT1) and redirects them to a print queue or network printer. For example, if you enter the command **CAPTURE** at the DOS prompt, everything that you print to the LPT1 port is instead sent to the default printer on the default server. To redirect print jobs to a local printer, enter **ENDCAP**.

A variety of options can be used with the CAPTURE command. For example, the following command statement intercepts print streams sent to the LPT2 port and routes them to print queue PRINTQ_2, printing three copies without a banner page:

```
CAPTURE L = LPT2 Q = PRINTQ_2 C = 3 NB
```

The CAPTURE and ENDCAP commands can also be executed from batch files or login scripts. This allows default printers to be set up for individuals or for everyone on the LAN.

PRINTING WITH PCONSOLE

Occasionally, users will need to print a file from outside an application program. One method of printing files to a network printer is by using the PCONSOLE utility. To illustrate this process, assume that you are user Krueger. Let's see how user Krueger PCONSOLE prints a file named TEST.TXT stored in the FS1:/SYS:PRIVATE\KRUEGER\WORDS subdirectory.

First execute PCONSOLE either by entering **PCONSOLE** at the DOS prompt or by selecting this command from a menu (if the network includes a menu with the PCONSOLE option). At the Available Topics menu, select the Print Queue Information option. From the next window that appears, select the desired print queue. This displays the Print Queue Information menu, where you can choose the Current Print Job Entries option to display a list of the print jobs currently in the queue.

To add jobs to the queue, press **Ins**. A prompt will ask you to select the directory to print from. You can enter the directory name directly, or you can press **Ins** to select the directory from entries in a pop-up window. After you choose the directory, press ⏎ to display a list of the available files. Select the file for printing—in this case, TEST.TXT. Then a window displaying the print job configurations will appear. You can now choose the print mode from the list.

The next screen that appears, shown in Figure 15.3, displays the default printing parameters. You can edit any of the entries if you

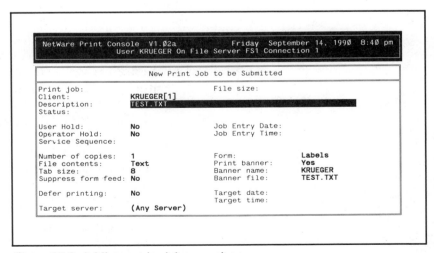

Figure 15.3: Adding a print job to a print queue

want to specify different parameters. When you are done setting the printing parameters for the print job, press **Esc** to add the job to the print queue.

Once the print job has been submitted, PCONSOLE will show the current status of the print queue, as in Figure 15.4. You can see that user Krueger's TEST.TXT file is the only job currently in the print queue.

To back out of PCONSOLE and return to the DOS prompt or the menu, press **Esc**.

WORKING WITH PRINT QUEUES

Users can also use PCONSOLE to delete print jobs that they submitted to the queue or to change the printing parameters. System supervisors or users designated as console operators (see Chapter 14) can delete or change any user's print jobs, and additionally, they can re-order the entries in the print queue.

Like adding print jobs to a queue, modifying existing entries is accomplished from the PCONSOLE Current Print Job Entries screen. To access the list of print jobs, enter **PCONSOLE** and then

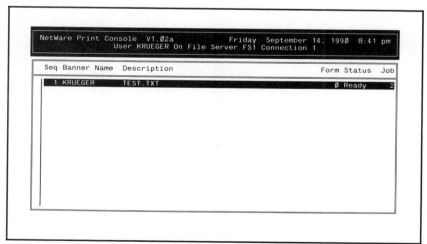

Figure 15.4: PCONSOLE print queue information screen

choose Print Queue Information from the Available Topics menu. Next, select the print queue that you want to modify from the list that appears in the pop-up window. Then select Current Print Job Entries from the Print Queue Information menu to display a list of every print job currently in the queue.

Users can delete one of their print jobs by highlighting the entry and pressing **Del**. NetWare prompts the user for confirmation of the deletion request. If the response is affirmative, NetWare then removes the print job from the queue. System supervisors and console operators can delete any users' print job.

The user can also modify the printing parameters for a print job from the list of items in the queue. To change a parameter, highlight the desired entry and press ←┘. This displays the Print Queue Entry Information screen (similar to Figure 15.4). The user can now move the cursor to any field to edit a printing parameter. Pressing **Esc** saves the revisions and returns the user to the list of print jobs. As with the delete function, users can modify the parameters only of their own print jobs, whereas system supervisors and console operators can change the parameters for any entry in the queue.

The Print Queue Entry Information screen can also be used to change the position of a job in the queue. The Service Sequence field lists the print job's current position in the queue. Changing this value moves the print job forward or backward relative to the other job entries. For example, changing the service sequence to 1 positions the entry as the next job sent to the network printer. This option is available only to system supervisors and console operators.

When the changes to the print jobs are complete, exit PCONSOLE by pressing **Esc** four times.

PRINTING FROM THE COMMAND LINE

Experienced network users can also send print jobs to a network printer from the DOS prompt. The NetWare NPRINT command works similarly to the DOS PRINT command, but it also permits the user to specify a variety of printing parameters.

For example, the following command prints three copies of user Krueger's TEST.TXT file to the printer managed by queue

PRINTQ_0 with the word *CONFIDENTIAL* printed at the bottom of the banner page:

```
NPRINT SYS:PRIVATE\KRUEGER\WORDS\TEST.TXT
Q = PRINTQ_0 C = 3
B = CONFIDENTIAL
```

SUMMARY

This chapter discussed how to prepare for the first network users. It also discussed the procedure that users follow when they first access the LAN and explored some of the various options available for printing on network printers.

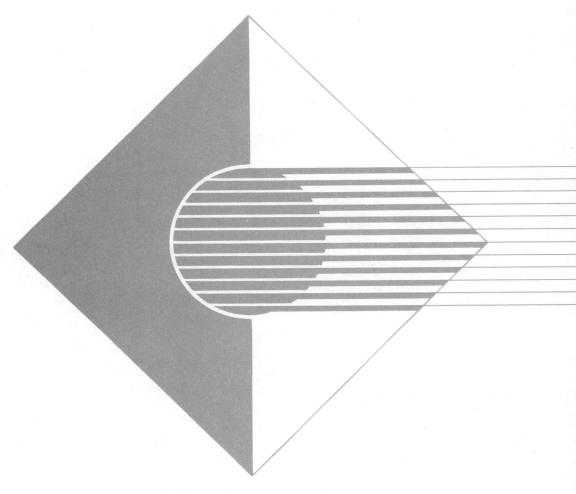

USER UTILITIES

FAST TRACK

Use the SYSCON utility for 233
   basic user maintenance, such as adding, changing, or deleting
   users or groups.

To add or delete drive maps 238
   use the SESSION utility.

To send messages to everyone in a group or to a single user, 239
   use the SESSION utility.

To view information about a user, 240
   select User List from the Available Topics menu. From the list
   of users, highlight the individual about whom you want to view
   information and press ←┘. Select Display User Info and type
   your message. Press ←┘ to view the user's full name, login
   name, network address, and node.

To maintain network files, 240
   use the FILER utility. Use FILER to view or change attributes
   associated with volumes, directories, and individual files.

To display information about a volume, 241
   select Volume Information from the FILER Available Topics

To display information about a directory, 242
   first make the directory about which you want information the
   current directory. Then choose Select Current Directory from
   the FILER Available Topics menu and then edit the name of
   the directory or press **Ins** to select the directory. Press **Esc** to
   return to the Available Topic menu and then choose Current
   Directory Information to display viewing options.

To add trustees with FILER,   243

    select Current Directory Information from the Available Topics
    menu. Choose Trustees and press ←⏎. Press **Ins** and choose the
    new user or group to act as trustee for the directory. Pressing
    ←⏎ one more time allows you to add or delete specific rights.

To view information about a file,   243

    choose File Information from the FILER Available Topics
    menu and highlight the file from the list of files displayed. Then
    press ←⏎ to select the file information to display or actions to
    perform.

To customize FILER options,   246

    choose Set Filer Options from the Available Topics menu.

To send a one-line message from DOS,   247

    use the SEND command. Be sure to surround your text with
    quotation marks (*"message"*).

To display currently logged in users,   248

    use the USERLIST command from the DOS prompt.

To change your password,   248

    type **SETPASS** at the DOS prompt and follow the instructions to
    enter your old and new passwords.

To display user information,   249

    type **WHOAMI** at the DOS prompt to list login and attachment
    information.

CHAPTER *16*

ALTHOUGH THE TYPICAL NETWORK USER MAY never need to venture beyond the menus and application programs on the network, NetWare does provide several menu-accessed utilities designed for the user. In this chapter, we'll examine three menu-accessed utilities: SYSCON, SESSION, and FILER. These programs provide information about the network and help users manage their work on the network. (The other menu-accessed utilities are VOLINFO, MENU, and COLORPAL. The COLORPAL utility lets you choose the colors for NetWare menus; the VOLINFO and MENU utilities are discussed in detail in other chapters. These utilities are of more interest to network administrators than to network users.) In addition, we'll look at several command-line utilities that many users will find helpful.

USING THE SYSTEM CONFIGURATION (SYSCON) UTILITY

When we set up our network, we used the SYSCON utility extensively for such functions as adding users, assigning trustee rights, and defining groups. Users without supervisor privileges can also access SYSCON, primarily to obtain information.

If SYSCON is included on the network menu, users can access it by selecting the System Configuration option or by entering **SYSCON** at the DOS prompt. The Available Topics menu that appears offers the same options as when SYSCON is executed by a network supervisor. The primary difference is that the supervisor options are not available to a user without supervisor equivalency status.

The SYSCON Available Topics menu offers these selections:

- Accounting
- Change Current Server
- File Server Information
- Group Information
- Supervisor Options
- User Information

If a user chooses the Accounting option, a submenu will appear with selections for viewing the rates for various network services. NetWare's accounting feature lets the supervisor assign rates for network activities. Then, if NetWare's accounting feature is turned on, these charges are deducted from the user's account balance when transactions occur. The accounting option can be used to review the current rates for activities such as blocks read and written, connect time, and disk storage space.

The Change Current Server option allows the user to change the default server, if the LAN uses more than one file server.

The File Server Information option provides information about the file server configuration. As shown in Figure 16.1, the screen lists the operating system version, the number of connections, the network address, and the node address of the file server.

The Group Information option displays a list of the user groups. When this list is on the screen, the user can position the cursor on a group name and press ← to display a submenu with options for viewing the group's full name and member list.

If a user without supervisor privileges chooses the Supervisor Options selection, the screen displays the message *No Supervisor Privileges on File Server FS1*. Access is then denied to the various supervisor options.

The last option on the Available Topics menu is User Information. This selection can be used to view another user's full name and group membership, as shown in Figure 16.2.

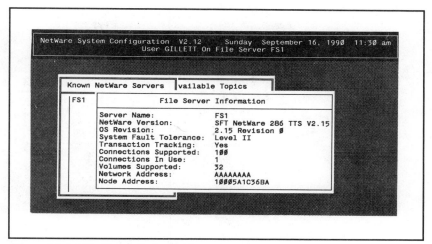

Figure 16.1: File Server Information screen

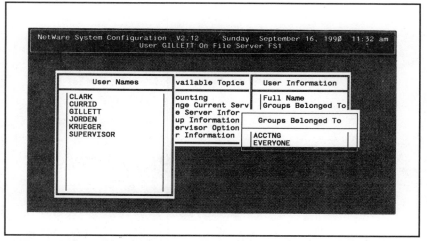

Figure 16.2: SYSCON User Information screen: viewing information about another user

If a user selects his or her own user name, then the window that appears contains an expanded list of options, as illustrated by Figure 16.3. In addition to displaying the user's full name and group membership, the screen displays the user's current account balance

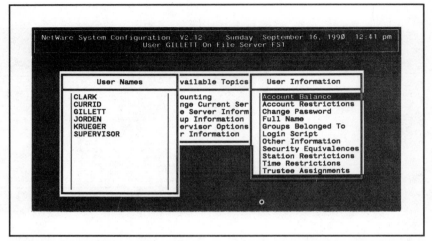

Figure 16.3: SYSCON User Information screen: viewing private information

and the restrictions and trustee rights assigned by the supervisor. The user cannot change these parameters, however, because only a network supervisor can change account restrictions, security equivalences, station restrictions, and time restrictions.

The user can, though, select the Change Password option to enter a new password. Likewise, the user can edit the login script by choosing the Login Script option.

USING THE SESSION MANAGEMENT (SESSION) UTILITY

Another utility that can be used by network supervisors and users alike is SESSION. The primary purpose of this utility is managing drive maps. SESSION also has functions for sending messages and viewing information about other users currently working on the network.

If the network menu includes the Session Management option, SESSION can be conveniently accessed by users. Alternatively, the utility can be executed by entering **SESSION** at the DOS prompt.

The first screen that appears when SESSION is executed is the Available Topics menu. This menu offers these six options:

- Change Current Server
- Drive Mappings
- Group List
- Search Mappings
- Select Default Drive
- User List

CHANGING AND DISPLAYING DRIVE MAP INFORMATION

Occasionally, advanced network users may want to modify the default drive maps set by the login script. For example, mapping a search drive to a different subdirectory may be necessary to execute a program. The drive maps can be changed from the DOS prompt, as we saw in Chapter 11. However, remembering the correct syntax for the MAP command can be difficult for even experienced NetWare users. SESSION provides a friendly interface for managing drive maps during the current session.

The Change Current Server selection allows users to attach, log in to, and log out of file servers when the LAN has more than one file server. In a single-file server network, the Change Current Server option can be used to log out. To use the option in this way, the user selects it from the Available Topics menu and, when the list of servers appears, presses **Del**. A prompt asks the user to confirm the action. If the user responds Yes, the user is then logged out of the file server.

The Drive Mappings and Search Mappings options let the user change the network drive maps. Both options operate in the same fashion, although as their names indicate, the first option modifies network drive maps, and the second option modifies search drive maps.

When the user selects Drive Mappings from the Available Topics menu, the screen displays a list of the current drive maps, as shown in Figure 16.4.

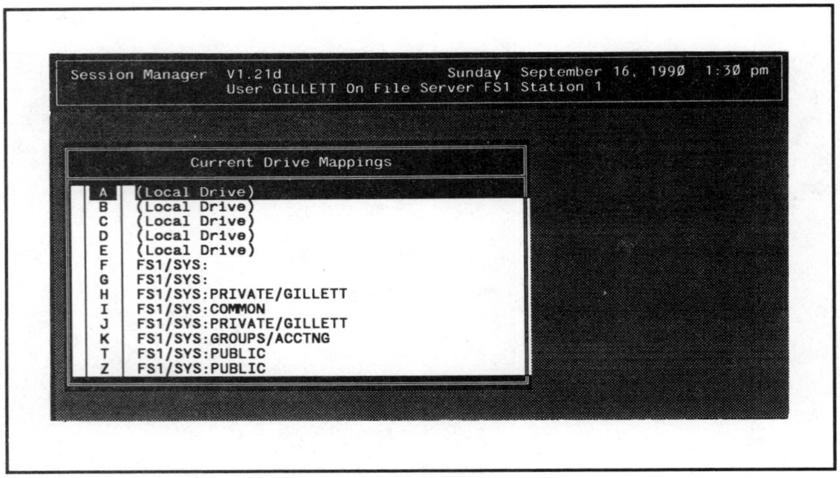

Figure 16.4: SESSION's Current Drive Maps screen

To delete a drive map, the user highlights the entry to be removed and presses **Del**. The screen will prompt for confirmation. If the user confirms the action, the specified drive map is deleted.

To add an additional drive map, the user presses **Ins**. A pop-up window then appears with the next available drive letter as the default value. The user can either edit the drive letter or accept it. To accept the drive letter, the user presses ←. The next window that appears prompts the user to select a directory. The default entry is the current directory. The user can either type the fully qualified directory name (for example, **FS1/SYS:PRIVATE/GILLETT**) and press ←, or press **Backspace** until the default entry disappears and then press **Ins**. Pressing **Ins** displays lists of the file servers, volume names, and directories to help define the drive map. After selecting the directory for the drive map, the user can press ← to add the directory to the list.

Existing drive maps can also be modified. To do this, the user highlights the entry to be changed and presses **F3**. When the "Select Directory" prompt appears, the user can change the drive map by following the same procedure used to add a new drive map.

Another feature available from the Current Drive Mappings screen lets users view the effective rights associated with a directory.

To list the effective rights of a directory, the user highlights the drive name and presses ←┘. A window similar to Figure 16.5 then appears.

Another drive map option on the Available Topics menu is Select Default Drive. This selection lets users change the drive currently designated as the default drive. When the Select Default Drive option is chosen, a list of the current drive maps appears on the screen. To change the default drive, the user simply highlights the desired drive map and presses ←┘.

USING GROUP AND USER OPTIONS

The Group List selection on the SESSION Available Topics menu provides two features. When selected, it displays a list of all of the user groups. It also lets users send a short message to everyone in the group who is currently logged in to the network.

For example, to send a message to everyone in the ACCTNG group to see if they are ready for lunch, the user highlights ACCTNG in the group list and presses ←┘. This displays a window similar to Figure 16.6, where the user can enter a message. When the user presses ←┘, the message is sent to all members of the ACCTNG

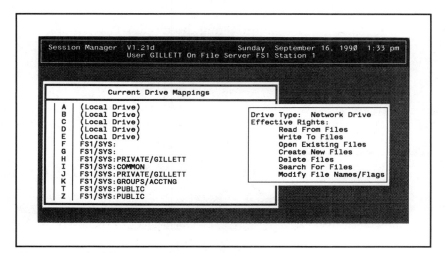

Figure 16.5: SESSION's Effective Rights screen

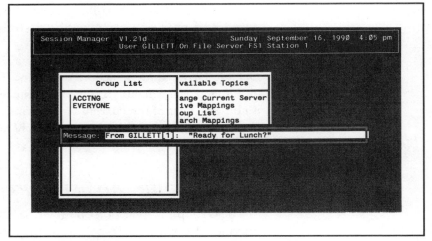

Figure 16.6: Sending a group message from SESSION

group. It will appear on the bottom row of their screens and stay there until they press the **Ctrl-** ⏎ key sequence.

The User List option on the Available Topics menu contains similar features. When this option is selected, the screen displays a list of all users currently logged in. Highlighting an entry and pressing ⏎ displays a submenu with two selections. The first option on the submenu is Display User Info and the second is Send Message.

Selecting the Display User Info option displays a window similar to Figure 16.7. This window contains the user's full name and login name and the network address and node. Selecting Send Message allows the user to route a message to the selected user.

SESSION is exited by pressing **Esc** four times.

USING THE FILE MAINTENANCE (FILER) UTILITY

A third menu utility with features available to the ordinary user is NetWare's file maintenance program, FILER. This utility provides an easy-to-use interface for viewing and changing the attributes associated with volumes, directories, and files. The tasks that can be accomplished through FILER are controlled by NetWare security.

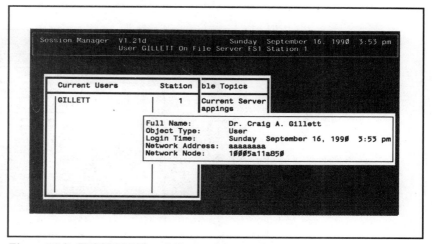

Figure 16.7: SESSION User Information screen

For example, a user can copy or view a file only if the user has trustee rights that allow these operations.

As with the other NetWare menu utilities, if the network menu contains the File Maintenance option, users can easily access it. Alternatively, users can enter **FILER** at the DOS prompt.

FILER's Available Topics menu offers six options:

- Current Directory Information
- File Information
- Select Current Directory
- Set Filer Options
- Subdirectory Information
- Volume Information

DISPLAYING VOLUME INFORMATION

Selecting Volume Information allows a user to view statistics related to the capacity and configuration of the file server's hard disk. The window that appears when this option is selected looks like Figure 16.8. The information includes the volume's total and remaining capacity as measured in bytes and directory entries.

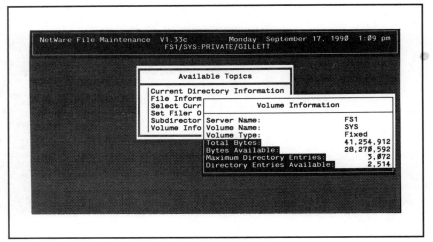

Figure 16.8: FILER's Volume Information screen

DISPLAYING DIRECTORY INFORMATION

The name of the current directory appears at the top of the FILER screen. To change directories, the user selects Change Current Directory. A window will appear prompting for the current directory path. The default entry in this window will be the current directory. Here the user can either edit the default directory path or press **Ins** to select volumes, directories, and subdirectories from the lists that appear in pop-up windows.

Once the directory has been selected, the Current Directory Information option can be chosen to view information about the directory. The submenu that appears when this selection is picked contains the following options:

- Creation Date

- Current Effective Rights

- Maximum Rights Mask

- Owner

- Trustees

Selecting any of these options displays a pop-up window that contains the requested information. For example, choosing the Maximum Rights Mask option displays a window similar to Figure 16.9. This window lists the maximum rights that the user has in the current directory.

The Trustees option is available only if the user has parental rights to the current directory. When the Trustees option is selected, a window appears listing the users and groups with trustee rights to the directory. The user can delete the trustee rights of other users or groups by highlighting the entry and pressing **Del**. Likewise, the user can add users and groups to the list of trustees by pressing **Ins**. Pressing **Ins** displays a list of the users and groups that do not have trustee rights to the directory, as shown in Figure 16.10. Any of these can be added by positioning the cursor on the user or group name and pressing ◄─┘.

Pressing **Esc** twice returns the user to the Available Topics menu. Selecting the Subdirectory Information option from FILER's

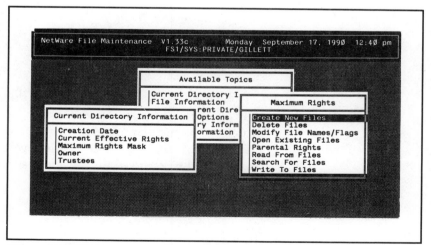

Figure 16.9: FILER's Maximum Rights screen

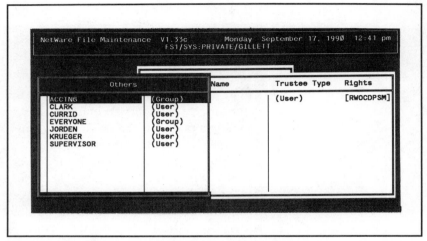

Figure 16.10: Adding trustee rights with FILER

Available Topics menu displays a list of the subdirectories in the current directory. Highlighting one of the subdirectories and pressing ◄─┘ displays a submenu with the following selections:

- Creation Date
- Maximum Rights
- Owner
- Trustees

If the user has parental rights to the directory, new subdirectories can be added by pressing **Ins**. Subdirectories and their contents can be deleted by highlighting the subdirectory name and pressing **Del**. Pressing **Del** displays a selection window, as shown in Figure 16.11, that allows the user to delete the entire subdirectory structure or just the subdirectory's files.

DISPLAYING FILE INFORMATION

The File Information option on the Available Topics menu lets users view information about the files in the current directory. In addition, users can change a file's attributes, copy or delete a file, and

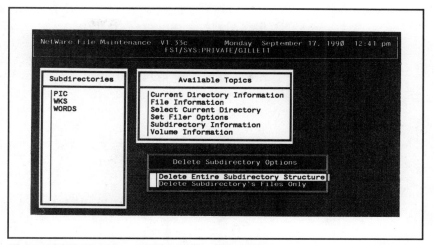

Figure 16.11: Deleting subdirectories with FILER

view a file's contents. As when working with directories and sub-directories, the appropriate trustee rights are required to perform these operations.

When File Information is chosen, a list of the files in the current directory appears. The user can delete a file by highlighting its name and pressing **Del**. Other functions are available through a submenu that appears when the user highlights a file name and presses ←. The File Information submenu offers these options:

- Attributes
- Copy File
- Creation Date
- Last Accessed Date
- Last Archived Date
- Last Modified Date
- Owner
- Size
- View File

These options allow you to view information about the selected file. The Attributes option displays a list of the characteristics associated with a file (for example, read only, nonshareable). Copy File permits you to create a duplicate of the file on a network or local drive. The next four options—Creation Date, Last Accessed Date, Last Archived Date, and Last Modified Date—provide information about when the file was created and any subsequent activity. The Owner option shows who owns the file, and the Size option displays the number of bytes in the file. The last option, View File, provides a utility for displaying the contents of the file.

CHANGING FILER OPTIONS

FILER also allows the user to customize several options. When Set Filer Options is chosen from FILER's Available Topics Menu, a submenu appears with the following options:

- Confirm Deletions
- Confirm File Copies
- Confirm File Overwrites
- Directories Exclude Pattern
- Directories Include Pattern
- File Exclude Pattern
- File Include Pattern
- File Search Attributes

Each of these options allow the user to change the parameters used by FILER when executing a request. For example, choosing the Confirm Deletions option displays the window shown in Figure 16.12. In this window, the user can specify whether FILER asks the user for confirmation before deleting a file.

USING COMMAND-LINE UTILITIES

In addition to the menu-driven utilities, several command-line functions are available to both users and system supervisors.

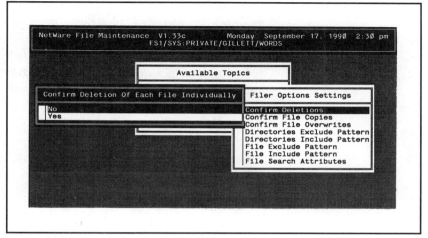

Figure 16.12: Changing FILER options

SENDING MESSAGES

We saw earlier how messages can be sent to users and groups from SESSION. The same type of message can be sent from the command line with NetWare's SEND command. For example, to send the "Are you ready for lunch?" message to user Clark and everyone in the ACCTNG group, the user can enter the following command at the DOS prompt:

```
SEND "Are you ready for lunch?" TO USER CLARK GROUP
ACCTNG
```

Two related commands are CASTOFF and CASTON. The CASTOFF command prevents messages from being received by the user. If one user attempts to send a message to the workstation of another user who has executed CASTOFF, a notice similar to the following appears on the screen:

```
Message NOT sent to FS1/CLARK (Station 3).
```

The CASTON command permits messages to be received by a workstation.

When a workstation is running certain applications, particularly mainframe emulation programs, conflict can occur when the workstation receives messages sent with the NetWare SEND command. To avoid such conflict, the CASTON and CASTOFF commands can be included in the batch files that call the program to prevent the workstation from receiving messages while the application runs.

LISTING USERS

Another handy utility is the USERLIST command. Executing **USERLIST** at the DOS prompt displays a list of users currently using the network, as shown here:

```
User Information for Server FS1
Connection   User Name      Login Time
-------------   ----------------------   -------------------------------
    1        * SUPERVISOR   9-17-1990 12:33 pm
    3          CLARK         9-17-1990 07:12 am
   10          JORDEN        9-17-1990 08:15 am
   11          CURRID        9-17-1990 09:24 am
```

The asterisk indicates the user logged in to the workstation from which the USERLIST command was executed.

CHANGING A USER PASSWORD

A user's password can be changed from the SYSCON utility. A user's password can also be changed by entering **SETPASS** at the DOS prompt. When **SETPASS** is entered, the screen displays the following prompts to guide the user:

```
Enter your old password:
Enter your new password:
Retype your new password:
Would you like to synchronize your passwords on all attached
    servers (Y/N) Y

Synchronizing all passwords...
Password on server FS1 synchronized.
```

DISPLAYING USER INFORMATION

The WHOAMI command provides users with information about their current status on the network. The screen lists the file servers to which the user is attached and the user's name on each server, login date and time, group membership, security equivalences, and effective rights. Entering the command **WHOAMI/A** at the DOS prompt displays information similar to the following:

```
You are user SUPERVISOR attached to server FS1 connection 1.
Server FS1 is running SFT NetWare 286 TTS V2.15.
Login Time:  Monday  September 17, 1990  12:33 pm
You are security equivalent to the following:
     EVERYONE (group)
You are a member of the following Groups:
     EVERYONE (group)
You have the following effective rights:
     [RWOCDPSM] FS1/SYS:
```

The /A parameter indicates that you want to view *A*ll of the available information. Other parameters are /G for listing *G*roup memberships, /S for displaying *S*ecurity equivalences, and /R for viewing directory *R*ights.

SUMMARY

Most of the utilities discussed in this chapter may never be used by the typical network user. However, as the users of your LAN become more sophisticated, some will demand increased control over network functions. The three menu-driven utilities discussed in this chapter—SYSCON, SESSION and FILER—provide a friendly interface for both system supervisors and ordinary users to control various network functions. Several command-line utilities can also be helpful to advanced LAN users.

PART V

NETWORK MAINTENANCE AND FINE TUNING

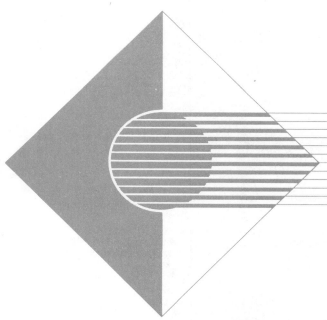

Now that the network is up and running, the real work begins. Local area networks, like any important business system, require considerable maintenance. Because networks are dynamic, changing each time a user saves a file, they must be monitored continuously.

The chapters in this part discuss some of the maintenance techniques, including troubleshooting and backup procedures, available to help keep your network running well. Because your network likely will grow, this part also discusses how to expand a network by adding communications options.

Note that beyond the NetWare functions discussed in this part, many good third-party maintenance tools are available. For further information about these tools, check with your local NetWare dealer.

CHAPTER 17

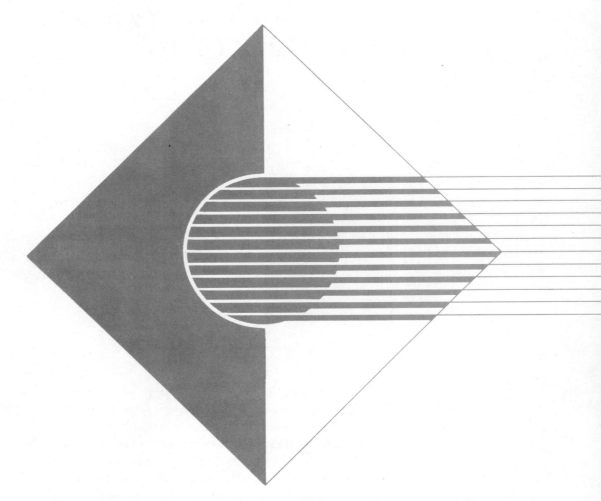

MAINTENANCE TECHNIQUES

FAST TRACK

Specific maintenance techniques depend   255

largely on users' demands on the system. Until you determine
the right sequence and frequency of maintenance, you should
review procedures monthly.

Check disk space utilization   255

weekly until you have a good feeling for activity. To view the
number of free kilobytes and directory entries, type **VOLINFO**
at the DOS prompt. When only 40 percent free disk space
remains, ask users to delete or archive unnecessary files.

Use NDIR to display specific information   256

about disk space use. To display information by user's login name,
for instance, enter **NDIR Z: SUBDIRECTORY OWNER = user's
login name.**

Use SYSCON to display space information   257

for each user by logging on as a supervisor, entering **SYSCON**,
selecting User Information, and highlighting the individual
user. To view total disk space in use for the user, select Other
Information.

Use BINDFIX to recover disk space   258

for each deleted user. BINDFIX recovers space and maintains
the MAIL subdirectories in the SYS volume.

You should periodically check common file areas   259

and remove files. You can write a small batch file to do this
automatically.

To monitor the file server statistics,   260
      use the FCONSOLE utility. Monitor current and peak use to
      make sure your settings are not at the maximums.

To check for possible network security problems,   262
      run the NetWare SECURITY utility. SECURITY is located
      in the SYS:SYSTEM directory. You must have supervisor
      rights to use this utility.

To recover from file server failures,   263
      use the VREPAIR utility. VREPAIR repairs any file allocation
      table errors after a server failure.

CHAPTER *17*

MANY PEOPLE WHO INSTALL LOCAL AREA NET-
works are surprised at how smoothly the process goes. Well-designed
and properly installed networks often seem so trouble-free that you
might think they never need maintenance.

Nevertheless, sooner or later, you'll run out of disk space on a volume, or your screen will display the message *Out of file handles*, or
you'll get a call from a user who can't find a file. All of these problems
can be corrected if your network uses appropriate maintenance procedures. The exact maintenance procedures you employ depend
largely on the users' demands on the system.

This chapter discusses some general maintenance techniques. You
can use these techniques to develop a maintenance program suitable
to your system. Until you determine the right sequence and frequency of maintenance for your network, you should review your
maintenance procedures monthly.

MONITORING DISK SPACE

No one can tell you how fast your network will use up the file
server disk space, but a few simple steps can give you some clues. For
the first few months the network is running, check the file server disk
space weekly. Enter the numbers in a spreadsheet and graph them.

To get a quick review of each volume on the file server and the
number of free directory entries and kilobytes that remain, run
the VOLINFO utility supplied with NetWare. You run this utility
from DOS. Begin running VOLINFO as soon as your network is set
up and all the software is loaded. Record the number of both free
kilobytes and free directories. Run VOLINFO weekly to see how
these numbers change.

Figure 17.1 shows a VOLINFO display.

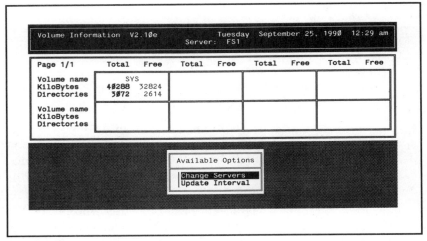

Figure 17.1: VOLINFO display

When you have finished recording the amount of free space, press
Esc and answer Yes to the prompt to exit VOLINFO. When free disk
space becomes 40 percent or less than the amount originally contained on the volume, you should ask network users to delete any
unnecessary files.

DISPLAYING SPECIFIC DISK-USE INFORMATION WITH NDIR

To quickly let users know how much disk space is in use and what
files are on the network, run the NetWare NDIR utility. You can
access the NDIR utility from the DOS prompt.

NDIR offers several parameters that let you select from, or filter,
the directory. We want to see how much disk space individual users
have used, so we enter the following command:

NDIR Z: SUBDIRECTORY OWNER = *user's login name*

This command searches the entire SYS volume (where drive Z is
located), including each subdirectory path, for the files owned by the
user specified by *user's login name*.

If you may want to print a copy of or create a file with this information, add a command to pipe the contents of the report to a file. Such a command would look like this:

NDIR Z: SUBDIRECTORY OWNER = *user's login name* >
TESTFILE.PRN

This command creates a file called TESTFILE.PRN. To send this command to the printer, enter the DOS command **PRINT TESTFILE.PRN**. To send this file to the screen, enter the DOS command **TYPE TESTFILE.PRN | MORE**.

REVIEWING USERS' DISK SPACE WITH SYSCON

You can also review users' disk space by using SYSCON. To use SYSCON in this way, follow these steps:

1. Log on to the server as a supervisor.
2. Enter **SYSCON** at the DOS prompt.
3. Select User Information from the menu that appears.
4. Select a user from the list on the screen.
5. Select Other Information from the menu.

The screen will list the time and date when the user last logged in to the network and whether the user is a file server console operator. The screen will also list the maximum file server disk storage space the user can use, the amount of disk space currently in use by the user, and the user's ID. For our purposes, the important numbers are those indicating the maximum disk space allowed and the disk space in use. (Note that the maximum disk space allowed is the space allowed to the individual user. If the Maximum Disk Usage field displays *Unrestricted*, the user has unlimited file server disk storage space.) Figure 17.2 shows a SYSCON user information screen.

RECOVERING SPACE FROM DELETED USERS

When you delete users, you should move the deleted users' files from the user directory to archive files.

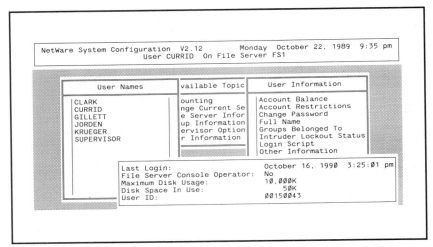

Figure 17.2: SYSCON user information screen

When you delete users, you also should run the NetWare utility BINDFIX from the SYSTEM subdirectory to recover space and maintain MAIL subdirectories in the SYS volume. BINDFIX performs a number of checks on the bindery.

For this example, we want to check active login IDs and compare these with the MAIL subdirectories. When BINDFIX finds MAIL subdirectories for users that no longer exist in the bindery, it will prompt you to delete them, as follows:

Delete mail directories of users that no longer exist? (y/n):

When you enter **Y** for Yes, the program removes MAIL subdirectories for users who are no longer active.

BINDFIX issues a separate prompt to delete the trustee rights for users no longer on the network. When you enter **Y** for Yes, BIND-FIX searches each file server volume and deletes trustee rights from directories.

You should run BINDFIX monthly or quarterly, depending on the frequency with which users are deleted.

MONITORING COMMON FILE AREA SPACE

You also need to monitor the disk space in the COMMON subdirectory. Users share files in this subdirectory, and they may neglect to delete files when they are finished with them.

You should periodically remove files from the COMMON directory. Generally, sweeping this directory once a month is adequate. You can write a small batch file to perform the entire process.

The batch file can be as simple as the one shown here. Using any text processor, create a file called ERASEI.BAT. It should contain the following lines:

```
ECHO OFF
: Batch file to remove files from the common directory
: * * * RUN with care, this program will delete all files
:           in the SYS:COMMON directory. * * *
:
ECHO * * * ERASING ALL FILES IN THE COMMON DIRECTORY * * *
MAP N: = FS1/SYS:COMMON
N:
DELETE *.* < Y.CMD
H:
ECHO * * * PROCESS COMPLETED * * *
```

For safekeeping, save this file in your PRIVATE directory. This will prevent anyone without proper security access from inadvertently running the program.

MONITORING DUPLICATE FILES

As users share information on the local area network, chances are they will duplicate files. File duplication can use up considerable disk space and confuse users.

You may want to find a third-party utility program to check for duplicate files. You can use either a program especially written for NetWare or a DOS-based program. If you use a DOS-based program, be sure to run it for each NetWare volume, because DOS-based software usually does not cross NetWare volumes.

MONITORING FILE SERVER STATISTICS

The number of users that log on to the LAN will start to grow almost as soon as the cables are laid. For this reason, you should periodically check some of the statistics provided by the FCONSOLE utility. You should monitor at least the number of open files, the number of connections, and dynamic memory 1. (Dynamic memory 1 is the file server memory that is allocated to keep track of drive maps and open files. This memory cannot be configured in NetWare 286. If you have a busy server with many users running multitasking programs, you can exceed dynamic memory 1, which can cause the file server to stop functioning abruptly.)

To access this information, make sure you are logged on to the network as a supervisor or an authorized console operator. To start the FCONSOLE utility, type **FCONSOLE** at the DOS prompt. Then select Statistics from the Available Options menu and choose Summary from the File Server Statistics menu, shown in Figure 17.3.

The screen displayed next, the File Server Statistics Summary screen, contains a wealth of information about the status of the file

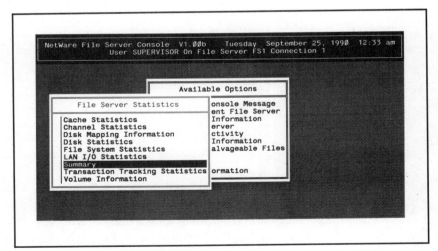

Figure 17.3: FCONSOLE File Server Statistics menu

server since the last time it was booted. Figure 17.4 shows an example of this screen.

When checking the statistics for open files, connections, and Dynamic Memory 1, note the three variables: Maximum, Peak Used, and Currently in Use. Be sure to compare the peak usage against the maximum figures. If the peak value is close to the maximum value, you should perform some maintenance. Such tasks may be as simple as changing the number of open files allowed or as complicated as bringing up a new server. The only parameter you can change is the number of open files allowed. If the number of open files reaches 70 percent of the maximum, you probably should change the maximum. To change this parameter, run the Install program. Be sure to back up the system before you change this parameter.

PERFORMING OTHER MAINTENANCE CHECKS

You should routinely perform several other checks on your network. For the most part, these are housekeeping chores that keep the system running smoothly.

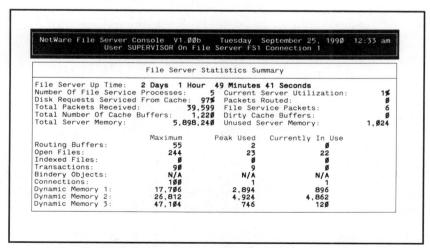

Figure 17.4: FCONSOLE File Server Statistics Summary screen

PERFORMING SECURITY CHECKS

You should periodically run the NetWare SECURITY utility. This utility is located in the SYSTEM subdirectory, and it requires supervisor rights. The SECURITY utility checks the bindery for users with supervisor security, short passwords, nonexpiring passwords, and other conditions that may make the network less secure.

To run the SECURITY program, make sure you have a drive mapped to the system subdirectory. You can do this by issuing the following commands from DOS:

```
MAP N: = SYS:SYSTEM
N:SECURITY
```

If you want to keep the output from this program on file, simply pipe the contents to a file. Do this by adding a greater-than sign and a file name on the command line, as follows:

```
MAP N: = SYS:SYSTEM
N:SECURITY  >  SEC0412.PRN
```

Now the contents of the security check will be sent to a file called SEC0412.PRN.

You may want to build a number of these files over time. Even though DOS places a time and date stamp on each file, a good way to identify each file is to make the date a part of the file name. In the preceding example, the numbers 0412 indicate that the file was created on April 12.

CHECKING THE ROOT DIRECTORIES

You should periodically check the root directory of each NetWare volume for extraneous files. NetWare security prevents most users from inadvertently placing files in these areas. Users with supervisor equivalency, however, are not restrained from leaving files in these areas. Although these files most likely will cause no harm, they could cause confusion in the search path, which could yield unexpected results during program execution.

RECOVERING FROM FILE SERVER FAILURES

Your file server may never have a problem and may never fail. However, if it does fail, data will be left unfiled, and program files will be left open, leading to problems in the file allocation table (FAT).

NetWare generally recovers problems by itself, and usually the server is restored without problems. Some error messages indicating file allocation table errors may appear on the console, however, though these problems may correct themselves over time. To help correct such problems, you can run the NetWare VREPAIR utility. Like other NetWare utilities, you can run VREPAIR from DOS. Before running VREPAIR, be sure to back up your files on the server, just for safety.

To execute the VREPAIR utility, simply type VREPAIR from the DOS prompt.

MONITORING NETWORK USE

NetWare by itself does not provide full network use statistics. It provides file server statistics, but it does not provide information about cable use and other activities. Generally, for small- to medium-sized networks these measures are not necessary. For large or busy networks, however, you may need to purchase a third-party diagnostic tool to measure network activity and performance.

Whatever diagnostic tool you use, you should use as part of the regular monthly maintenance cycle. Monthly monitoring will give you benchmark statistics while the network is operating under regular conditions.

SUMMARY

This chapter discussed some maintenance procedures you should use to keep your network running smoothly.

Generally, the busier the network, the more maintenance it needs. Although NetWare provides some maintenance functions, other, third-party network maintenance utility programs can facilitate the maintenance process. You should discuss these products with your NetWare dealer.

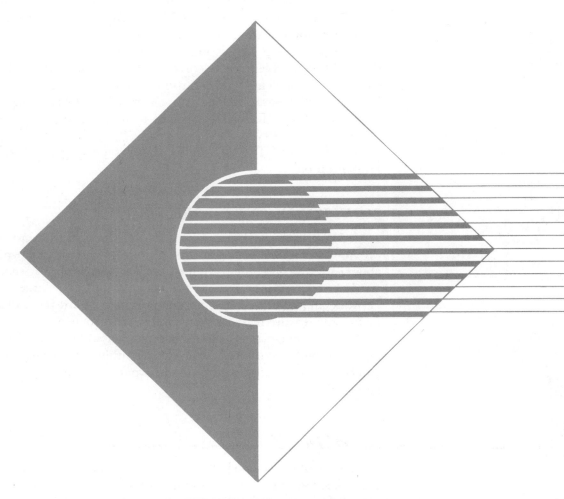

MONITORING SYSTEM PERFORMANCE AND TROUBLESHOOTING

FAST TRACK

To establish a benchmark of network performance,   **267**
> run the NetWare PERFORM utility. Run PERFORM when
> the network is new. Then record the results and run the utility
> again as the network becomes busier.

To monitor selected server statistics,   **270**
> use the FCONSOLE utility. Watch for changes in the percent-
> age of disk requests serviced from cache.

If disk request services from cache fall below 95 percent,   **271**
> you may examine server utilization patterns. The network may
> need adjustment to avoid degradation of performance.

To check current server utilization,   **272**
> monitor the server from FCONSOLE. Server use is updated
> frequently, and the figure displayed reflects the current activity.
> Generally, the server utilization rate should be less than 25 per-
> cent except during momentary peaks.

To monitor open files,   **272**
> use the FCONSOLE utility. Certain software applications
> open many files at one time. Monitor the peak number of open
> files to make sure the number remains within the maximum
> number set. Application software will not run correctly if the
> server reaches its maximum for open files.

When troubleshooting problems,   **272**
> be sure to change no more than one element at a time.

If you suspect a software problem,   273
    first check users' security rights. Make sure users have proper
    access to read, write, create, delete, or open files as required by
    the software.

A list of common software-related problems   274
    appears in Table 18.2.

A list of common hardware-related problems   275
    appears in Table 18.3.

If a new workstation fails to operate,   275
    check the network adapter card and other cards in the work-
    station for possible conflicts.

Check cabling   276
    as a potential source of problems. Look especially for damaged,
    loose, or bent pins.

Check wire centers   276
    for problems if one or more workstations fails to operate.

CHAPTER **18**

BECAUSE THE SIZE AND SHAPE OF YOUR NETWORK changes every day, system performance changes over time. Changes may be slight, or a component may fail completely. To avoid problems, you should monitor your network regularly. Keeping a careful eye on certain performance areas can help you detect problems before they become serious.

MONITORING KEY SYSTEM PERFORMANCE AREAS

You can evaluate system performance by monitoring such factors as the amount of time the system takes to retrieve programs from the file server hard disk, sort a database, and run a program. Changes in performance, however, often occur so gradually that users don't notice a deterioration in performance until something is seriously wrong with the network.

Because performance changes are difficult to detect by sight, you need to use special performance measuring tools, such as Novell's PERFORM utility. Good third-party programs also are available for measuring performance changes in the file server or in the network in general.

Table 18.1 summarizes common maintenance tasks.

USING NOVELL'S PERFORM UTILITY

The Novell PERFORM utility helps you measure network throughput. PERFORM uses common DOS functions, such as creating, opening, reading, and writing to files, to monitor performance. You can run PERFORM for the entire network or for a standalone computer.

Table 18.1: Common Maintenance Tasks

TO CHECK	DO THE FOLLOWING
Workstation performance	Run the PERFORM utility to determine workstation speed. If speed drops 30 percent or more, check for problems. (Note: You must have benchmark PERFORM information for each type and speed of workstation. PERFORM results vary by workstation processor speed. Therefore, if a workstation that normally clocks 104 K/sec drops to 60 K/sec, you can confirm that something has gone wrong.)
Cache statistics	Check the FCOSOLE file server statistics. If the disk requests serviced from cache measurement is below 95 percent, consider doing one of the following: • Add additional memory to the file server. • Move applications or data to local disk drives. • Add another server for high-volume applications.
Server use	Check the FCONSOLE file server statistics. If the current server utilization regularly exceeds 60 percent, consider upgrading the server memory or reconfiguring applications
Number of open files	Check the FCONSOLE file server statistics. If the peak number of open files begins to approach 70 percent of the maximum configuration, consider raising the maximum number. (Note: Each open file requires 100 bytes of file server memory.)

Note: Be sure to keep benchmark statistics for the file server that show how the network runs when everything is all right. Then, when you suspect a problem, you can compare current performance to the benchmarks to see what areas are affected.

PERFORM provides data about the number of kilobytes per second that the system can read and write. When using PERFORM to monitor system performance, you should not alter system parameters or options. The results of PERFORM vary considerably, depending on configured settings such as whether records are both read from and written to, the types of files in the system, and the record size used. The type of default disk drive used—network drive, local hard disk, or local floppy disk drive—also affects PERFORM results.

To use PERFORM, place an executable file in a search path, such as in the X:\UTIL subdirectory. This allows anyone on the network to use PERFORM. When executing PERFORM to record a performance benchmark, make sure the network is quiet (with no users logged on).

To start, make sure your default directory is a network directory. Log on to a network drive, such as drive X. Then type **PERFORM** at the DOS command prompt and press **F1** to begin the first measurement. When the test is over, the results will appear in a box in the center of the screen, as shown in Figure 18.1. Be sure to record these results.

Note that if you compare the network results against those for a local hard disk drive or floppy disk drive, you will find significant

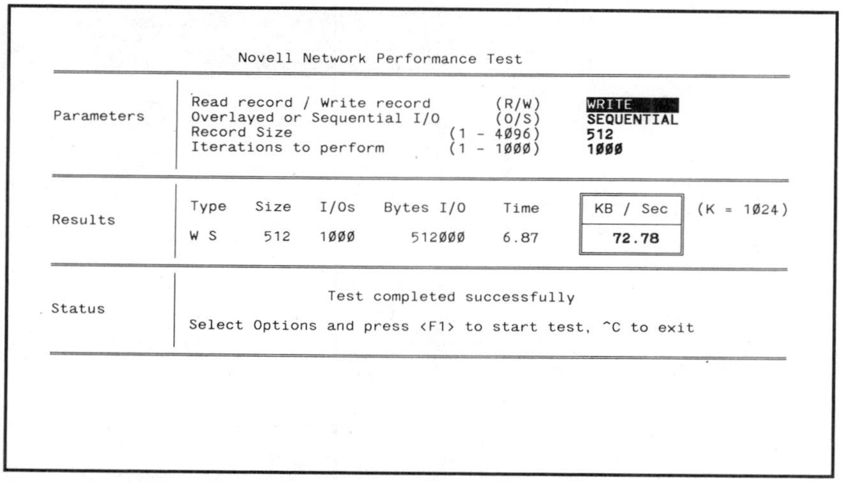

```
                    Novell Network Performance Test

                 Read record / Write record      (R/W)    WRITE
 Parameters      Overlayed or Sequential I/O      (O/S)    SEQUENTIAL
                 Record Size              (1 - 4096)       512
                 Iterations to perform    (1 - 1000)       1000


                 Type   Size   I/Os   Bytes I/O    Time    KB / Sec   (K = 1024)
 Results
                 W S    512    1000     512000     6.87      72.78


 Status                        Test completed successfully

                 Select Options and press <F1> to start test, ^C to exit
```

Figure 18.1: Novell network performance test results

differences in performance. Generally, because of the way the network operating system works, network performance is better than that of locally attached drives.

Continue to monitor system performance regularly with the PER-FORM utility. Using the benchmark measurement, you'll be able to see changes in performance as the network gets busier. PERFORM results may be your first clue when system performance starts degrading because of high activity levels or other causes.

USING FCONSOLE INFORMATION

The NetWare FCONSOLE utility can also help you monitor network performance. FCONSOLE provides detailed information about the network. For monitoring performance, some of the summary statistics are the most useful.

To access the FCONSOLE summary screen, make sure you are logged on as a user with either supervisor or console operator rights. Then type **FCONSOLE** at the DOS prompt. Select Statistics from the first menu and Summary from the next menu. The file server statistics summary screen will appear, as shown in Figure 18.2.

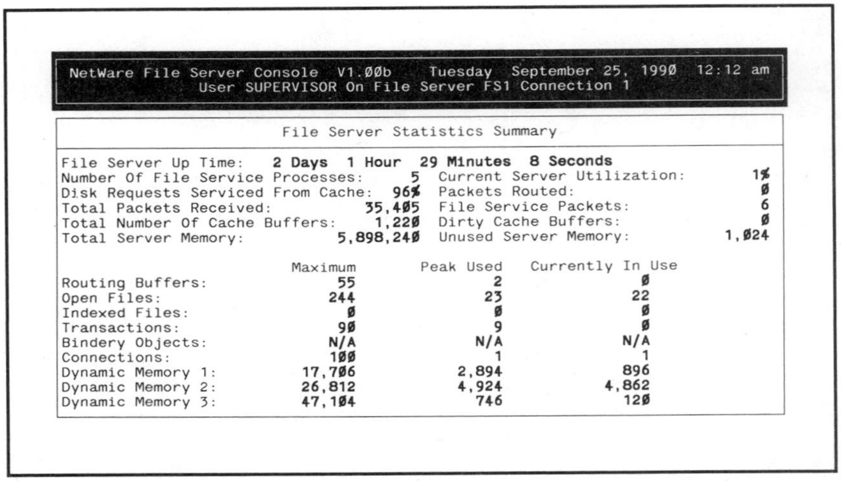

```
NetWare File Server Console   V1.00b    Tuesday  September 25, 1990  12:12 am
                 User SUPERVISOR On File Server FS1 Connection 1

                       File Server Statistics Summary

File Server Up Time:    2 Days 1 Hour 29 Minutes 8 Seconds
Number Of File Service Processes:        5   Current Server Utilization:      1%
Disk Requests Serviced From Cache:     96%   Packets Routed:                   0
Total Packets Received:             35,405   File Service Packets:             6
Total Number Of Cache Buffers:       1,220   Dirty Cache Buffers:              0
Total Server Memory:             5,898,240   Unused Server Memory:         1,024

                         Maximum      Peak Used    Currently In Use
Routing Buffers:            55            2              0
Open Files:                244           23             22
Indexed Files:               0            0              0
Transactions:               90            9              0
Bindery Objects:           N/A          N/A            N/A
Connections:               100            1              1
Dynamic Memory 1:       17,706        2,894            896
Dynamic Memory 2:       26,812        4,924          4,862
Dynamic Memory 3:       47,104          746            120
```

Figure 18.2: File server statistics screen

To evaluate performance, pay particular attention to the following items on the summary screen:

- Disk Requests Serviced from Cache
- Current Server Utilization
- Open Files

DISK REQUESTS SERVICED FROM CACHE   A good indicator of efficient system performance is a high number of disk requests serviced from the file server cache memory, instead of from the file server hard disk. The Disk Requests Serviced from Cache measurement on the summary screen indicates the percentage of requests serviced from the cache since the last time the server was activated. For meaningful results, you should monitor this figure after the server has been online for several weeks or months.

Generally, the percentage of disk requests serviced from the cache should be between 95 and 99 percent. If your system shows a lower percentage, you have several options for increasing performance:

- You can add memory to the file server.
- You can move certain applications to local disks.
- You can add another server for especially taxing applications.

The easiest of these solutions is to add more memory to the file server, thus increasing the available memory in the cache.

Moving applications to local disks helps if certain applications do not require sharing of information. Large data files often can be processed faster on a local disk, but moving them to local disks may not be efficient if the files need to be shared across the network.

Adding another server is, by far, the most expensive solution, but it can be a practical one for important applications. Database applications are especially taxing to a file server. A number of client-server database products are becoming available. These are serviced by an independent server, not the mail file server, and so do not strain the rest of the network.

CURRENT SERVER UTILIZATION   Current Server Utilization indicates how busy the file server is at the current time. This measurement varies widely with the type of activity on the network. Generally, file server use should be under 25 percent except during momentary peaks of activity.

Certain activities and applications, such as databases, electronic mail systems, and other programs that copy large files to the file server, can greatly increase file server use. If you observe sustained periods of time where server use exceeds 60 percent, you should investigate the activities being performed and determine whether the server or network needs upgrading.

OPEN FILES   As network use increases, you should monitor the number of open files. Certain applications, such as databases, electronic mail systems, and sometimes word processing packages, can cause many files to be open at once. In addition, users who employ multitasking environments (such as DesqView or Windows/386) use many open files.

During file server installation for our example system, we set the maximum number of files that can be open by all users on the network at one time. Depending on the number of users logged in and the types of applications the network runs, however, the number we set may be inadequate. When users attempt to open more files than we have allowed, results are unpredictable. Files and application software can be damaged or may not run correctly.

To monitor the number of open files, periodically use the file server statistics summary screen to record the number of open files during peak use. Divide this number by the number of connections during peak use (obtained from the same screen). If the peak-use number approaches 70 percent of the maximum number of open files, you need to change the system configuration.

TROUBLESHOOTING

Although most networks are stable, from time to time something will go wrong. Diagnosing problems, however, can be difficult. You will find diagnosis easier if you follow this rule: Change only one element at a time. If you change more than one element at a time, you may never know what corrected the problem or what the problem really was.

Most problems are either hardware or software problems. Hardware problems are usually (but not always) limited to a workstation or a group of workstations connected to the same device. Software problems, on the other hand, usually occur in all similarly configured workstations that run the software application.

TROUBLESHOOTING SOFTWARE PROBLEMS

Software problems are usually caused by improperly installed software. Generally, these problems affect only one software package. They may or may not affect all users who use the package.

If you suspect a software problem, first check the security levels of the people who are having problems. A common mistake of many network administrators is to install and test the software using high-level or supervisor rights. Because the supervisor has the rights to read, write, create, delete, and open all files in the directory, security-related problems rarely surface.

If security rights are not the cause of the problem, check the configuration of the software. Most software packages contain both executable files and configuration or overlay files, so you should make sure the programs are located in a searched path. Then all files will be accessible.

If the preceding steps do not resolve the problem, try reinstalling the software. Install it into a brand new subdirectory so you don't skip any steps.

Table 18.2 summarizes procedures for troubleshooting common software problems.

TROUBLESHOOTING HARDWARE PROBLEMS

Troubleshooting hardware problems starts at the workstation. When hardware problems occur, you should first inspect the network adapter card, the network cable, and the wire closet connections. Table 18.3 summarizes troubleshooting procedures for common hardware problems.

Table 18.2: Troubleshooting Common Software Problems

PROBLEM	SOLUTION
A software package does not run properly on the network.	Check to see if the software is installed correctly. • Check security access rights to the files in the program directory. • Check drive maps to the files in the program directory. (Note: For most software packages, the program directory should be in the search path.) • Check software installation parameters. Make sure all configuration files are in place (the configuration varies by software package; check the software package installation manual). • If all else fails, reinstall the software (from scratch) in another program directory. Note: A few packages exist that do not run properly on a network. If problems persist, contact the software vendor for assistance.
Some (but not all) users cannot run a software package.	Check security levels and drive maps of the users who cannot run the software properly. Adjust these if necessary.
A new workstation will not work on the network.	Check cables first, then the network adapter card, then the connection in the wire closet. Replace items as necessary, being sure to change just one item at a time.
A (previously installed) workstation will not work on the network.	Check cables first, then the network adapter card, then the connection in the wire closet. Replace items as necessary, being sure to change just one item at a time.

Table 18.2: Troubleshooting Common Software Problems (continued)

PROBLEM	SOLUTION
A group of workstations will not work on the network.	Check the multistation access unit (MAU). Move the workstation patch cables to another unit.

Table 18.3: Troubleshooting Common Hardware Problems

PROBLEM AREA	POSSIBLE SYMPTOM AND SOLUTION
Network adapter card	A single workstation fails to operate, but other workstations on the network function normally. Remove the old card and replace it with a new card.
Cable	A single workstation fails to operate, but other workstations on the network function normally. Remove the cable that connects the workstation to the wall. If the problem still exists, remove the cable that connects the patch panel (or other wire-room device) to the multistation access unit (MAU).
Wire centers (MAUs or concentrators)	One or more workstations do not function on the network. Move the cable connection in the wire room to another port on the multistation access unit.

CHECKING NETWORK ADAPTER CARDS If a workstation fails to operate when it is first placed on the network, make sure your network adapter card is properly seated in the computer. A poor connection can yield unpredictable results.

If the workstation still fails, check the setting of the network adapter card. All network adapter cards require the use of an interrupt and some memory addresses. Other cards and boards, such as bus mouse boards, extra serial or parallel adapters, and video adapter boards, also use interrupts. Make sure your network adapter does not use the same interrupt or memory addresses as other boards.

You should know what interrupts and addresses your specific network adapter card uses. Sometimes, the card can be configured, so you must know the settings if you are using settings other than the factory default values.

If you suspect that another adapter card is conflicting with the network adapter card, check the settings of the other boards. More often than not, however, you will not know what addresses your other adapter boards use. If that is the case, your best approach is trial and error. First remove all nonessential boards from the computer. Then place the network adapter card in the computer and attempt to log in to the network. If you can log in, then begin replacing the other boards until you find the one that makes the workstation fail.

CHECKING CABLES   Cabling problems can be difficult to diagnose. If you suspect a cable problem, first check that the cable is seated properly in the network adapter card or wire center port. Then check for bent or loose pins in each cable. These can cause certain workstations on the network to have problems, but not to fail.

If the cable itself is damaged or broken, you may be able to replace it yourself, or you may need to call a cable specialist. An outright break in the cable will stop a workstation from accessing the network. A damaged cable may allow a workstation to function, but to function poorly.

CHECKING WIRE CENTERS   All network topologies have a wire center device. The name of the device that joins your network connections together depends on the topology you use. For Ethernet this device is called the concentrator, for ArcNet it is called the active hub, and for Token Ring networks it is called the multistation access unit.

If the entire device malfunctions, all workstations connected to the device (and potentially all others that follow it on the network) will not function. If a single port on the device breaks, only the workstations connected there fail.

Wire centers can cause only certain workstations on the network to fail, or failures to occur only at certain times of the day, especially if the wire center device uses an electronic repeater to boost the network signal over long distances. If you suspect a wire center problem and the device uses a repeater, ensure that the repeater has an active source of power.

You can also diagnose wire center problems by removing or bypassing the suspected device. If just a single port seems to be involved, plug the workstation into another port. Even if only one port is involved, however, you should replace the entire wire center device.

CHECKING OTHER HARDWARE   Network-specific hardware, such as the cards, cables, and wire centers, are not always responsible for hardware problems. Sometimes the problem is in the file server or in the workstations themselves.

The file server is the key component of the network, so you should have ready access to parts that might fail. This means keeping supplies on hand or having a service contract with a specified turnaround time.

The three file server components most likely to fail are the hard disk controller card, the hard disk, and memory.

The file server's hard disk and controller card are used constantly and so eventually may fail. When the controller card malfunctions, the server may or may not display an error message. (Usually it does not.) When the hard disk fails, usually an error message appears when the server is activated.

Memory problems also may or may not be reported by error messages. Sometimes an error message will report a memory problem that causes the server to shut down, but then this message (and the problem) may not recur for a period of time.

If you suspect memory problems, you should replace memory boards and move suspect boards out of the server where they could cause problems for everyone on the network. If you suspect memory problems, it is best to call a qualified technician to help diagnose and correct the problem.

SUMMARY

This chapter discussed several techniques for monitoring your network's performance and performing first-line troubleshooting. Keep in mind, though, that networks are relatively new, and sophisticated tools and monitors still do not exist for them. As local area network technology matures, more effective monitoring devices will emerge.

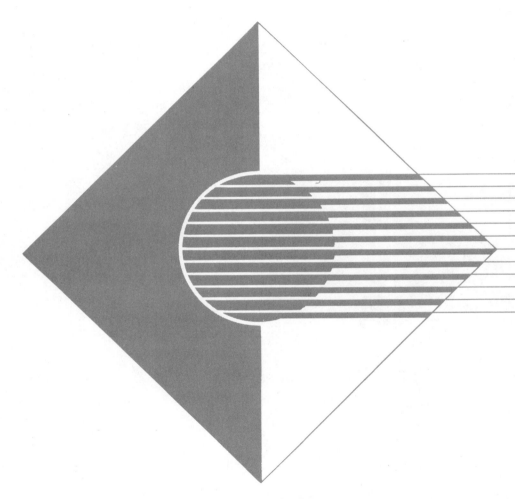

BACKING UP AND
ARCHIVING THE NETWORK

FAST TRACK

The first step in backing up the network   283
is deciding who is in charge. Backup processing should be
assigned to one individual.

The difference between backup files and archive files   284
is in their purposes. Backup files protect network files from
mechanical and human errors. Archive files are previous versions of files that you intend to keep over time.

Hardware and software for making backup copies   284
should be fully compatible with Novell NetWare.

NetWare provides four backup and restore utilities   285
for backing up network files and trustee rights: NARCHIVE,
NRESTORE, LARCHIVE, and LRESTORE.

Perform backup processing when the network is   285
quiet and not many files are open. Most backup utilities do not
back up open files.

A good schedule for backup processing is   286
to back up changed files nightly and back up the entire system
once a week.

A good archive procedure   287
backs up only files or directories that you want to keep generations of over time.

Use the NARCHIVE utility to   289

back up files to another network directory. You must have supervisor rights to back up bindery files. From DOS, make an ARCHIVE directory to hold the NARCHIVE files. To keep a log of the activity, respond Yes to the log file prompt.

Use the NRESTORE utility to   290

restore some or all files backed up with NARCHIVE.

Use the LARCHIVE utility to   294

back up files to a local hard or floppy disk. LARCHIVE works much the same way as NARCHIVE. However, LARCHIVE directs backup files to a local drive.

You can make a automatic archive program   294

by creating a small text file that is piped in as a command file. This file helps automate the archive process.

Use the LRESTORE utility to   297

restore some or all files backed up with the LARCHIVE utility. Follow the prompts to restore the files.

CHAPTER **19**

A FREQUENTLY OVERLOOKED REQUIREMENT OF managing local area networks is backing up and archiving the system. Backing up and archiving the system means making copies of your file server programs, files, and bindery and storing them someplace else. If something goes wrong with the file server or any of the backed-up files, you'll be able to restore the system by using your copies.

We configured our example system so that all programs and files are directed to the file server hard disk. This architecture places considerable importance on the file server hard disk. If the file server hard disk fails, the network is useless until the files can be restored or re-created. Too often, however, people don't realize the importance of backing up their system until a major catastrophe, such as a failed hard disk, occurs.

This chapter discusses various backup strategies and options. It discusses the difference between backing up and archiving and then examines the types of backup procedures important for average networks. Finally, it provides a suggested procedure for backing up the file server using the NetWare backup and archiving commands.

DETERMINING WHO BACKS UP THE SYSTEM

Before any discussion of the technical options for backing up your system takes place, you need to determine who is in charge of backing up your system.

Some network administrators leave the backup process to individual users. This requires every user on the system to take responsibility for safeguarding his or her own files. In practice, this is not a good idea. Realistically, most users will not take the time to adequately back up files. Some studies indicate that, when making backup copies is left to users, fewer than 10 percent perform the task regularly.

Many network administrators thus opt to perform all backup tasks as a part of their routine maintenance of the system. The network administrator is responsible for keeping the system running, maintaining program files, and performing other housekeeping functions. Performing all file backup procedures is a logical addition to these tasks. Realistically, too, the network administrator can perform backup tasks more efficiently than users, who perform such tasks less frequently and often without the same expertise as the network administrator.

BACKING UP VERSUS ARCHIVING

Most networks require two different types of protection: backup copies and archives. The basic difference between making backup copies and making archive copies is purpose. Generally, you back up your system to protect your network from mechanical or human error. Backup copies protect the network from hardware problems, such as a failed network hard disk. They are also helpful when users inadvertently erase files or programs.

Archive files, however, are usually created to maintain certain files over time. For example, you might want to archive your monthly spreadsheets or status reports. Users may want to archive files in much the same way they archive paper copies of documents over time.

A good archiving procedure also helps manage disk space. Certain files do not need to be kept online over long periods of time. Correspondence files, for example, generally do not need to be stored online indefinitely. Because you may not want to delete these files entirely, you should have a procedure that stores these files elsewhere.

Often, you'll use the same tools to get both jobs done. Most utilities intended for backing up files can be used for archiving them as well.

CHOOSING HARDWARE AND SOFTWARE

You can use either NetWare's own utility programs to back up and archive your system, or you can use third-party software. The software you choose affects the hardware options available.

If you choose third-party software for backing up and archiving your system, make sure it will fully back up your files and also the NetWare trustee rights and bindery. That way, should you ever need to restore files, you'll not have to recreate trustee rights.

Especially for large networks, the best device for backing up your system usually is a tape unit that has been certified for NetWare. Tape units are quick and efficient. They don't require floppy disks or hard disks. Most tape backup units that are made for networks have all the utility software and timer software you need to automate the backup process. Tape cartridges also can be used as backup devices. Tape cartridges are relatively inexpensive, so you'll be able to keep several generations of backup files. Products of various sizes and capacities are available. Check with your NetWare dealer for a specific product recommendation.

USING NETWARE UTILITIES

You can also use NetWare's own utilities to back up and archive your system. The NetWare operating system includes the backup utilities NARCHIVE, NRESTORE, LARCHIVE, and LRESTORE.

NARCHIVE backs up files to another network disk area. Its counterpart, NRESTORE, restores the files and trustee rights.

LARCHIVE backs up files to a local hard or floppy disk. Its counterpart, LRESTORE, restores the files and trustee rights.

ESTABLISHING PROCEDURES

In general, you should reserve time every day for backing up your system. You don't have to back up the entire system every day, but you should at least back up data files that have been changed.

Most back up utilities do not back up open files, so you should schedule backup processing for times when the network is quiet, usually at night, when all the users have gone home. Many network administrators write simple batch files to start the backup procedure and purchase small utility programs that start the backup process during the middle of the night.

Here are some general guidelines you should follow:

- Back up selected files daily.
- Back up the entire system weekly.
- Archive files monthly.
- Perform backup processing at night (or when most users are off the network).
- Assign the backup and archiving process to one individual.
- Make one person responsible for restoring files.

BACKING UP FILES DAILY

For all but the smallest network, backing up every file every night is too time consuming. Therefore, you need to set up procedures for backing up important files daily and other files less frequently.

First, determine what files on the network should be backed up. Generally, program and operating system files don't change often, so these files need not be backed up daily. User data files and configuration files, however, are prime candidates for nightly backup processing.

Depending on how large your network is and how often files are revised and updated, you may want to back up only files that have been modified since the last backup processing. The system can determine this, so many LAN administrators only back up changed files.

Backing up only changed files is efficient, but this procedure can cause problems when you need to restore a file quickly. The user may not remember the last time the file was changed, so you might need to search through multiple backup logs to find the file. Most LAN administrators prefer to back up only changed files for three to five days and then back up the entire system because this schedule speeds up the restoration process. A file can be restored more quickly when you have only a few tapes to search.

BACKING UP THE ENTIRE SYSTEM WEEKLY

Most network administrators find that backing up the entire system weekly is appropriate. Then no more than a week's worth of files need be searched if you need to restore the system to its most recent state. A tape backup unit facilitates this process because tape backup units are much faster than disk units. Although this extra speed may not mean much to small networks, it will save a lot of time as the network grows.

The following is an example schedule for backing up the system:

Monday	Back up changed files. Back up bindery and trustee rights.
Tuesday	Back up changed files. Back up bindery and trustee rights.
Wednesday	Back up changed files. Back up bindery and trustee rights.
Thursday	Back up changed files. Back up bindery and trustee rights.
Friday	Back up *all* files. Back up bindery and trustee rights.
Sunday	Back up changed files. Back up bindery and trustee rights.

Using this schedule, if the file server hard disk were to fail on Wednesday, you would have to restore only four sets of backup files: Friday, then Sunday, then Monday, and then Tuesday.

Note that you must restore files in the proper order. Depending on how your users use the network, certain files will change daily. Working from the last complete backup to the day the system failed will ensure that the most current version is restored.

ARCHIVING FILES MONTHLY

Generally, archiving needs to be performed only once a month. Make sure you place archived files on different media (tape, disk, or disks) from backup copies.

The purpose of archives is different from backup files, so you should follow different procedures. The following are example procedures for archiving files:

- Determine the directories and files to be archived.
- Determine whether files should remain on the server after archiving.
- Perform the archiving process.
- Erase archived files no longer needed on the server.
- Print a list of the archived files.
- Store the media that contains the archived files in a safe place.

Another technique that many network administrators use is compressing files before archiving them. Several good utilities are available that compress files and package them into a single file. Compressing reduces the amount of disk space you need for archives. Files often can be compressed by 50 to 80 percent. When your archive takes up less space, your archive disk space goes further, thus reducing the cost of archiving.

USING NETWARE BACKUP AND ARCHIVING UTILITIES

As mentioned previously, NetWare provides several utilities that facilitate the backup and archiving processes. These utilities are NARCHIVE and its counterpart, NRESTORE, and LARCHIVE and its counterpart, LRESTORE.

Both sets of utilities not only make copies of files, but also save the directory rights and trustee lists. They also produce a record of the files backed up.

THE NARCHIVE AND NRESTORE UTILITIES

NARCHIVE and NRESTORE back up or restore files to another network directory. These utilities can be used by anyone on the network with read, search, open, and modify rights. Certain files, such as the network security files (NET$BIND.SYS and NET$BVAL.SYS) can be backed up only if you are logged on as a supervisor or have rights equivalent to supervisor rights. The examples here assume that you are logged on as a supervisor equivalent.

Because NARCHIVE copies your files and network information to another area of the network, it doesn't protect you from a hardware failure, such as a disk failure. NARCHIVE is useful, however, when you have plenty of disk space and want to protect certain files from human errors, such as when a user accidentally deletes important files.

USING NARCHIVE TO BACK UP FILES   In order to use the NARCHIVE utility, you must first log on to the network drive that contains the files. Then you execute the utility and indicate where you want the files stored. To use the utility, you first must create an archive directory. We will map an unused drive to the area where the users' private files are located, create the archive directory, and then log on to the PRIVATE directory. From DOS, type the following commands, pressing ◄─┘ at the end of each line:

```
MAP N: = FS1/SYS:PRIVATE
MAP M: = FS1/SYS:
M:
MD ARCHIVE
N:
```

We can now direct all our backed up files to the archive directory (on drive M).

Log on to the N:\PRIVATE directory and execute the NARCHIVE utility. First check the DOS prompt to be sure you are at the N:\PRIVATE directory. If you are not, NARCHIVE will not back up the proper files.

Next, type **NARCHIVE**. The first prompt asks you to enter the names of the directories to which files should be archived. We want to place all the PRIVATE files in the SYS:ARCHIVE directory, so enter **SYS:ARCHIVE**, as shown in Figure 19.1.

```
N:\PRIVATE>narchive
Advanced NetWare NARCHIVE V2.16b -- Archive DOS files to Network Volume
Copyright (c) 1987 Novell, Inc.  All Rights Reserved.


Enter names (separated by commas) of directories to which files should be
archived (destination directories).
You must specify a complete directory name including the volume.
> SYS:ARCHIVE
```

Figure 19.1: Selecting the archive directory for NARCHIVE

We will not be adding other destination directories, so press ← to respond to the next prompt. A series of questions then appears, one at a time, asking if you want to print a log of the session, use a local or a network spooler for the report, save directory rights and trustee lists, and archive the system's user and group definitions. Generally, you should keep both a printed and a file log of the backup session, so respond Yes to the first prompt. For our example, respond to the other prompts as in Figure 19.2.

NARCHIVE next asks whether you want to select or ignore any specific files. This feature lets you filter some files out so you can back up just certain files. For example, we want to maintain all files in the PRIVATE directories, so we will select the third option: Back Up All Files. Once we make this selection, the backup procedure begins. The screen will list the files being backed up, and your printer will print a detailed log of the files being backed up. Your screen will look like Figure 19.3.

USING NRESTORE TO RESTORE FILES   To restore files backed up with the NARCHIVE utility, NetWare provides the NRESTORE utility. You can use this utility no matter what directory you are logged on to, because the archive records indicate the proper directory locations and files.

```
N:\PRIVATE>NARCHIVE
Advanced NetWare NARCHIVE V2.16b -- Archive DOS files to Network Volume
Copyright (c) 1987 Novell, Inc.  All Rights Reserved.


Enter names (separated by commas) of directories to which files should be
archived (destination directories).
You must specify a complete directory name including the volume.
> SYS:SYSTEM
>
Do you want to print a log report of this session? (Y/N)  Y
Print to Local printer or Network spooler? (L/N) L
Do you want to save directory rights and trustee lists? (Y/N)  Y
Do you want to archive the system's user and group definitions? (Y/N)  Y
```

Figure 19.2: NARCHIVE prompts

```
Select specific directories to be backed up?
(N = Back up all directories)  N

Select the backup mode for ALL directories from the following:

1) Back up ALL qualified files in each directory
2) Back up ONLY qualified files that have been modified since last backup

Select Option: (1, 2) 1

Do you want to:
 1)   Select specific files
 2)   Ignore specific files
 3)   Back up all files
 Select Option: (1 - 3) 3
    Archiving: +***
SYS:PRIVATE
    Archiving: +*******
SYS:PRIVATE/GILLETT
    Archiving: +**********
SYS:PRIVATE/GILLETT/WKS
    Archiving: +*
SYS:PRIVATE/GILLETT/WORDS
    Archiving:+***************************
```

Figure 19.3: NARCHIVE in progress

To see how to use the NRESTORE utility, suppose that user Gillett inadvertently erases all the files in WORDS, his word processing directory. To restore just these files, and no others, first log on to the network as a user with supervisor equivalency. Then, at the DOS prompt, type **NRESTORE**.

The first prompt asks if you want to restore security information with the directories. Enter **Y** for Yes. NRESTORE then asks if you want to select specify directories to restore. We want to restore only one user's files, so again enter **Y** for Yes.

The next instruction asks you to enter the name of the directory. Specify the directory name and path to be restored. For this example, enter **SYS:PRIVATE/GILLETT/WORDS**, as shown in Figure 19.4.

The NRESTORE file then restores every file to the specified directory. If the program finds a file of the same name in the directory, it will ask you whether to overwrite the file or bypass it.

CREATING ARCHIVE LOGS The NARCHIVE utility creates a file called ARCHIVE.LOG, which is similar to the printed log. This file is useful for searches because it lists every file backed up. A sample listing of this file is shown here:

```
$SYS:SYSTEM
    Monday, Oct 1, 1990  2:00 pm  | 5a a 1 e 0 c 1


    ARCHIVERLOG LOG
    NET$BINDSYS SYS 6
    NET$BVALSYS SYS 6
```

```
N:\PRIVATE>NRESTORE
Advanced NetWare NARCHIVE V1.Ø3 -- Restore from Network Volumes
Copyright (c) 1987 Novell, Inc.  All Rights Reserved.

Do you wish to restore security information with the directories? (Y/N)  Y

WARNING: To guarantee proper restoration of directory rights, trustee lists,
and file flags, you should be logged in as a SUPERVISOR user.  This is
especially true if you are going to do a full system restore.  If you are not
logged in as a SUPERVISOR, press ^C at the next question to exit.


Select specific directories to be considered for restoration? (Y/N)
(N = Consider all archived directories) Y

Enter full names of directories to be restored (only ONE per line).
To select a directory AND its subdirectories, just give the name of the
directory (e.g., SYS:SALES/REPORTS).  To select ONLY the subdirectories of
a given directory, include a slash ('/') but no subdirectory names (e.g.,
SYS:SALES/REPORTS/).  To select ONLY a given directory and ignore its sub-
directories, precede the directory's name with an equals sign ('=') (e.g.,
=SYS:SALES/REPORTS).
> SYS:GILLETT/WORDS
```

Figure 19.4: NRESTORE screen for restoring a directory

$SYS:PRIVATE
    Monday, Oct 1, 1990 2:00 pm | 5a a 1 e 0 d 1

    ARCHIVERLOG 000
    SCREEN09CAP CAP20
    SCREEN08CAP CAP20
    SCREEN07CAP CAP20
    SCREEN06CAP CAP20
    SCREEN05CAP CAP
    SCREEN04CAP CAP

$SYS:PRIVATE/GILLETT
    Monday, Oct 1, 1990 2:00 pm | 5a a 1 e 0 f 1

    ARCHIVERLOG 001
    TEST
    CHAP16 2 2
    SCREEN05CAP 000
    SCREEN04CAP 000
    SCREEN03CAP CAP
    SCREEN02CAP CAP
    SCREEN01CAP CAP
    SCREEN00CAP CAP
    CHAP16

$SYS:PRIVATE/GILLETT/WKS
    Monday, Oct 1, 1990 2:00 pm | 5a a 1 e 011 1

    ARCHIVERLOG 002

$SYS:PRIVATE/GILLETT/PIC
    Monday, Oct 1, 1990 2:00 pm | 5a a 1 e 011 1

    ARCHIVERLOG 003

$SYS:PRIVATE/GILLETT/WORDS
    Monday, Oct 1, 1990 2:00 pm | 5a a 1 e 013 1

    ARCHIVERLOG 004
    MORE   TUT TUT
    RESTART TUT TUT

```
PRINTB  WPM WPM
WILL    WPM WPM
MEMO    TUT TUT
    ...
```

Note that a date and time stamp appears in the log for each directory, but not for each file. The log also lists each directory backed up. The NARCHIVE utility does not tell you the last date and time that the individual files were saved.

THE LARCHIVE AND LRESTORE UTILITIES

The second set of NetWare backup utilities is LARCHIVE and LRESTORE. These utilities are functionally equivalent to NARCHIVE and NRESTORE, except they copy the files to a local hard drive or floppy drive. This approach is safer because it protects against hardware failures, such as failure of a file server disk drive.

AUTOMATING THE BACKUP PROCESS WITH LARCHIVE

With LARCHIVE, as with NARCHIVE, you need to set up archive directories before you begin the backup process. For example, log on to the system as a supervisor equivalent and enter the following commands at the DOS prompt:

```
MAP M: = FS1/SYS:PRIVATE
C:
CD\
MD FS1SAVE
CD FS1SAVE
M:
LARCHIVE
```

These commands position you at the proper place on the file server to back up the PRIVATE directories. They also create a new directory, called FS1SAVE, on local drive C.

The LARCHIVE utility displays a set of prompts similar to those displayed by the NARCHIVE utility. Enter the responses shown in Figure 19.5.

```
M:\PRIVATE>LARCHIVE
Advanced NetWare LARCHIVE V2.16b -- Archive DOS files to Local Disks
Copyright (c) 1987 Novell, Inc.  All Rights Reserved.

If you want to archive to a floppy disk drive (or other removable media),
    insert a new diskette NOW, before proceeding.

Enter the letter of the LOCAL disk drive on which to archive files: C
Do you want to print a log report of this session? (Y/N) Y
    Print to Local printer(L) or Network spooler(N)? (L/N) L

Do you want to save directory rights and trustee lists? (Y/N) Y
Do you want to archive the system's user and group definitions? (Y/N) Y

Select specific directories to be backed up? (Y/N)
(N = Back up all directories) N

Select the backup mode for ALL directories from the following:
    1) Back up ALL qualified files in each directory
    2) Back up ONLY qualified files that have been modified since last backup

Select Option: (1, 2) 2
```

Figure 19.5: LARCHIVE prompts

These responses direct all files to the drive C directory most recently logged on to, print a log of the backup session on a local printer, save directory rights and trustee lists, archive the system's user and group definitions, and back up all directories.

LARCHIVE next asks whether you want to select specific files for backup, or to back up all files. After you respond to that prompt and press the space bar, the archiving process begins. Your screen should look like Figure 19.6.

Note that when you back up to a floppy disk, LARCHIVE stops when the disk becomes full and prompts you for another disk. Thus, when you use disks, you cannot run the utility unattended.

If your local hard disk has sufficient capacity, you can easily set up a DOS batch file that automatically responds to the LARCHIVE prompts.

First, you must make a text file with the LARCHIVE responses and place this file on a search drive. In our example system, we keep our utilities in the SYS:UTIL directory, so at the DOS prompt enter the following commands to place the file in the proper directory:

```
MAP M: = FS1/SYS:UTIL
M:
```

```
Do you want to:

    1) Select specific files
    2) Ignore specific files
    3) Back up all files

Select Option: (1-3) 3

SYS:SYSTEM
      If you are archiving to a floppy disk drive (or other removable media),
      insert a diskette.
Press the space bar to continue.
      Archiving: +***
SYS:PRIVATE
      Archiving: +**
SYS:PRIVATE/GILLETT
      Archiving: +******
SYS:PRIVATE/GILLETT/WKS
      Archiving: +*
      No files in this directory changed since they were last archived.
SYS:PRIVATE/GILLETT/PIC
      Archiving: +*
      No files in this directory changed since they were last archived.
SYS:PRIVATE/GILLETT/WORDS
      Archiving: +*
```

Figure 19.6: LARCHIVE in progress

These commands map the M drive to the UTIL directory and log you on to that directory.

The next step is to create the text file. You can use any text editor or word processor that can save a plain ASCII text file, or you can use the DOS copy CON function to create the file. If you use the DOS function, enter the following, pressing ⏎ at the end of each line:

```
COPY CON LAUTO.CMD
C
Y
L
Y
Y
N
2
3
^N
```

(For the last entry, type one blank space and press **F6**.)

The preceding code enters exactly the same responses you entered in the example used in the discussion of LARCHIVE. The first line of this code tells DOS to copy the contents of the console (CON) to a file named LAUTO.CMD. The next lines enter every response, followed by ◀━┘. The last line issues a **Ctrl-N** or end-of-file marker (we typed a blank space and pressed **F6**).

You can check the file by typing it to the screen. Enter **TYPE LAUTO.CMD** to display the file on the screen.

Next, you'll need a batch file to properly position all the directories and execute the LARCHIVE utility. Again, place this file in the FS1/SYS:UTIL directory so it can be executed from anywhere on the network. To create this file, you can use your text editor or the COPY CON command. Name the file **FS1SAVE.BAT**.

Enter

```
ECHO OFF
ECHO * * * * * * * * BEGINNING BATCH FILE, PLEASE WAIT
: BATCH FILE TO LARCHIVE PRIVATE DIRECTORIES TO DISK
: Copies all files in PRIVATE directories to C:\FS1SAVE
: Make sure C:\FS1SAVE directory exists
: * * * * * * * * * * * * * * * * * * * * * * * * * * * * * * * * * *
MAP M: = FS1/SYS:PRIVATE
C:
CD\FS1SAVE
M:
LARCHIVE < LAUTO.CMD
ECHO * * * * * * * * END OF ARCHIVE * * * * * * * *
```

You can then set up this batch file to run unattended by using a third-party timer utility. Be sure, though, that your C drive has enough free space to handle all the files.

USING LRESTORE TO RESTORE FILES LRESTORE is similar to NRESTORE. The difference between the two utilities is that for LRESTORE, your local drive and directory must be in the proper position before the utility can find the files.

Practice using LRESTORE as you did with NRESTORE. Use some test files to make sure you understand the procedure for restoring files so that when a problem occurs, you'll be able to restore files with ease.

SUMMARY

This chapter discussed the importance of backing up the file server and offered some suggested backup procedures. This chapter also discussed the NetWare backup utilities.

Smart network administrators begin backup procedures on the first day the network is in place and continue to perform them regularly. Then, when an accident or hardware failure occurs, the system can be restored with minimal disruption.

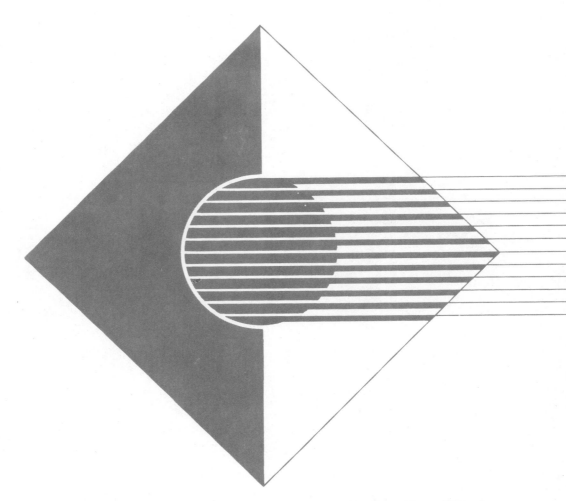

EXPANDING YOUR NETWORK COMMUNICATIONS OPTIONS

FAST TRACK

Expanding single-site communications can be accomplished   303
through local bridging if the local bridges operate within the
cable limitations of the networks.

LAN-to-LAN internal bridging in a local building   303
can be accomplished as easily as placing multiple network
interface cards in the file server and running NETGEN to configure the operating system to recognize the cards.

LAN-to-LAN external bridging in a local building   304
requires the use of special bridge software. NetWare, as well
as third-party software, provides the required utilities. The
NetWare utility is called BRGEN, for *bridge generation*.

Asynchronous outbound communications can be performed   304
with various types of modem-pooling devices. The NetWare
asynchronous communications server allows the sharing of
modems through a dedicated communications server.

Remote-control software options can   306
let users dial into the network from homes or hotel rooms. The
limitation of this approach is that a dedicated workstation is
required for each concurrent remote computer dialing into the
network.

Other approaches for dial-in network access can be accomplished   307
by an inbound access server. The NetWare access server, which
runs on a 80386-based computer with multitasking software,
allows multiple dial-in connections.

Large, geographically dispersed networks can be constructed   310
through the use of wide area network (WAN) hardware and software. WANs can be constructed using dial-up lines, public data networks, T-1 leased lines, or satellite communications.

Three techniques commonly used for remote bridging are   310
using asynchronous bridge software, using X.25 protocols, and using T-1 leased lines.

Asynchronous bridging is   312
inexpensive but supports relatively slow communications (up to 10.9 kilobits per second).

X.25 bridging requires   312
an external bridge on each LAN and the use of an X.25 circuit. Up to 11 remote LANs can be connected through one bridge.

T-1 bridging requires   314
the use of internal or external bridges and a WAN interface card and driver.

LAN-to-host communications can be used for   314
access to mainframe or minicomputers. Such communications provide terminal emulation, such as 3270 emulation, to the host computer.

SNA gateways can be used as   317
either locally attached or remote-access vehicles to mainframe computers on an SNA network.

CHAPTER *20*

AS THE USE OF YOUR LOCAL AREA NETWORK
expands, almost inevitably users will demand increased connection
capabilities. A traveling professional will want to access the LAN
remotely from a laptop computer. The accounting department will
want to send electronic mail to LAN users in the sales department
and to remote regional offices. Other users will want direct access
to the company mainframe or minicomputer from their LAN
workstations.

This chapter examines some of the popular options for expanding
NetWare local area network communications. Because connection
technology is rapidly changing, this discussion is not exhaustive.
Rather, this chapter offers an overview of some of the alternatives
currently available.

EXPANDING SINGLE-SITE COMMUNICATIONS

As discussed in Chapter 2, you can connect two or more LANS at
the same physical location. Doing so lets you expand network capacity and link existing networks into an internetwork.

You can also permit users of the network (or internetwork) to
share modems for outbound asynchronous communications. The
NetWare asynchronous communications server (NACS) provides
this capability.

LAN-TO-LAN BRIDGING

Connecting two or more NetWare local area networks through
local bridging is relatively easy. Recall from Chapter 2 that a local
bridge operates within the cable limitations of the network. (A bridge
that operates outside of the cable limitations of the network's topology is called a remote bridge.)

Because all traffic on a NetWare network communicates via IPX (the protocol for exchanging network packets), you can bridge LANs that use different topologies and cables. For example, you can connect a Token Ring network running on twisted-pair cable to an Ethernet LAN that uses coaxial cable.

The bridge software comes bundled with NetWare. If you are using internal bridging (that is, multiple LAN boards in a single file server), the NETGEN utility allows the operating system to recognize multiple network interface cards.

External bridging requires the generation of specialized bridge software using the BRGEN (bridge generation) utility. BRGEN operates similarly to NETGEN and SHGEN. The utility is menu driven and includes a default configuration option to simplify the installation process.

The use of bridging can expand a departmental LAN into an organization-wide network. The strategic placement of external bridges can overcome the limitations imposed by cable distances. You can even consider using microwave and laser technologies to link network resources in separate buildings where running a cable is difficult or impossible (for instance, between buildings separated by a highway).

MODEM SHARING

Within a single site, you can also use modem pooling for asynchronous communications. The NetWare asynchronous communications server (NACS) allows the sharing of modems through a dedicated communications server (a personal computer) running special control software.

Figure 20.1 illustrates modem pooling using NACS. The communications server runs the NACS control program. The interface to the modems is provided by wide area network interface modules (WNIM). Each WNIM can support four asynchronous ports, and up to four WNIM's can be installed in the NACS communications server. Workstations access the NACS server by running the NetWare asynchronous interface (NASI) program.

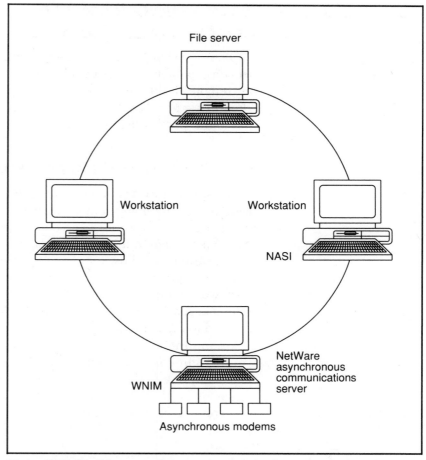

Figure 20.1: NetWare asynchronous communications server processing

NACS supports both outbound and inbound communications. Thus, network users can dial out to services such as Dow Jones and CompuServ, and remote users can dial in to the LAN with remote communications software. The NetWare asynchronous communications server is a cost-effective alternative to equipping individual workstations with modems and dedicated phone lines.

EXPANDING REMOTE COMMUNICATIONS

Often, the first request to a LAN administrator for expanded connection capability is for network access from another location. Without remote communication facilities, traveling personnel and those who work at home cannot use the network. Providing dial-in capabilities to the LAN is relatively easy and inexpensive.

USING REMOTE-CONTROL SOFTWARE

The simplest means of allowing remote network connection is by using one of the many remote-control software packages marketed by third-party companies. These applications use a standard asynchronous modem in the remote computer to access a network workstation running the host version of the remote control software. The remote computer then can control and monitor the activities of the LAN workstation. The commands are entered on the remote computer's keyboard, and the processing is performed on the computer attached to the network.

Among the popular remote-control software are NETremote, from Brightwork Development, Inc.; Carbon Copy Plus, from Microcom Inc.; and Close-Up, from Norton-Lambert Corp. These packages can be purchased for about $200 (one copy is required for each computer). Their primary limitation is that a dedicated workstation is required for each concurrent remote computer dialing into the network.

USING NOVELL REMOTE-ACCESS PRODUCTS

Novell offers two products that permit LAN access from remote computers: NetWare AnyWare and the NetWare access server.

NETWARE ANYWARE   The NetWare AnyWare program permits remote computers to communicate through the NetWare asynchronous communications server to a workstation attached to the LAN. Similar to the way remote-control software operates, keystrokes are entered at the remote computer, and a dedicated workstation attached to the network performs the processing.

Figure 20.2 illustrates NetWare AnyWare operation. As the figure shows, the locally attached network computers run AnyWare, and the remote computers run the access program, ATerm. The asynchronous communications between the two computers are managed by NACS, with only the keystrokes and screens of data being transmitted back and forth.

Because NetWare AnyWare requires a dedicated computer on the LAN for each remote user, it suffers from the same major limitation as other remote-control software. It is an expensive option when many remote users require network access.

NETWARE ACCESS SERVER The NetWare access server was designed to overcome the drawback of requiring a dedicated LAN workstation for each remotely attached computer. By capitalizing on the multitasking capabilities of the 80386 processor, the access server divides the computer into 640-kilobyte virtual CPUs. This allows up to 12 dial-in connections, depending on the amount of random-access memory (RAM) in the access server computer. (Every four sessions requires 3 megabytes of RAM.) As with other remote approaches, keystrokes and screen updates are communicated through asynchronous dial-up lines, and processing is performed on the access server attached to the LAN.

Figure 20.3 shows how the access server operates. The access server software runs on a computer with 80386 industry-standard architecture (ISA) connected to the LAN. Novell's WNIM cards provide the communications interface, with each adapter supporting up to four modems. Remote computer users run Novell's OnLAN/PC software and dial the access server through locally attached modems. A similar program, OnLAN/Mac, is available for Apple Macintosh users.

Another advantage of the access server is that it introduces an incremental security layer to the network. In addition to the existing NetWare security, the access server has its own security features. For example, you can implement dial-back capability that lets the user log in to the LAN only after the access server dials back the user (at a number specified by the network supervisor) following the initial

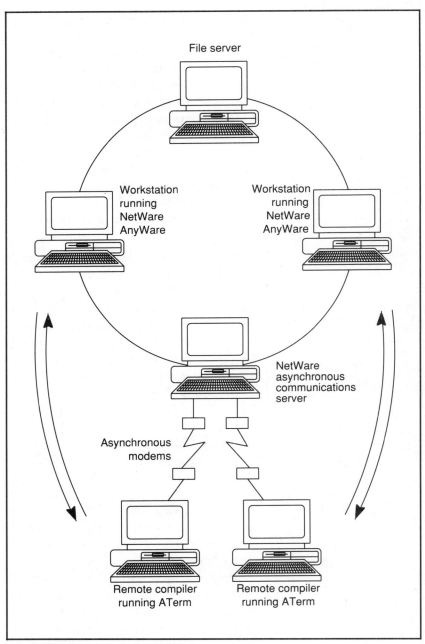

Figure 20.2: NetWare AnyWare processing

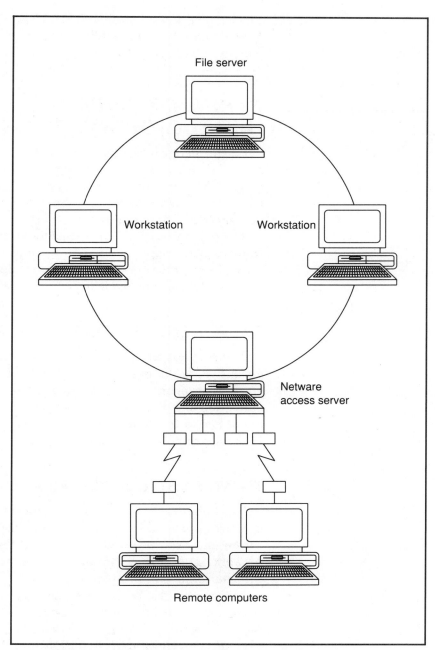

Figure 20.3: NetWare access server processing

contact. The access server also maintains audit trails and has various utilities that allow the network supervisor to monitor and control remote activities.

EXPANDING WIDE AREA NETWORK (WAN) COMMUNICATIONS

Large, geographically dispersed organizations may want to expand their LAN to allow wide area network (WAN) communications. WANs present a new set of challenges to the network manager because the trade-offs between the performance and cost of connection alternatives are significant.

The approaches that can be used for WAN communications range from regular telephone lines to satellite transmissions. The right choice for your network depends on the applications you run and the amount of traffic anticipated.

USING DIAL-UP LINES

The simplest telecommunications method, and usually the least expensive, is the use of voice-grade dial-up lines. This approach employs asynchronous modems to transmit data packets over standard telephone lines. If only a limited number of users need infrequent access to the network, a dial-up system may be adequate. However, response time on dial-up lines is relatively slow.

USING PUBLIC DATA NETWORKS

For sophisticated WANs, public data networks (PDNs) are a more effective approach. PDNs, such as Tymnet or Telenet, use the X.25 communications protocol to send data through a packet-switched network. The X.25 communications protocol was developed as an international communications standard for accessing packet-switched networks. Service users access the packet-switched network (sometimes called the cloud) through a dedicated line or by dialing the network using a standard modem. You can use an X.25 gateway to connect an entire LAN to a PDN.

An X.25 strategy is most appropriate for companies with remote offices that need occasional connection to LANs and hosts at a head-quarters facility. Because most users will have only 9600-baud modems or 19.2 kilobits-per-second lines to the PDNs, running LAN applications interactively will be too slow for many users.

USING LEASED LINES AND T-1

Digital leased lines can provide fewer errors and greater reliability than voice-grade lines, but at a higher cost. A leased line can provide transmission speeds of up to 56 kilobits per second. For networks with a medium amount of traffic, the leased-line approach can be attractive. However, as demands on the network increase, the limited transmission speed may create bottlenecks.

A higher-speed alternative is T-1 service that offers two-way communication at 1.544 megabits per second. T-1 service is usually obtained from the local telephone company, which installs twisted-pair wire from each office on the WAN to the telephone company's switching equipment. T-1 is frequently employed by companies for their private voice networks. T-1 can transmit voice, data, facsimile, and even compressed video signals for teleconferencing over the same line at the same time.

A relatively new offering by telecommunications companies is fractional T-1. This service allows companies to purchase T-1 capabilities in increments of 64 kilobits per second each. For cost-conscious companies that do not require full T-1 capacity, fractional T-1 is an attractive option.

USING SATELLITE COMMUNICATIONS

In a few situations, satellite communications may be the only alternative available for a WAN. For instance, remote offices in areas without high-quality data circuits may require satellite communications. Satellite communication is expensive. It requires a satellite bridge, an earth station, and a satellite. In addition, because an earth station may be more than 22,000 miles away from its satellite, a long delay occurs between transmission and reception.

EFFECTING LAN-TO-LAN COMMUNICATIONS

Three remote bridging techniques are commonly used, according to the type of wide area communications used: asynchronous bridging, X.25 bridging, and T-1 bridging.

ASYNCHRONOUS BRIDGING   The NetWare asynchronous remote bridge software permits the linking of two or more LANs to create a simple WAN. The bridge software currently supports transmission speeds up to 19.2 kilobits per second through standard dial-up lines.

The NetWare asynchronous bridge supports three configurations. You can install a WAN interface module into a NetWare file server, thus turning the file server into an internal remote bridge. You can also install a WNIM in a workstation, thus using the workstation as a nondedicated internal remote bridge. Finally, you can configure a computer as an external remote bridge and connect through either the COM1 or COM2 port.

The preferred configuration is usually an external bridge. Although economically internal bridging looks attractive, you need to consider that the operation of the file server or workstation that houses the WNIM + will be interrupted or slowed during the communication process.

Figure 20.4 illustrates external asynchronous remote bridge operation. Each network has an external bridge, with the bridges connected to each other by asynchronous modems and dial-up lines. Other than the slower transmission speed, the connection is completely transparent to users of both networks, thus allowing users to access information and other resources as if they were at a local workstation on either network.

X.25 BRIDGING   Implementing an X.25 WAN requires an external bridge on each LAN included in the network. The NetWare X.25 multipoint bridge permits a LAN to be connected to up to 11 remote LANs. Each LAN uses only a single X.25 circuit, and the public data network multiplexes transmissions and routes them to their proper destinations. By adding additional bridges, the limitation of 11 remote LANs can be exceeded.

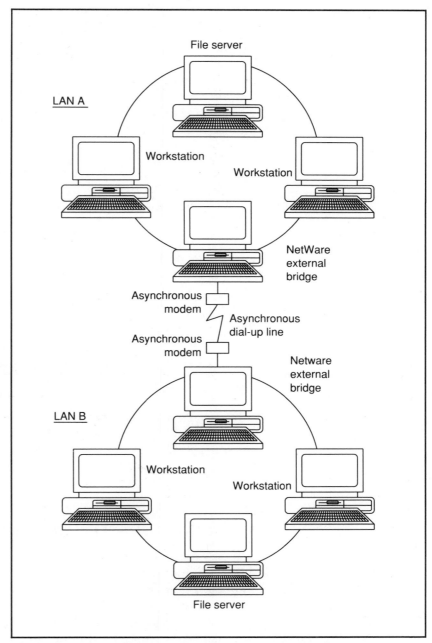

Figure 20.4: NetWare asynchronous remotely bridged WAN

Figure 20.5 shows an X.25 WAN using NetWare X.25 multipoint bridges. Each LAN has an external bridge that communicates to the public data network through a dial-up X.25 connection using synchronous modems. As with an asynchronous WAN, the connection is transparent to the network users, allowing them to access resources on other file servers as if they were locally attached.

Using X.25 bridging is usually preferable to using asynchronous bridging, where users require continuous access to multiple LANs.

T-1 BRIDGING   The third approach to connecting geographically separate LANs is through T-1 bridging. The NetWare T-1 bridge consists of a WAN driver for either internal or external bridges and a WAN interface card that resides in the file server or external-bridge computer.

Figure 20.6 illustrates a typical T-1 WAN. A bridge (either internal or external) connected to the LAN passes the remote traffic through a T-1 multiplexer to the telephone company's switching equipment via twisted-pair cable. The local telephone company then sends the signal to a long-distance carrier for delivery to the local telephone company on the other end.

EXPANDING LAN-TO-HOST COMMUNICATIONS

In most large organizations, a mainframe or minicomputer serves as the central repository for business information. LAN users frequently need to communicate with the host computer to run applications and to upload and download data. Such communication usually requires LAN-to-host connection.

EFFECTING SINGLE-USER CONNECTION

If only a few network users need access to the host, direct connections with coaxial cable may be adequate. In this approach, terminal emulation software, such as NetWare 3270 Multi Workstation, is run on the computer that requires host access. Figure 20.7 shows a typical configuration with a direct coaxial connection from a workstation to a mainframe computer through an IBM cluster controller.

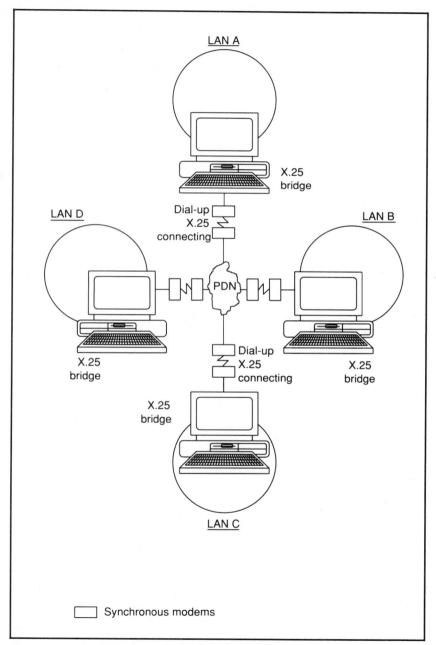

Figure 20.5: NetWare X.25 multipoint-bridged WAN

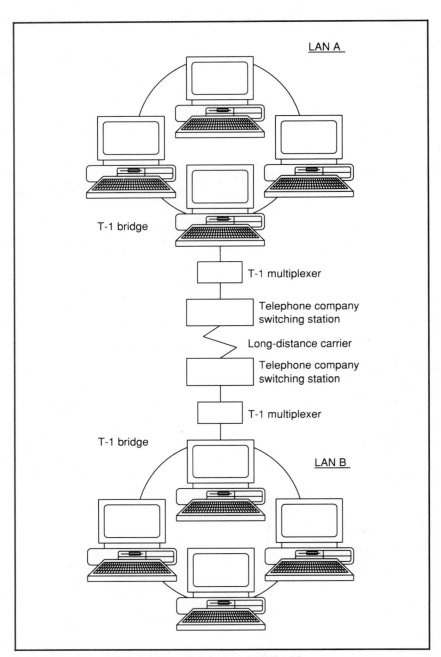

Figure 20.6: T-1 service connecting two remote LANs

The obvious limitation to this approach is that only the workstations with the coaxial connections can access the host. In addition, the emulation software and the LAN shell may occasionally conflict and cause operating problems.

USING SNA GATEWAYS

SNA gateways can be used in environments where more than a few users require connection to the host. An SNA gateway provides simultaneous multiple-user access. An SNA gateway works similar to a bridge in managing communications between the host computer and multiple workstations on the LAN.

USING REMOTE SNA GATEWAYS If the host computer is not located at the site of the LAN, then a remote connection is required. Figure 20.8 illustrates how a remote SNA gateway operates. Gateway software, such as the NetWare SNA gateway software, is run on a LAN computer, thus turning this computer into an SNA gateway server. An SDLC line connects the LAN to the host's front-end processor via synchronous modems. Every workstation can now run the terminal emulation software and communicate with the host device. The NetWare SNA gateway can support up to 97 users through a single SNA gateway.

USING COAXIAL SNA GATEWAYS If the host computer is local, then the SNA gateway can be attached to the cluster controller via a coaxial cable. As shown in Figure 20.9, the configuration (and functionality) is very similar to that of a remote SNA gateway. The primary difference is that coaxial cable connects the gateway computer to the front-end processor through a cluster controller.

SUMMARY

This chapter outlined some of the alternatives for expanding your LAN through connections to other computers and networks. The flexibility of NetWare lets you expand your network as dictated by the user needs.

Through bridging, you can link multiple networks to form an internetwork. Other approaches allow users to dial in and out of the

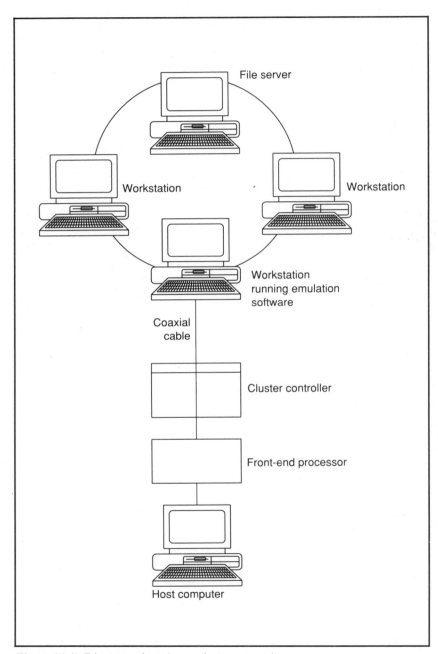

Figure 20.7: Direct workstation-to-host connection

LAN using asynchronous modems. You can expand your LAN to include wide area communications. WANs permit you to connect LANs in geographically dispersed offices into an integrated network. Finally, through terminal emulation and SNA gateways, network users can access both the company mainframe computer and LAN resources.

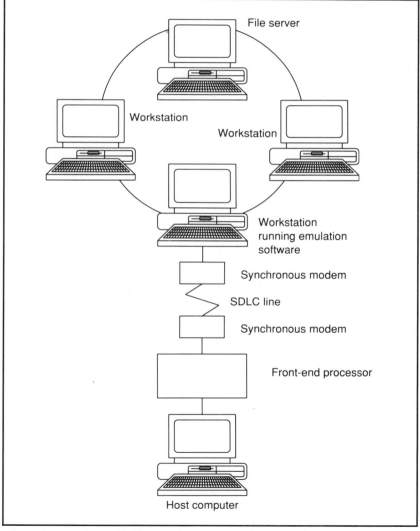

Figure 20.8: Remote SNA gateway

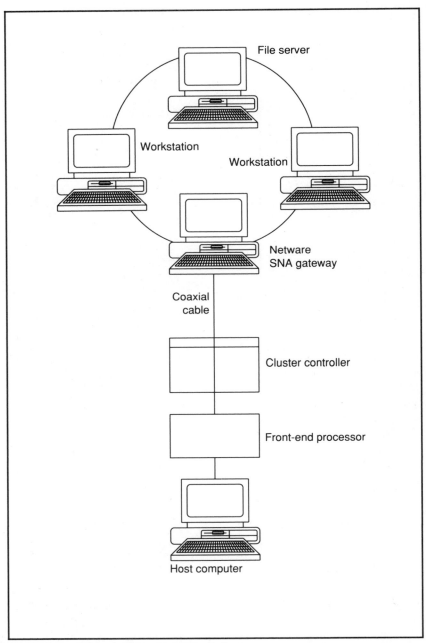

Figure 20.9: SNA gateway coaxial connection

PART VI

NETWARE COMMANDS

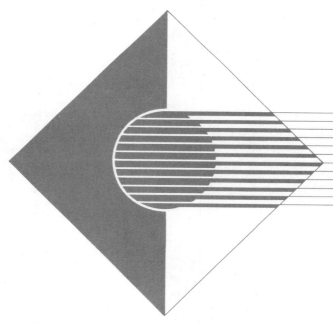

This part discusses the NetWare command-line utilities. The first chapter in this part presents an overview of the NetWare command-line utility. The second chapter in this part provides a quick reference to NetWare command-line utilities.

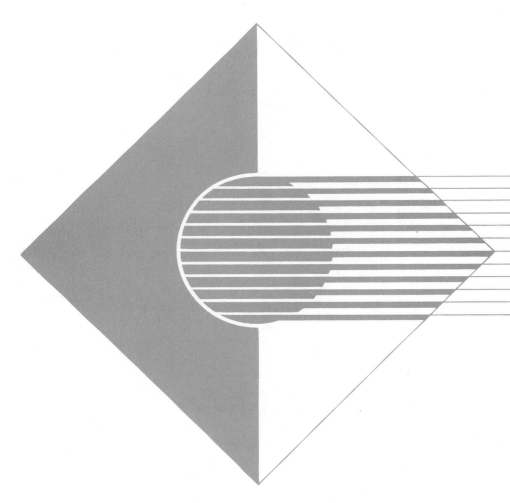

INTRODUCTION
TO NETWARE COMMANDS

FAST TRACK

NetWare commands can be divided into two groups: **325**
those that can be executed from a workstation, and those that must be executed from the file server console. Some commands are available to all users, and others are intended primarily for system operators and supervisors. Console commands can be entered only at the file server console. Console commands are available to anyone with physical access to the file server.

Workstation commands intended for users   **326**
are listed in Table 21.1.

Workstation commands intended for system operators   **327**
are listed in Table 21.2.

Console commands   **328**
are listed in Table 21.3.

Special console commands for printer control   **328**
let you quickly start, change, or stop printer action. These commands include PRINTER *xx* FORM MOUNT *yy*, PRINTER *xx* REWIND, PRINTER *xx* START, and PRINTER *xx* STOP.

Status information commands   **329**
display information about the status of directories, security, and resources. These commands include CHKVOL, NVER, PSTAT, and TLIST.

CHAPTER *21*

THIS BOOK INTRODUCED SOME OF NETWARE'S MANY, powerful commands as relevant to the discussions at hand. However, NetWare offers many other commands as well. This chapter outlines some of the other NetWare commands commonly used in day-to-day network activities in addition to providing an overview of NetWare command-line utilities in general.

TYPES OF NETWARE COMMANDS

Some NetWare commands can be executed from the workstation, and others must be executed from the file server console. Sometimes, workstation and console commands perform the same function, a feature which may seem confusing, but which allows flexible network maintenance.

Some workstation commands are available to all users. These commands are located in the SYS:PUBLIC directory. Generally, these commands add some function to the workstation environment. Another set of workstation commands is intended primarily for system operators. These commands require higher security privileges and are located in the SYS:SYSTEM directory. Workstation commands must be entered from a workstation.

Console commands, by contrast, cannot be typed at a workstation. They can be entered only at the file server. Console commands are available to anyone with physical access to the file server. They are typed directly into the file server keyboard and do not require a password.

Note that some console commands have a major impact on the network. Messages can be sent to every workstation, and the file server can be brought down by anyone with access to the console. Thus, access to the file server should be appropriately limited.

In addition, some commands can be considered supervisor or operator commands, and others can be considered user commands.

Although there is some overlap between these two types of commands, the groupings reflect the type of person most likely to use a command. Most of the supervisor or operator commands perform file server maintenance. Most of the user commands manage a single network session.

Table 21.1 lists user workstation commands, Table 21.2 lists supervisor or operator workstation commands, and Table 21.3 lists console commands.

COMMONLY USED COMMANDS

In addition to the commands discussed in previous chapters of this book, you will find certain other commands especially useful. These commands control the file server, workstation use of the file server, and network printers. Other commands provide status information.

Overall, NetWare commands have one of two purposes. Some commands provide information about the current status of the file server or network. For example, the file server command CONFIG displays information about how the file server is configured. This command cannot, however, change the file server configuration.

Other commands cause an action to be taken. For example, the file server command DISABLE LOGIN prevents anyone from logging into the network. This condition remains in effect until the ENABLE LOGIN command is entered from the file server console.

Table 21.1: User Workstation Commands

ATTACH	LOGIN	SEND
CAPTURE	LOGOUT	SETPASS
CASTOFF	MAP	SLIST
CASTON	NCOPY	SYSTIME
ENDCAP	NDIR	USERLIST
HOLDOFF	NPRINT	WHOAMI
HOLDON	NSNIPES	
LISTDIR	RIGHTS	

Table 21.2: Supervisor or Operator Workstation Commands

CHKVOL	NRESTORE	SALVAGE
FLAG	NVER	SETTTS
FLAGDIR	PSTAT	SLIST
GRANT	PURGE	SMODE
LARCHIVE	REMOVE	TLIST
LRESTORE	RENDIR	VERSION
NARCHIVE	REVOKE	

Table 21.3: Console Commands

BROADCAST	NAME
CLEAR MESSAGE	OFF
CLEAR STATION	REMIRROR
CONFIG	SEND
CONSOLE	SET TIME
DISABLE LOGIN	TIME
DISK	UNMIRROR
DISMOUNT	VAP
DOS	*Printer-Specific Commands:*
DOWN	FORM
ENABLE LOGIN	PRINTER
MONITOR	QUEUE
MOUNT	SPOOL

FILE SERVER COMMANDS

The CONFIG, DISK, DOWN, MONITOR, NAME, OFF, and SETTIME commands monitor or direct network resources. Although these commands must be issued from the file server itself, much of the information they display can be obtained from a workstation logged on to the network and running the FCONSOLE utility.

WORKSTATION CONTROLS

The BROADCAST, CLEAR STATION, DISABLE LOGIN, ENABLE LOGIN, and SEND commands control access by the workstations on the network. These commands can be issued only from the file server keyboard. They control some (or all) of the workstations on the network.

PRINTER AND PRINT QUEUE COMMANDS

Note that most printer queue and printer setup operations can be accomplished from the server itself, by using the PRINTDEF utility discussed earlier in the book. PRINTDEF offers a friendlier approach to printer management than do the PRINTER commands, so you should use PRINTDEF for your major printer setup work.

Certain PRINTER commands, however, are handy when some immediate action is necessary. These commands perform such functions as starting and stopping the network printer. These commands especially can be helpful when a printer problem, such as a paper jam or broken ribbon, occurs. Other useful PRINTER commands tell the file server that you've changed form types. These commands are helpful when you want to change paper types; for example, to load letterhead or special types of long paper. (Of course, to change forms, you must first set up the form definitions correctly in the PRINTDEF utility.)

In particular, the PRINTER xx STOP, PRINTER xx START, PRINTER xx REWIND xx PAGES, PRINTER xx FORM MOUNT yy, PRINTER xx MOUNT FORM yy, and PRINTER xx FORM yy MOUNTED commands help manage network printers. These commands are important when quick action is needed. They provide controls directly from the file server console keyboard. They do not require a workstation to be logged on to the network.

STATUS INFORMATION COMMANDS

The CHKVOL, NVER, PSTAT, and TLIST commands display information about the status of directories, security rights, and other resources. These commands are available to both users and administrators.

Note that you can save the output of these commands in a file by adding a greater-than sign (>) and a file name to the command. For example, to save the output of the CHKVOL command to a file named TEST, you enter

```
CHKVOL > TEST
```

This command causes the contents that normally appear on the screen to go to the file named TEST. The screen then will not display the results of the command.

SUMMARY

This chapter introduced some of the more helpful NetWare commands grouped according to their functions. These commands provide an effective way to check the network or take action.

The next chapter takes a closer look at the NetWare command-line utilities and the proper syntax for using them.

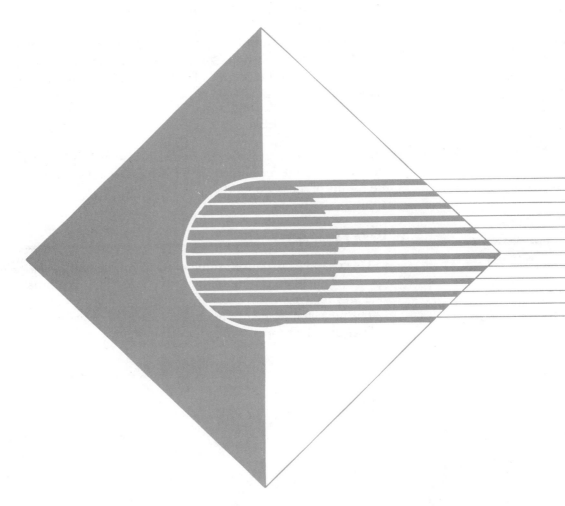

NETWARE COMMANDS

FAST TRACK

To enter NetWare commands, 333
follow the syntax presented in this chapter for each command.

CHAPTER **22**

THIS CHAPTER PROVIDES A QUICK REFERENCE TO the NetWare commands.

COMMAND CONVENTIONS USED IN THIS CHAPTER

This chapter describes NetWare commands using the same format as in the NetWare documentation. For example, the format shown for the NDIR command is as follows:

NDIR (*path* | *filespec option*) [...]

The portion of the command in all uppercase letters is a command constant and must be included when the command is executed. Although constants appear in all uppercase letters, NetWare commands are not case sensitive. That is, you can enter the command in any combination of uppercase and lowercase letters.

The command elements shown in lowercase italic characters are variable parameters. In the NDIR command, *path*, *filespec*, and *option* are the command's variables. When you enter the command, you can replace *path* with the appropriate directory path, *filespec* with the appropriate directory path and file name, and *option* with appropriate options.

Square brackets ([ ]) indicate an optional parameter in the command. Any data contained within a set of square brackets is not required to execute the command, but can be used to further qualify the command instructions.

Some commands have nested square brackets: for example, [[ ]]. Nesting indicates that the command has levels of optional items. However, the options within the innermost brackets can be used only in conjunction with the items in the outermost brackets.

A vertical bar (|) between two command parameters indicates that you can use one or the other, but not both, parameters. In the NDIR command, you can enter either a *path* or a *filespec*. Parentheses are used for clarity to group command choices.

An ellipsis (...) means that the command variable immediately preceding the ellipsis can be used more than one time. In the NDIR command, you can specify several *option* parameters.

NETWARE COMMANDS

The following section presents the Netware commands in alphabetical order.

ATTACH

General Description   ATTACH allows you to connect to another file server on an internetwork when your workstation is already logged in to a file server.

Syntax

ATTACH [*server*[/*user*]]

Options   The *server* option lets you specify the desired file server when you enter the ATTACH command. If you do not specify a server, NetWare will prompt you for the file server name. The *user* option works in a similar fashion. If you do not specify a user when you enter the command, NetWare will prompt you for the user name.

Examples   User KRUEGER can connect to file server FS2 with either of the following commands:

ATTACH

or

ATTACH FS1/KRUEGER

BROADCAST

General Description   The BROADCAST command is a workstation or console command. This command allows you to send up to a 60-character message to all workstations attached to the file server. It displays a message on line 25 of the screen and stops the activity of the workstation until the user clears the message by simultaneously pressing **Ctrl** and ◄─┘.

The BROADCAST command is much like the SEND command that can also be entered from either the workstation or the console. However, there are two notable differences. First, BROADCAST does not include the login name of the user who is sending the message, thus allowing you to send a longer message than the SEND command. Second, BROADCAST does not allow you to specify the users, groups, or workstations to send the message to. It sends the message to everyone on the network.

Syntax

BROADCAST *message*

Options   The message does not need to be surrounded by quotation marks.

Note that BROADCAST does not interrupt all workstations. Generally, Windows-based or graphical user interface (GUI) software, certain types of terminal-emulation software (such as 3270 emulation software), and ACS software do not receive broadcast messages until after the user exits the software package.

Examples   To send a message about the weekly staff meeting to all workstations, enter

BROADCAST The weekly staff meeting has been changed to May 21.

CAPTURE

General Description   The CAPTURE command redirects print jobs from a workstation's parallel printer port to a network printer.

Syntax

CAPTURE [*option* ...]

Options   Twenty options can be used with the CAPTURE command. Some of the most commonly used are listed here.

OPTION	MEANING
SH	Shows the status of the workstation's parallel ports: that is, whether they are captured and are routed to a file or to a network printer. (This option cannot be used with any other option.)
TI = *n*	Timeout option; specifies the number of seconds between the time that the print key is pressed and the time that a print job is queued for printing. Replace *n* with the number of seconds (specify any whole number between 1 and 1,000).
L = *n*	Specifies the local LPT (parallel) port to capture. Replace *n* with the LPT port number.
S = *server*	Directs the print job to a printer on a server other than the default file server. Replace *server* with the file server name.
P = *printer*	Directs the print job to a specific network printer. Replace *printer* with the printer number.
C = *n*	Indicates the number of copies to print. You can print up to 256 copies. Replace *n* with the number to print.
A	Autoendcap option; leaves the LPT port set to the network printer. This option stays in effect when you enter or exit a file. To

OPTION	MEANING
	disable this option, enter an ENDCAP or CAPTURE NA command, which resets the LPT port to the local printer port.
NA	NoAutoendcap option; inhibits data from being sent to the network printer when you enter or exit an application.
J	Print job option; allows you to specify a particular print job definition (if print jobs are set up with the PRINTCON utility).
Q = *n*	Queue option; allows the printed output to be sent to a specific queue. Replace *n* with the queue name.
F = *n*	Form option; allows the printed output to use a specific form. (Forms are defined by the PRINTDEF utility.) Replace *n* with the form number or form name.
T = *n*	Tabs option; searches the printed document for tab characters and inserts *n* number of blank spaces.
NT	NoTabs option. Sends tabs in the printed document unchanged.
NAM = *name*	Replace the user name on the banner page. Replace *name* with the name that you want to appear. The default name is the login name.
Banner = *banner*	Custom banner option; allows you to enter up to 12 characters as a custom banner in the lower portion of the banner page. Replace *banner* with the banner contents. (Note: Use an underscore character to insert a blank space between words: for example, TEST_MESSAGE.)
NB	No banner option; prevents a banner page from being printed in between print jobs.

OPTION	MEANING
FF	Form-feed option; forces an extra page to be inserted between print jobs.
NFF	No form-feed option; stops an extra page from being inserted between print jobs.
CR =*filespec*	Create file specification option; captures everything that would have been sent to the network printer in a file. Replace *filespec* with the name of the file to be used.

Examples   The following command displays the current status of the workstation's LPT ports:

CAPTURE SH

The following command reroutes print jobs sent to LPT 2 to printer 1 and prints five copies:

CAPTURE L = 2 P = 1 C = 5

CASTOFF

General Description   CASTOFF prevents messages from being received from other workstations.

Syntax

CASTOFF [A]

Options   Specify A to prevent all messages, including BROADCAST messages from the console, from being received at the workstation.

Examples   To prevent all messages from being received at a workstation, enter the following command:

CASTOFF A

CASTON

General Description   CASTON permits messages to be received at a workstation. (The default setting is CASTON enabled.)

Syntax

```
CASTON
```

Options   This command does not have any options.

Examples   The following command allows messages to be received at a workstation:

```
CASTON
```

CHKVOL

General Description   The CHKVOL command displays information about a network volume. The data displayed includes the file server name, volume name, total storage capacity, and remaining storage space.

Syntax

```
CHKVOL [path ...]
```

Options   Entering CHKVOL without designating a path returns information about the current volume. You can also enter one or more paths by designating either a drive letter or the volume name.

Examples   To view information about the volume to which drive X is mapped, enter

```
CHKVOL X:
```

To check the data for several volumes—SYS, VOL1, and VOL2—on file server FS1, enter the following command:

```
CHKVOL FS1/SYS: FS1/VOL1: FS1/VOL2:
```

The following is sample CHKVOL output:

```
Statistics for fixed volume FS1/SYS:
        41254912 bytes total volume space,
        7614464 bytes in 454 files,
        33640448 bytes remaining on volume,
        33640448 bytes available to user SUPERVISOR,
        2618 directory entries available.
```

CLEAR STATION

General Description   The CLEAR STATION command is a console command. It breaks the connection between a file server and a workstation. CLEAR STATION is useful when a problem occurs on a workstation that prevents the workstation from properly logging out of the system. If the workstation fails, open files may be left on the file server. The CLEAR STATION command closes all open files and removes the internal tables that the file server was using to keep track of the workstation.

Syntax

CLEAR STATION *xx*

Options   Replace *xx* with the connection number of the workstation to be cleared.

Use this command with caution; you could inadvertently clear the wrong connection number. Many network managers prefer to use the FCONSOLE utility from a workstation instead of the CLEAR STATION console command to clear a network connection. The FCONSOLE command is more friendly, as it lists the user's login name as well as the connection number.

Note that as with other console commands, you can type the command incorrectly and not see an error message. For example, if you enter the command **CLEAR STATION 7** and no one is logged on to station 7, nothing will happen. The screen will not display an error message, nor will any workstation be cleared from the network.

Examples   To break the connection between workstation 3 and the file server, enter

    CLEAR STATION 3

CONFIG

General Description   The CONFIG command is a console command. It provides handy information about the networks supported by the file server. If you have multiple network cards in your server, CONFIG provides information about each.

The CONFIG command can be issued only from the file server console. It provides the following information:

- Number of service processes
- Configuration of LAN A:

    Network address setting

    Hardware type

    Hardware settings (including adapter board and I/O address)

Syntax

    CONFIG

Options   This command does not have any options.

Examples   CONFIG command output depends on how the server is set up. It looks something like the following:

    Hardware Configuration Information for Server FS1

    Number of Service Processes: 05
    LAN A Configuration Information:
    Network Address: [1986BEEF] [AAAAAAAA]
    Hardware Type: NetWare RX-Net
    Hardware Settings: IRQ = 2, I/O Base = 2E0h, RAM Buffer at
        D000:0

DISABLE LOGIN

General Description   The DISABLE LOGIN command is a console command. It prevents users from logging in to the file server. It is most often used when the supervisor wants to stop the server or perform maintenance on the server. The command prevents new users from logging in to the server, but it does not affect users who are already logged in.

Once DISABLE LOGIN has been entered, no one can log in to the server until the ENABLE LOGIN command is entered from the console.

Syntax

DISABLE LOGIN

Options   This command has no options.

Examples   To prevent new users from logging into the server, enter

DISABLE LOGIN

Now if a new user attempts to log in to the server, the screen will display the message

Access denied. The Supervisor has disabled logins.

DISK

General Description   The DISK command is a console command. It is available for advanced versions of Netware. It gives you a quick report on the status of the disks installed in the file server. The output lists such information as the channel used, the physical drive number of the disk drive, the number of I/O errors that have occurred, the free blocks available in the disk's redirection area, and the number of blocks used.

Syntax

DISK *
DISK *volumename*

Two variations of the DISK command are available with the SFT version of Netware. Entering **DISK** * displays information about each volume, the physical drive, and the mirror drive (if any).

Entering **DISK** *volumename*, where *volumename* indicates a specific volume, displays detailed information about each volume.

Examples   To display information about the volume SYS, enter

DISK SYS

The screen will display the following information about SYS:

Physical drive number
Physical drive type
IO errors on the drive
Redirection blocks available
Redirection blocks used

DOS

The DOS console command is used only with nondedicated versions of NetWare, such as ELS. It is not a functional command in other NetWare versions.

The command, executed at the console, switches from console mode to a local DOS session.

Syntax

DOS

Options   This command has no options. To return from DOS back to console mode, type **CONSOLE**.

Examples   To switch from file server mode to a local DOS session, enter

DOS

DOWN

General Description   The DOWN command is a console command. It shuts down the system. Use DOWN before turning off the file server power to close down the system in an orderly way. The command closes all open file, writes cache buffers to disk, and updates file directory and allocation tables.

   To ensure that all files are properly closed, all users must log off the system before the DOWN command is issued. If a workstation remains logged into the server, it will receive a message from the file server when the DOWN command is issued.

Syntax

DOWN

Options   This command has no options.

Examples   To shut down the entire system, enter

DOWN

ENABLE LOGIN

   The ENABLE LOGIN command is a console command. It is used after the DISABLE LOGIN to allow users to log into the file server. This command must be used to reenable users to log into the server.

Syntax

ENABLE LOGIN

Options   This command has no options.

Examples   To reenable users to log on to the file server after the server has been disabled, enter

    ENABLE LOGIN

ENDCAP

General Description   ENDCAP terminates the capture of one or more of the workstation's parallel printer ports.

Syntax

    ENDCAP [*option* ...]

Options   The following options can be used with the ENDCAP command:

OPTION	MEANING
L = *n*	Terminates the capture of a specific parallel port. Replace *n* with the number of the LPT port.
ALL	Terminates the capture of all parallel ports.
C	Terminates the capture of LPT1 and discards any print jobs without printing them.
CL = *n*	Terminates the capture of a specific parallel port and discards any print jobs without printing them. Replace *n* with the number of the LPT port.
C ALL	Terminates the capture of all parallel ports and discards any print jobs without printing them.

Examples   To end the capture of LPT2, enter this command:

    ENDCAP L = 2

FLAG

General Description   Use the FLAG command to view or modify file attributes.

Syntax

FLAG [(*path* | *filespec*) [*option* ...]]

Options   Entering FLAG without any of the optional parameters displays a list of the files in the current subdirectory and their corresponding file attributes. If you enter a path or file specification, you can view the attributes of files in another location on the network's hard disk.

If your effective rights in a directory include search and modify, you can change the attributes of files by including one or more of the following options in the command:

OPTION	MEANING
S	Sharable
NS	Nonsharable
RO	Read only
RW	Read-write
N	Normal (nonsharable and read-write)
T	Transactional (used with SFT NetWare)
I	Indexed
SUB	Includes all subdirectories of the current directory

Examples   Enter the following to view the attributes of all files in the FS1/SYS:PROGRAMS directory:

FLAG FS1/SYS:PROGRAMS

To change the file attributes of all files in the current subdirectory to nonsharable and read-write, enter

FLAG N

To change the attributes of all drive P directory files with the .BAT extension to sharable and read only, enter

FLAG P:*.BAT S RO

FLAGDIR

The FLAGDIR command lets you change the following subdirectory attributes: Normal, Hidden, System, and Private. This command also lets you view attributes. To use FLAGDIR, you must have supervisor rights or parental and modify rights to the parent directory, and you must be logged into or attached to the file server.

Syntax

FLAGDIR [*path* [*option...*]]

Options   You can enter FLAGDIR for any subdirectory by referring to the subdirectory by its mapped drive letter. For example, if drive M is mapped to FS1/SYS:PRIVATE, then entering **FLAGDIR M:** returns the attributes of the directory.

You can also look for subdirectories subordinate to the current directory by entering **FLAGDIR ***. This command displays the status of any subdirectory under the current directory. You can also fully qualify the subdirectory in a FLAGDIR search. For example, you can enter **FLAGDIR FS1/SYS:PRIVATE/CURRID/*** to display the status of subdirectories subordinate to the SYS:PRIVATE/CURRID subdirectory.

You can change the directory attributes in your directories with FLAGDIR by using one of the supported attributes, including the following

OPTION	MEANING
Hidden	Hides the directory or subdirectory from directory searches using the DIR or LISTDIR commands. Note: Users can change to a hidden directory and access its files if they know that the directory exists and they have access rights to the directory and files.
Normal	The default directory attribute. You can also use this option to reset or cancel other attributes.
Private	Prevents users from seeing the contents of a subdirectory. If users have the search right to the

OPTION   MEANING

parent directory, however, they can see the files. As with the Hidden attribute, users can change to the subdirectory if they know its name.

System   Specifies a subdirectory needed for the system to function. As with other attributes, a directory search will not display the subdirectory.

You can change one or more attributes at a time. You specify changes for directories by entering the attributes after the path.

Examples   If drive P is mapped to FS1/SYS, entering

FLAGDIR P:

displays the following information:

FS1/SYS:
        PRIVATE   Normal

Entering

FLAGDIR SYS:PRIVATE/CURRID/* PH

applies the Private and Hidden attributes to the subdirectories directly under SYS:PRIVATE/CURRID.

Note that FLAGDIR does not automatically apply attributes to the subdirectories subordinate to those you specify. Therefore, the preceding command hides SYS:PRIVATE/CURRID/WORDS, but it does not hide SYS:PRIVATE/CURRID/WORDS/TEMP. The directories subordinate to those hidden can be searched with both the DIR and LISTDIR commands.

GRANT

General Description   GRANT assigns trustee rights to users and groups. You can use this command in lieu of assigning trustee rights through SYSCON.

The user who executes the GRANT command must have parental rights in the directory to which the rights are to be assigned.

Syntax

GRANT *option* ... [FOR *path*] TO ([USER] *user* | [GROUP] *group*)

Options   For you to use the GRANT command, the users and groups specified must exist.

The GRANT options correspond to the eight NetWare trustee rights:

OPTION	MEANING
R	Read
W	Write
O	Open
C	Create
D	Delete
P	Parental
S	Search
M	Modify
NO RIGHTS	Revokes all trustee rights
ALL	Grants all eight trustee rights

Examples   To grant read, write, and open rights to user Hull in the current directory, enter

GRANT R W O TO USER HULL

To grant the same rights to the accounting (ACCTNG) group in the TEST directory on file server FS1, volume SYS, enter the following command:

GRANT R W O FOR FS1/SYS:PROGRAMS TO GROUP ACCTNG

HOLDOFF

General Description   The HOLDOFF command cancels the effects of the HOLDON command (which prevents other users from accessing a file being used by the workstation).

Syntax

    HOLDOFF

Options   This command does not have any options.

Examples   To execute the HOLDOFF command, enter

    HOLDOFF

HOLDON

General Description   The HOLDON command prevents other users from accessing a file that is currently being used by a workstation. (Most application software performs this function automatically.)

Syntax

    HOLDON

Options   This command does not have any options.

Examples   To hold open any files that are accessed by a work-station, enter the following command:

    HOLDON

LARCHIVE

General Description   The LARCHIVE command backs up network files and attributes to a local disk drive (either a floppy or hard disk). As discussed in Chapter 19, the LARCHIVE utility can be used for both backing up and archiving certain files.

To use the LARCHIVE utility, you must be logged on to the server with at least read, open, search, and modify rights to the directories and files you want to back up.

Syntax

> LARCHIVE [*path* | SYSTEM]

Options   You can specify the directories or subdirectories that you want to back up by specifying *path* using either the fully qualified path name or the drive letter. To back up the entire system, specify SYSTEM.

Once activated, the LARCHIVE program displays a series of prompts to determine the destination disk for the backup, whether to print a log file, and whether to save directory rights and trustee rights of the backed-up files and directories. Then LARCHIVE asks whether you want to back up all qualified files in the directory or only those modified since the last backup operation.

Examples   To back up the SYS:COMMON directory mapped to drive I, enter either

> LARCHIVE SYS:COMMON

or

> LARCHIVE I:

LISTDIR

General Description   LISTDIR displays a list of all of the subdirectories in a directory along with any other information specified by *option*.

Syntax

> LISTDIR [*path*] [*option* ...]

Options LISTDIR can be executed to view subdirectories of the default directory or, by specifying the *path* option, to view subdirectories of another directory.

The following options can be specified for *option*:

OPTION	MEANING
/S	In addition to the current subdirectories, also displays all subordinate subdirectories.
/R	Displays the maximum rights mask for the subdirectories.
/D	Displays the creation date for the subdirectories.
/T	Displays the creation time for the subdirectories.
/A	Makes all options effective: that is, lists subsequent subdirectories and displays subdirectories' maximum rights masks and creation dates and times.

Examples The following command lists the subdirectories in the default directory:

LISTDIR

To view the subdirectories in the PROGRAMS directory of volume SYS1 on file server FS1 and display the subdirectories' maximum rights masks and creation dates, enter the following command:

LISTDIR FS1/SYS:PROGRAMS /R /D

LOGIN

General Description Once the NetWare shell is loaded, the LOGIN command permits a network user to access a file server and invoke the system and user login script.

Syntax

LOGIN [*server/[user]*]

Options   LOGIN entered without the optional parameters accesses the default file server. The system prompts for the user name. To access a file server other than the one that is logically closest on the network and to specify a user name without waiting for a prompt, use the server and user variables.

Examples   To gain access to the default file server, enter the following command:

LOGIN

User Jorden can access file server FS2 by entering this command:

LOGIN FS2/JORDEN

LOGOFF

General Description   LOGOFF terminates access to one or more file servers.

Syntax

LOGOUT [*server*]

Options   LOGOUT logs out of all file servers if you do not specify the optional server variable.

Examples   To log out of all file servers, enter

LOGOUT

To log out of file server FS1 only, enter

LOGOUT FS1

LRESTORE

General Description   The LRESTORE utility restores files and directories backed up with the LARCHIVE utility. You must have appropriate rights to the directories and subdirectories before you can restore files. You must have at least create, delete, open, write, and search rights.

Syntax

    LRESTORE

Options   Although the LRESTORE command has no parameters, LRESTORE displays a series of prompts. First, you are asked to select the drive from which to restore files. Next, you are asked if you want to restore security information. (You must be logged in as a supervisor to restore security information.) Next, you are prompted to select specific directories to restore.

During the restore process, LRESTORE stops at any file that is already in the network subdirectory. It prompts you, *File already exists. Recreate? (Y/N)*. You can then choose to overwrite the file or to leave it as is.

Examples   To restore a file backed up with LARCHIVE, go to the directory that contains the files and enter

    LRESTORE

Then respond to the prompts on the screen to restore the file.

MAP

General Description   Use the MAP command to view and modify drive maps.

Syntax

MAP [*drive:*]	Displays the current drive maps.
MAP *path*	Maps or remaps the default drive.
MAP *drive:* = [*drive:* | *path*]	Maps or remaps any network drive.

MAP [INS] *drive:* = [*drive:path*]   Maps a search drive.

MAP DEL *drive:*   Deletes a drive map.

Options   When mapping or remapping drives with the MAP command, you can replace the *drive* variable with a network drive letter (for example, **F:** or **T:**) or a search drive number (for example, **S1** or **S4**). The *path* variable should include the volume, directory, and subdirectory names.

Examples   To list the current drive maps, enter the following command:

MAP

To display the drive map currently assigned to drive T, enter

MAP T:

Enter the following command to change the map of the default drive to FS1/SYS:PROGRAMS:

MAP FS1/SYS:PROGRAMS

Enter the following command to map (or change the map of) drive T to FS1/SYS:PROGRAMS:

MAP T: = FS1/SYS:PROGRAMS

If file server FS1 is the default server, the preceding command can be shortened to

MAP T: = SYS:PROGRAMS

To add a search drive (S3) to the FS1/SYS:PROGRAMS/ LOTUS subdirectory, enter either of the following commands:

MAP S3: = FS1/SYS:PROGRAMS/LOTUS

or

MAP INS S3: = FS1/SYS:PROGRAMS/LOTUS

The difference between the preceding two commands is the way in which NetWare handles search drive S3 if such a search drive already exists. The first command changes the existing search drive to a regular network drive—designated drive X—and adds the new search drive (S3) as drive W. The second command inserts the new search drive between search drive S2 and the previous search drive S3, which becomes search drive S4.

The following command deletes drive R from the drive maps:

MAP DEL R:

MONITOR

General Description The MONITOR command is a console command. It displays one of NetWare's most familiar screens. The display shows the activity of six workstations as well as information about operating system performance. You can monitor any workstation on the network by specifying its connection number.

Syntax

MONITOR *xx*

Options You can monitor any station by replacing the *xx* with the station number. Typing **MONITOR** alone displays information about the workstations currently logged to connections 1 through 6.

In addition to the connection information, the following other information is available from the MONITOR screen:

- NetWare version number and revision date
- Current file server use rate (updated every second)
- Amount of disk I/O pending (based on the cache buffer space in the file server's memory that has changed but has not been written to disk)
- Station number and any of 44 request messages
- List of open files and status information for each file

The messages displayed in the request area show what is going on at the specified workstation at that moment. Forty-four messages can be displayed, as shown in Table 22.1.

Table 22.1: MONITOR messages

Aloc Resource	Get File Size	Release File
Begin Trans	Lock File	Release File Set
Clear File	Lock Phy Rec Set	Release Record
Clear File Set	Lock Record	Rename File
Clear Record Set	Log Out	Search Next
Close File	Log Pers FIle	Semaphore
Clr Phy Rec	Log Phy Rec	Set File Atts
Clr Phy Rec Set	Log Record	Start Search
Copy file	Open File	Sys Log
Create File	Pass File	Unlock Record
Dir Search	Read File	Win Format
End of Job	Rel Phy Rec	Win Read
End Trans	Rel Phy Rec Set	Win Write
Erase File	Rel Record Set	Write File
Floppy Config	Rel Resource	

The MONITOR screen also provides two other pieces of information: files currently in use and status messages about the files. The header portion of the screen displays *File* and *Stat*. The names of up to five of the most recently opened files are shown with a code indicating the current status of the files. The possible status codes are as follows:

CODE	MEANING
n	DOS task number.
P	File is protected from being read by other workstations.
R	File is open for reading.

CODE	MEANING
P	File is protected from being read by other workstations.
W	File is open for writing by other workstations.

Codes are listed in the format *n*PRPW.

Two other identifiers can be displayed: Pers and Lock. Pers indicates that the file is logged on to but not locked. Lock indicates that the file is locked. If the file server is running the SFT version of NetWare with the transaction tracking system (TTS) turned on, two other status letters can by displayed: T and H. When T is displayed in the first column, the transactional file is open. When H is displayed in the second column, the transactional file is on hold.

Examples   To display information about workstation 12, enter

    MONITOR 12

NAME

General Description   The NAME command is a console command. It simply identifies the file server name.

Syntax

    NAME

Options   This command has no options.

Examples   To display the name of the file server to which you are attached, enter

    NAME

NARCHIVE

General Description   The NARCHIVE utility backs up network files and attributes to another network drive. As discussed in

Chapter 19, the NARCHIVE utility can be used for both backing up and archiving certain files.

To use the NARCHIVE utility, you must be logged on to the server with at least read, open, search, and modify rights to the directories and files you want to back up.

Syntax

> NARCHIVE [*path* | SYSTEM]

Options   You can specify the directories or subdirectories that you want to back up by specifying *path* using either the fully qualified path name or the drive letter. To back up the entire system, specify SYSTEM.

Once activated, the NARCHIVE program displays a series of prompts to determine the destination disk for the backup, whether to print a log file, and whether to save directory rights and trustee rights of the backed-up files and directories. Then NARCHIVE asks whether you want to back up all qualified files in the directory or only those modified since the last backup operation.

Examples   To back up the SYS:COMMON directory mapped to drive I, enter either

> NARCHIVE SYS:COMMON

or

> NARCHIVE I:

NCOPY

General Description   NCOPY copies files from one network directory to another. You can also use the NCOPY command to copy files to and from local drives.

Syntax

> NCOPY *filespec* [TO] [*path*] [*filename*] [/V]

Options   Use the /V option to verify that the original file and the newly created file are identical. The DOS wildcard characters (* and ?) can also be used with the NCOPY command.

Examples   To copy a file named MEMO.TXT from network drive G to the FS1/SYS:/PRIVATE/GILLETT/WORDS subdirectory, enter

    NCOPY G:MEMO.TXT TO
    FS1/SYS:/PRIVATE/GILLETT/WORDS

or

    NCOPY G:MEMO.TXT FS1/SYS:/PRIVATE/GILLETT/WORDS

The following command copies all of the files with a .DOC extension in the FS1/SYS:COMMON subdirectory to network drive T and changes the extension to .TXT. This command also verifies that the copied files are identical to the source files.

    NCOPY FS1/SYS:COMMON/*.DOC T:*.TXT /V

NDIR

General Description   NDIR displays information about subdirectories and the files within subdirectories. Information that can be listed about subdirectories includes the directory name, creation date, maximum rights mask, and creator, plus the user's effective rights. File information includes the file name, the file size (in bytes), the date and time that the file was last updated and accessed, the date that the file was created, the file attributes, and the file's creator.

Syntax

    NDIR [path] | [filename]   For use without options.
    NDIR (path | filespec) option [...]   For use with options.

Options   The following options can be used in conjunction with the NDIR command:

OPTION	*MEANING*
File Selectors:	
FILENAME [NOT] = *file*	Displays files that contain the specified file name (wildcard characters are allowed). Use the optional NOT to exclude specified file names. Replace *file* with the desired file name.
OWNER [NOT] = *name*	Displays files created (or not created) by the same user.
CREATE [NOT] (BEF | = | AFT) *mm-dd-yy*	Displays files created (or not created) before, on, or after the specified date.
SIZE [NOT] (GR | = | LE) than *nnn*	Displays files with a size in bytes (or without a size in bytes) greater than, equal to, or less than a specified size.
ACCESS [NOT] = BEF | = | AFT *mm-dd-yy*	Lists the files that were last accessed on, before, or after the date. Replace *mm-dd-yy* with the date.
UPDATE [NOT] = BEF | = | AFT *mm-dd-yy*	Displays the files that were last updated on, before, or after the date. Replace *mm-dd-yy* with the date.
Files Sorted By:	
[REVERSE] SORT FILENAME	Sorts files by file name in ascending or descending (reverse) order.
[REVERSE] SORT OWNER	Sorts files by their creator in ascending or descending (reverse) order.
[REVERSE] SORT ACCESS	Sorts files by the date each was last accessed, from earliest to latest date or in reverse order.

OPTION	MEANING
[REVERSE] SORT UPDATE	Sorts files by the date each was last updated, from earliest to latest date or in reverse order.
[REVERSE] SORT CREATE	Sorts files by creation date, from earliest to latest date or in reverse order.
[REVERSE] SORT SIZE	Sorts files by size, from smallest to largest file or in reverse order.

Selection Filters:

DO	Displays only the subdirectories in a specified directory.
SUB	Displays the subdirectories, and any subsequent subdirectories, in a specified directory.
FO	Files-only option. Displays just the files in the directory or subdirectory.
BR	Brief description option. Lists just a limited amount of information. Shows only the size and last update date of the files.

Archiving Selections:

BACKUP	List files and shows the date each was last modified and last archived. This option uses a slightly different format than other NDIR selections.
WIDE	Displays information in NDIR's default wide format.
[NOT] ARCHIVED	Displays files that have (or have not) been backed up. The date will be shown.
A D BEF | = | AFT *mm-dd-yy*	Lists files that have an archive date before or after the date specified by *mm-dd-yy*.

OPTION	*MEANING*
CHANGED	Displays files that have been changed since the last backup operation.
[NOT] A B	Lists files in which the DOS archive bit has (or has not) been set.
TOUCHED	Lists files modified since the last archiving operation. The option checks both the DOS archive bit and the date and time of the last archive processing.
HELP	Displays a help message showing the command format and options of the NDIR command.

Examples   To display a help message for the NDIR command, enter

NDIR HELP

Enter the following command to list all subdirectories and files in the current directory:

NDIR

The following command displays all files stored on network drive T that have the .TXT extension, that were created by owner GILLETT, and that are larger than 100,000 bytes. The command then displays these files sorted by file name.

NDIR T: FILENAME = *.TXT OWNER = GILLETT SIZE GR 100000 SORT FILENAME

NPRINT

General Description   The NPRINT command prints files to a network printer.

Syntax

NPRINT *filespec* [*option* ...]

Options   Fourteen options can be used with the NPRINT command. Among the most commonly used are the following:

OPTION	MEANING
S = *server*	Designates the file server to which the print job should be routed. Replace *server* with the file server name.
J = *job*	Specifies the name of the print job configuration to be used when printing. Replace *job* with the print job name.
P = *printer*	Indicates the printer to be used when printing the print stream. Replace *printer* with the printer number.
C = *copies*	Designates the number of copies to print. Replace *copies* with the number of copies.
D	Automatically deletes a file after it is printed.

Examples   To print a file named DOCUMENT.TXT in the default directory to the default printer on the default file server, enter the following command:

NPRINT DOCUMENT.TXT

To print three copies of a file named WORDS.TXT stored in the FS1/SYS:COMMON directory to printer 2, enter the following command:

NPRINT FS1/SYS:COMMON/WORDS.TXT P = 2 C = 3

NRESTORE

General Description   The NRESTORE utility restores files and directories backed up with the NARCHIVE utility. You must have appropriate rights to the directories and subdirectories before you restore files. You must have at least create, delete, open, write, and search rights.

Syntax

NRESTORE

Options   Although the NRESTORE command has no parameters, NRESTORE displays a series of prompts to restore files. First, you are asked to select the drive from which to restore files. Next, you are asked if you want to restore security information. (You must be logged in as a supervisor to restore security information.) Next, you are prompted to select specific directories to restore.

During the restore process, NRESTORE stops at any file that is already in the network subdirectory. It prompts you, *File already exists. Recreate? (Y/N)*. You can then choose to overwrite the file or to leave it as is.

Examples   To restore a file backed up with NARCHIVE, go to the directory that contains the file and enter

NRESTORE

Then respond to the prompts on the screen to restore the file.

NSNIPES

General Description   NSNIPES executes an interactive network game for one or more users.

Syntax

NSNIPES [*option*]	For use with a monochrome monitor.
NCSNIPES [*option*]	For use with a color monitor.

Options   Specify *option* to set the difficulty level of the SNIPES game. Enter a value between 4 and 10. The default value is 4.

Examples   To play SNIPES with a moderate degree of difficulty on a color monitor, enter the following command:

    NCSNIPES 6

NVER

General Description   The NVER command displays the version numbers of several file server and workstation network software pieces. It displays the version number of NetBIOS (if loaded), IPX, SPX, the LAN driver, the shell, and the workstation.

Syntax

    NVER

Options   This command has no options.

Examples   To display information about file server and workstation software, enter

    NVER

at the DOS prompt. Sample output looks like this:

    NetBIOS: A NetBIOS error has occurred,
    unable to obtain the NetBIOS version information.

    IPX Version: 2.12
    SPX Version: 2.12

    LAN Driver: IBM Token Ring Network V1.00
    Self Configurable.

    Shell: V2.12 Rev. B
    DOS: MSDOS V3.31 on COMPAQ

    FileServer: FS1
    Novell SFT NetWare 286 TTS V2.15 Rev. A 12/11/88

As this example shows, if NetBios is not loaded, the screen displays an error message instead of NetBios information.

OFF

General Description   The OFF command is a console command. It clears the console screen. For efficiency and to prevent images from being burned into the monitor, you should turn the console display off when it is not needed for viewing.

Syntax

OFF

Options   This command has no options.

Examples   To turn off the console display, enter

OFF

PRINTER XX FORM

The PRINTER *xx* FORM command tells the file server what form number is mounted in the printer. If the printer receives a job from a workstation that requires another form, the file server displays a message asking you to mount the required form. The file server halts the print job until you type the proper PRINTER *xx* FORM command at the console.

Syntax

COMMAND	*SHORT FORM*
PRINTER *xx* FORM MOUNT *yy*	P *xx* FORM *yy*
PRINTER *xx* MOUNT FORM *yy*	P *xx* MOUNT *yy*
PRINTER *xx* FORM *yy* MOUNTED	P *xx* FORM *yy*

Options   The three forms of the PRINTER *xx* FORM command are identical in function. Replace *xx* with the printer name. Replace *yy* with the name of the form.

Examples   If you've identified letterhead paper as form 5 and a print job comes to the server asking for letterhead, the console displays the following message:

> Mount form 5 (UNKNOWN) in printer 0. Then use PRINTER 0 MOUNT FORM 5.

The print job will not be printed until you enter the following command at the file server console:

> P 0 FORM 5

Then the print job will print from the network printer. All other jobs (if any) directed to that printer and calling for form 5 will also print. If the next print job comes in and calls for form 0, you will again be prompted to change the form number at the file server console.

PRINTER XX *REWIND* YY *PAGES*

General Description   The PRINTER *xx* REWIND command is a console command. It lets you reprint up to the last 10 pages of a print job. This command is helpful when you need to reprint part of a document.

Syntax

> PRINTER xx *REWIND* yy *PAGES*

Options   Replace *xx* with the printer name. Replace *yy* with the number of pages to be reprinted.

Examples   To reprint the last two pages printed by printer 0, enter

> PRINTER 0 REWIND 2 PAGES

This command can be shortened to

P 0 REWIND 2 PAGES

PRINTER XX START

General Description   The PRINTER *xx* START command is a console command. It restarts a printer that has been stopped with the PRINTER *xx* STOP command.

Syntax

PRINTER *xx* START

Options   Replace *xx* with the printer name.

Examples   To restart the printer named printer 0 stopped with the PRINTER *xx* STOP command, enter

PRINTER 0 START

This command can be shortened to

P 0 START

PRINTER XX STOP

General Description   The PRINTER xx STOP command is a console command. It stops the server from sending anything to the printer. The command is useful when you need to stop the printer to, for example, change a ribbon or correct a paper jam.

Syntax

PRINTER *xx* STOP

Options   Replace *xx* with the printer number. You must know the printer number to use this command.

The PRINTER xx STOP command halts the printer until the PRINTER xx START command is issued.

Examples   To stop the printer named printer 0, enter

    PRINTER 0 STOP

This command can be shortened to

    P 0 STOP

PSTAT

General Description   Execute PSTAT to view information about network printers. The information displayed includes the printer number, the printer status, and the type of paper being used.

Syntax

    PSTAT [*option* ...]

Options   Two options can be used in conjunction with the PSTAT command:

OPTION	MEANING
S = *server*	Use this option to view information about printers on a file server other than the default server.
P = *printer*	Use this option to view information about a specific printer.

Examples   To view information about all network printers on the default file server, enter

    PSTAT

To display the same information about printer 1 on file server FS2, enter the following command:

PSTAT S = FS2 P = 1

Sample PSTAT output looks like this:

Server FS2: Network Printer Information
Printer   Ready   Status   Form: number, name
━━━━━   ━━━━━   ━━━━━   ━━━━━━━━━━━━━━━━━━━
1   On-Line Active   0, Labels

PURGE

General Description   The PURGE command permanently deletes from the current workstation files erased from the file server's hard disk by the DOS DEL or ERASE command or NetWare FILER menu utility. Unless PURGE is specified, these files can be recovered with the SALVAGE command.

Syntax

PURGE

Options   This command does not have any options.

Examples   To render erased files irrecoverable, enter the following:

PURGE

REMIRROR

The REMIRROR console command is used with SFT versions of Netware only. It restores system fault tolerance (SFT) disk mirroring or duplexing that either failed or was turned off.

REMIRROR first cycles through both drives to make sure that all data is copied onto the mirrored drive. A status message appears as the remirroring process proceeds.

Syntax

REMIRROR *xx*

Options   Replace *xx* with the number of the drive to which everything is copied.

Examples   To copy the contents of physical disk drive 0 to physical disk drive 1, enter

REMIRROR 01

During the remirroring process, a status message tells you what block is being copied. When the process is complete, the message *Remirroring successfully completed* appears.

REMOVE

General Description   REMOVE deletes a user or group from the list of trustee rights in a directory.

Syntax

REMOVE ([USER] *user* | [GROUP] *group*) [[FROM] *path*]

Options   The words USER, GROUP, and FROM are optional in the command statement. You can remove rights from the current directory, or you can remove rights from another directory by specifying a path.

Examples   To remove the trustee rights of user Pierce from the current directory, you can enter either of the following commands:

REMOVE USER PIERCE

or

REMOVE PIERCE

To remove the trustee rights of the ACCTNG group from the TEMP directory on volume SYS of the FS1 file server, enter

REMOVE GROUP ACCTNG FROM FS1/SYS:TEMP

or

REMOVE ACCTNG FS1/SYS:TEMP

RENDIR

General Description   Use RENDIR to change the name of a directory on a file server's hard disk.

To use the RENDIR command, the user must have parental and modify effective rights in the directory being renamed.

Syntax

RENDIR *path* [TO] *directory*

Options   The word TO in the command statement is optional.

Examples   Enter the following command to change the name of the current directory to DEFAULTS:

RENDIR . TO DEFAULTS

or

RENDIR . DEFAULTS

In this example, the period (.) indicates the current directory.

To change the name of the PROGRAMS directory in the SYS volume of file server FS1 to PROG, you can enter

RENDIR FS1/SYS:PROGRAMS TO PROG

REVOKE

General Description   REVOKE rescinds trustee rights previously granted to users and groups. You can use this command instead of SYSCON to delete trustee rights.

The user executing the command must have parental rights in the directory for which the rights are to be rescinded.

Syntax

REVOKE *option* ... [FOR *path*] TO ([USER] *user* | [GROUP] *group*)

Options   For the REVOKE command to be effective, the specified users or groups must exist.

Any of the eight NetWare trustee rights can be specified for *option*, as follows:

OPTION	MEANING
R	Read
W	Write
O	Open
C	Create
D	Delete
P	Parental
S	Search
M	Modify
ALL	Grants all eight trustee rights

Examples   To revoke the read, write, and open rights for user Hull in the current directory, enter

REVOKE R W O TO USER HULL

To revoke the same rights for the ACCTNG group in the TEST directory on file server FS1, volume SYS, enter

REVOKE R W O FOR FS1/SYS:PROGRAMS TO GROUP
ACCTNG

RIGHTS

General Description   The RIGHTS command displays a user's effective rights in a directory.

Syntax

RIGHTS [*path*]

Options   Specify *path* to view the user's effective rights for a directory other than the current directory. If you do not specify a path, the effective rights for the current directory are displayed.

Examples   To display the effective rights for the default directory, enter the following command:

RIGHTS

Enter the following command to display the user's effective rights in the FS1/SYS:PROGRAMS directory:

RIGHTS FS1/SYS:PROGRAMS

SALVAGE

General Description   Under certain conditions, the SALVAGE command recovers files that are inadvertently erased from the file server's hard disk.

The SALVAGE command can be executed only from the workstation that deleted the file to be recovered. Before SALVAGE is executed, no other files can have been created or erased from the same volume, and the workstation cannot have been logged out of the file server.

Syntax

SALVAGE [*path*]

Options   SALVAGE can be executed for the default volume, or the optional *path* variable can be specified to restore a file on another volume.

Examples   To restore the last file erased on volume VOL1 of file server FS1, enter the following command from the workstation that deleted the file:

SALVAGE FS1/VOL1:

SEND

General Description   The SEND command allows network users to send brief messages to other users and groups. Messages can be up to 45 characters long, including your login name and connection number. The messages appear at the bottom of the screen.

Unlike the BROADCAST command, SEND lets you send your message just to specific workstations.

Syntax

SEND *"message"* [TO] [USER] *user* [GROUP] *group*

Options   Messages can be sent to any combination of users and groups. The word TO in the command is optional.

SEND requires you to enclose messages in quotation marks to indicate the beginning and end of the message.

Examples   To send a message about today's 4:00 o'clock staff meeting to users Krueger, Provost, and Gillett and to everyone in the ACCTNG group, enter the following command:

SEND "Staff Meeting Today a 4 p.m." TO USER KRUEGER
PROVOST GILLETT GROUP ACCTNG

SETPASS

General Description   The SETPASS command allows users to change their network password from the command line.

Syntax

SETPASS [*server*]

Options   The *server* option lets users change their password on a file server other than the default server (if they are logged on to another server).

Examples   To change the password on the default server, enter

SETPASS

To change the user password on file server FS2, enter

SETPASS FS2

SET TIME

General Description   The SET TIME command is a console command. It sets the file server date and time.

Syntax

SET TIME [*mm/dd/yy*][*hh:mm:ss*]

Options   Replace *mm/dd/yy* with the month, date, and last two digits of the year. Replace *hh:mm:ss* with the hour, minute, and second. If you omit both the date and time, the command simply displays the file server date and time.

Examples   To set the file server time to September 23, 1990, 9:40 PM, enter

SET TIME 09/23/90 21:47:47

SETTTS

General Description   The SETTTS command is used only with the system fault tolerance (SFT) versions of NetWare. It replaces the logical level of record locks that the transaction tracking system (TTS) lets pass by before TTS starts tracking.

You use SETTTS only if your specific software calls for it and the TTS feature has been installed on your file server. The command can be issued from DOS or placed in a batch file to be executed at certain times.

Syntax

SETTTS [*logical level* [*physical level*]]

Options   Specify the *logical level* and *physical level* using a number from 1 to 255.

Examples   To view the current TTS setting, simply enter

SETTTS

at a DOS prompt.

Generally, the logical level is set for 1 lock and the physical level is set for two locks. To change this setting, enter

SETTTS 2 2

This command changes both the logical and physical levels to a two-record-lock threshold before the system begins to track the transaction.

SLIST

General Description   SLIST displays a list of the file servers running on an internetwork.

Syntax

SLIST

Options   This command does not have any options.

Examples   To list the file servers on the internetwork, enter

SLIST

SMODE

General Description   The SMODE utility views or assigns a search mode to executable files. Search modes are helpful when a program needs to open or access data files in directories other than the ones that contain the executable files.

Syntax

SMODE [*path* | *filespec* [*option*]]

Options   Specify the path if it is other than the default directory. Specify *path* using either a drive letter or a fully qualified directory name, such as SYS:PRIVATE/GILLETT.

To assign a search mode to a file, specify a number from 0 to 7 to represent the search mode you want to use. You can assign the following search modes to files:

SEARCH MODE	*MEANING*
0	This is the default setting for all executable files. The executable file (or program) looks for instructions (if any) contained in the SHELL.CFG file.
1	The executable file searches the default directory and then all search drives.
2	Only the default directory is searched.
3	If no path is specified, the executable file searches only the read-only files in the default directory and all search drives.

SEARCH MODE	MEANING
4	Reserved for future use.
5	The executable file searches all search drives and the default directory, even if the path is not specified in the executable file.
6	Reserved for future use.
7	If only read-only files are searched, the executable file searches the default directory and all search drives.

Examples   To view the current SMODE setting for a given directory, type **SMODE** and the directory path. For example, to return the mode for every executable program (.EXE and .COM file) in the subdirectory SYS:PROGRAMS/WP, enter

    SMODE SYS:PROGRAMS/WP

This command also displays the current mode setting for each of the executable files.

SYSTIME

General Description   SYSTIME displays the day, date, and time set on any file server on the internetwork.

Syntax

    SYSTIME [*server*]

Options   The *server* option displays the system time for file servers other than the default server.

Examples   To display the system time on file server FS2, enter

    SYSTIME FS2

TLIST

General Description   The TLIST command displays a list of the trustee assignments for a specified directory.

To use the TLIST command, the user must have parental rights to the directory.

Syntax

TLIST [*path* [USERS | GROUPS]]

Options   You can execute TLIST for the current directory, or you can specify a directory with the *path* option. By specifying USERS or GROUP, you can limit the display to either user or group trustee assignments.

Examples   To display both user and group trustee assignments for the default directory, enter the following command:

TLIST

To display only user trustee assignments for the current directory, enter the following command statement:

TLIST . USERS

The period indicates that the current directory is to be displayed.

To display group trustee assignments for the PROGRAMS directory of volume SYS on file server FS1, enter

TLIST FS1/SYS:PROGRAMS GROUPS

UNMIRROR

The UNMIRROR console command is used with SFT versions of Netware only. It turns off disk mirroring.

Syntax

UNMIRROR *xx*

Options   Replace *xx* with the number of the drive that was used to mirror the contents.

Examples   If you execute the command

UNMIRROR 01

then the contents of physical disk drive 0 will no longer be copied to physical disk drive 1. The screen displays the status message *Mirroring turned off on volume SYS* when the command has finished execution.

USERLIST

General Description   The USERLIST command displays a list of the users currently logged on to a file server.

Syntax

USERLIST [*server/*] [*user*] [/A]

Options   Use the *server/* option to display the users of a file server other than the default server (if you are connected to another file server). Use the *user* option to display only the information about a specific user. Use the /A option to expand the information displayed to include network numbers and node addresses.

Examples   To list the users on the default file server, enter the following command:

USERLIST

To display expanded information for the users on file server FS2, enter

USERLIST FS2/ /A

VERSION

General Description   The VERSION command displays the version number of any NetWare utility and tells you whether the program uses overlays.

Syntax

    VERSION [*path* | *filespec*]

Options   Specify the path only if the executable files are not in a search directory. Specify a file name for *filespec*.

Examples   To see which version of the NetWare user list is being used, enter

    VERSION USERLIST

WHOAMI

General Description   The WHOAMI command lets users view information about who they are on the network. By selecting the appropriate options, you can display the following information: the file servers to which you are currently attached, your user name on each server, your login dates and times, your group memberships, your security equivalences, and your effective rights in every directory on the internetwork.

Syntax

    WHOAMI [*server*]
    [*option* ...]

Options   In addition to specifying the file server for the user information, you can select from among the following options:

OPTION	MEANING
/G	Displays group membership.
/S	Displays security equivalences.

OPTION	*MEANING*
/R	Displays the effective rights in every directory.
/A	Displays all available information.

Examples   To display the file servers to which you are attached, along with your user names, connection numbers, and login times, enter the following command:

WHOAMI

The following command provides user access information, including group membership and security equivalences, about file server FS1:

WHOAMI FS1 /G /S

APPENDICES

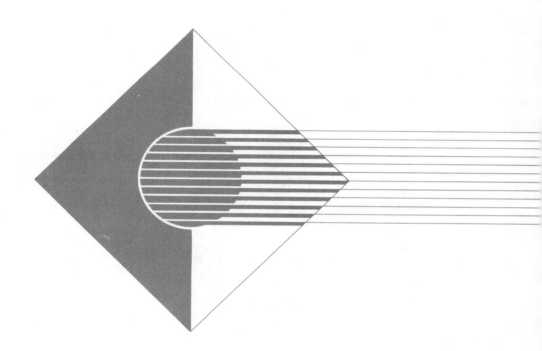

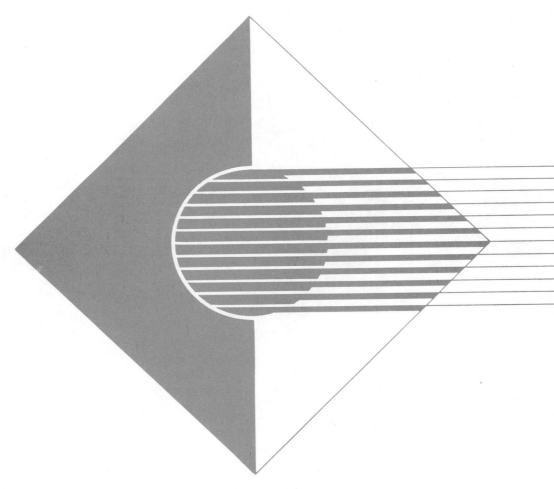

NETWARE 386

APPENDIX A

NETWARE 386 IS ESPECIALLY DESIGNED FOR YOU TO take advantage of the 80386 processor chip. Although NetWare 386 is the most expensive version of NetWare, it also is the version with the largest number of features. NetWare 386 features include the capability for more active users on the file server, enhanced security, more printer options, and the capability to configure itself to meet network demands.

NetWare 386 is designed for large or complex network installations. However, even though it is more sophisticated than earlier versions of NetWare, in many cases NetWare 386 is easier to install and maintain.

This appendix discusses the design philosophy and new features of NetWare 386 and how to upgrade to this version. This discussion assumes that many networks will not begin with this version of the NetWare operating system, but instead will grow to need it.

NETWARE 386 DESIGN PHILOSOPHY

NetWare 386 is a completely rewritten version of the NetWare operating system. It features a redesigned modular architecture that makes expansion easier than in previous versions. For the network manager, this means a technology platform that can easily be expanded or changed. NetWare 386 can operate with computers using many different types of local operating systems, such as workstations based on MS-DOS, OS/2, Apple Macintosh, or UNIX. The modular design also facilitates connection to larger systems, such as to IBM or DEC hosts.

NetWare 386 also allows more flexible configuration and security. This lets networks set up classes of users, such as workgroup managers, who have the capability to perform many of the supervisor maintenance tasks, but who are responsible for only a certain group of users on the network.

NetWare 386 is a more robust operating system than NetWare 286 or other NetWare versions. It is flexible and easy to install and configure. For networks with more than 30 users and the need for flexible security and user controls, NetWare 386 offers a superior operating environment.

DIFFERENCES BETWEEN NETWARE 386 AND PREVIOUS VERSIONS

A number of differences exist between NetWare 386 and its predecessors. In large networks, NetWare 386 provides tangible benefits over previous versions.

INCREASED CAPACITY

NetWare 386 can address larger amounts of memory in the server and larger amounts of disk storage space. This increased capacity is especially helpful in large and busy networks, where users quickly consume file server disk storage space and tax server memory with many file read and write requests. Increased capacity also facilitates management of large database applications (which can be a problem for NetWare 286).

The following list compares the maximum capacities of NetWare 386 and 286.

	NETWARE 286	*NETWARE 386*
Maximum file server RAM	16 MB	4 GB
Maximum disk storage space	2 GB	32 TB
Maximum volume size	256 MB	32 TB

(Note that MB = megabytes, GB = gigabytes, and TB = terabytes.)

Realistically, the hardware limitations of today's microcomputer technology do not currently allow full implementation of the 386 maximums.

DYNAMIC RESOURCE ALLOCATION

Another welcome feature of NetWare 386 for large networks is dynamic reallocation of memory to different processes while the network is operating. The System Executive portion of Netware 386 handles all major resource allocation automatically. This feature facilitates changing certain server settings. For example, the network administrator does not have to manually reset the amount of server memory allocated to directory caching and routing buffers.

Resources allocated dynamically include the following:

- Directory cache buffers
- Directory hash tables (nonconfigurable tables the server uses to find files)
- Directory table entries
- Disk elevator size (an elevator is a buffer that is filled before a write operation is performed)
- FAT tables
- File locks
- File service processes
- Kernel processes
- Loadable modules
- Maximum number of open files
- Router or server memory
- Routing tables
- TTS transactions
- Turbo FAT index tables

In essence, the file server constantly tunes itself for optimum performance. The network administrator does not have to become an expert in tuning parameters.

MORE FLEXIBLE PRINTER CONNECTION

Another feature of NetWare 386 is a print server that allows up to 16 printers on the network. Unlike with previous versions of NetWare, printer servers can be attached to either workstations or the file server.

Aside from the convenience and flexibility that workstation-attached printers offer to users, this feature also gives network administrators the option of placing the file server in a secured room.

ENHANCED SECURITY

NetWare 386 offers enhanced security through password encryption and enhanced file access security. Both these improvements help network administrators create a more secure environment for the network.

PASSWORD SECURITY   The password security feature actually encrypts a password at the workstation before sending the password to the file server. Only the file server can decode the password. This feature prevents anyone with special line trace equipment from reading passwords from the network.

FILE ACCESS SECURITY   File access security is enhanced by modifications in user access rights and file attributes.

In NetWare 386, eight rights can be assigned:

- Supervisor
- Read
- Write
- Create
- Erase
- Modify
- File scan
- Access control

These rights are similar to those of NetWare 286, but there are some notable differences, summarized here.

RIGHT	*NETWARE 286*	*NETWARE 386*
Supervisor	N/A	Grants all rights in a directory and its subdirectories. (Rights cannot be revoked in the subdirectories.)
Open	Opens a file.	No longer used. The rights to open files come automatically with other rights, such as read, write, or create.
Search	Looks for a file.	Replaced by the file-scan right.
Parental	Creates rights.	Replaced by the access-control right.
Delete	Deletes files.	Renamed Erase.

These changes in file access rights help the network administrator more tightly control files on the network, if necessary.

Certain rights can be granted at either the directory level or the file level, as follows:

Access control
Directory level: Allows users to modify the trustee rights of other users. All rights, except supervisor rights, can be granted in a directory or subdirectory. If the directory has restricted disk space, the user's portion of the disk can be allocated.
File level: All rights, except supervisor rights, can be granted in individual files.

Create
Directory level: Allows users to create files and subdirectories.
File level: Allows users to create files or to salvage a file after it has been erased. *Note*: For security-conscious applications, these rights

	allow the network administrator to create a "mail slot" directory. Users can then be given only create rights, which allow users to drop files in the directory, but not to read them or erase them.
Erase	**Directory level:** Allows users to erase subdirectories and files. Users can delete the entire directory and all of its files, plus any subdirectories and files subordinate to the directory. **File level:** Allows users to erase a file. *Note*: If the erase right is granted for a certain file, but not for the directory that contains the file, the user can erase only the specific file and no others in the directory.
File scan	**Directory level:** Allows users to see the file names of each file in the directory and any subdirectories subordinate to it. **File level:** Allows users who don't have file scan rights in the directory to see selected files only, and not any others.
Modify	**Directory level:** Allows users to change the attributes or rename a directory and any subordinate file, subdirectory, or file within the subdirectory. **File level:** Allows users to modify attributes or rename specific files, even if users don't have rights to modify the directory attributes.
Read	**Directory level:** Allows users to open and read any file in a directory. **File level:** Allows users to read specific files in a directory, even if they do not have read access at the directory level.
Supervisory	**Directory level:** Allows users all rights and the ability to grant all directory or file access rights to other users. **File level:** Grants all rights to specific files.

Write   **Directory level:** Allows users to open and
                           change the contents of any file in a directory.
                           File level: Allows users to open and write to
                           specific files.

To remove or revoke rights, NetWare 386 uses the inherited rights mask, which differs from the NetWare 286 maximum rights mask. The inherited rights mask causes users to inherit rights from preceding directories in the path. The inherited rights mask doesn't grant rights; it only revokes them. Once a right is revoked, it can be granted again only by a new trustee assignment.

The effective rights to the files in a directory can be viewed at any time by using the NetWare utility WHOAMI /R. The /R parameter displays all rights to directories and to the volume. A sample listing is shown here:

```
You are user CCC attached to server FS1A, connection 1.
Server FS1A is running NetWare 386 V3.00 Rev. A.
Login time: Saturday  October 7, 1990  10:34 pm
[         ] SYS:
[ R     F ] SYS:LOGIN
[ R     F ] SYS:PUBLIC
[   C     ] SYS:MAIL
[ RWCEMF ] SYS:MAIL/5000009
[ R     F ] SYS:TEST
[ RWCEMF ] SYS:TEST/SUB2
[ RWCEMFA] SYS:TEST/SUB3
[SRWCEMFA] SYS:TEST/SUB4
```

NetWare 386 also offers new or changed file attributes. These attributes can be used to prevent users from performing tasks even if they have trustee rights in a subdirectory. For example, if a user has erase rights granted in a subdirectory, but a specific file is flagged "delete inhibit," then the user cannot delete the file.

NetWare 386 offers fourteen file attributes:

ATTRIBUTE	*SPECIFICATION*	*MEANING*
Archive needed	A	Indicates that the file has changed since it was last backed up.

ATTRIBUTE	*SPECIFICATION*	*MEANING*
Copy inhibit	C	Does not allow the file to be copied.
Delete inhibit	D	Does not allow the file to be erased.
Execute only	X	Prevents the file from being copied. This attribute cannot be removed once it has been applied. X should be used for files only after they have been backed up, because backup utilities will not back up these files.
Hidden	H	Hides the file so that it doesn't appear in a DIR listing. The file will appear on an NDIR listing, however.
Indexed	I	Indexes the file so that NetWare can access it more quickly. NetWare automatically indexes files with more than 64 regular FAT entries.
Purge	P	Automatically purges the file after it has been deleted. The SALVAGE command cannot be used to restore a purged file.
Read audit	Ra	Not implemented in version 3.0. This attribute will record the login ID of the last user to read a file.

ATTRIBUTE	SPECIFICATION	MEANING
Read only	Ro	Allows the file to be read only.
Read-write	Rw	Allows the file to be both read from and written to.
Rename inhibit	R	Prevents users from renaming the file.
Sharable	S	Allows more than one user at a time to read the file.
System	Sy	Hides the file from a DIR command and prevents the file from being copied. An NDIR listing displays these files.
Transactional	T	Indicates that the file is protected by the NetWare TTS (transactional tracking system).
Write audit	Wa	Not implemented in NetWare 3.0. This attribute will list the user who last opened and wrote to a file.

File attributes can be converted from NetWare 286 to NetWare 386 by using the UPGRADE utility. This utility comes with NetWare 386.

UPGRADING TO NETWARE 386

There are two ways to upgrade from NetWare 386. You can install a new server, build a new bindery and new trustee lists, and then copy your program and data files. Alternatively, you can use the UPGRADE utility provided with NetWare 386. Each approach has its merits.

BUILDING A NEW SERVER

The primary reason for installing NetWare 836 by building a new server is to go through the entire installation process and make sure everything is the way you want it. This approach is a good one if you want to clean up your group and user definitions and trustee rights. Building a server from the ground up takes a little longer than running UPGRADE, but because the NetWare 386 installation process is so simple, a well-planned installation and conversion can be completed in an hour or two.

If you decide to build a new server, follow these steps:

- Back up the old file server completely.
- Activate the new server with the SERVER program.
- Create users and groups.
- Create work group managers (if you use work groups).
- Restore all program files and directories.
- Restore all data files.
- Keep the old server on hand for 30 days.

USING THE UPGRADE UTILITY

The NetWare 386 UPGRADE utility translates all NetWare 286 rights and attributes, bindery information, maps, and object IDs from the old file server to the new file server. This utility can save you time, and using it is a good approach if your old file server is set up more or less the way you want it to be. The UPGRADE process can be accomplished by transferring data from one file server to another or, if a second file server is not available, by using a DOS device to store backup data. No matter which approach you use, be sure you have a current backup copy of your system, just in case anything goes wrong.

SUMMARY

This appendix provided an overview of NetWare 386 and the differences between this version and NetWare 286.

All versions of NetWare offer options for building robust and stable networks. NetWare 386 is most appropriate for large or complex networks.

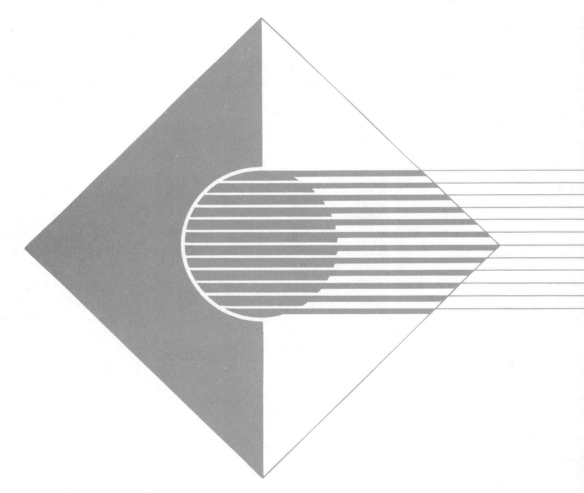

GLOSSARY OF NETWORKING TERMS

APPENDIX **B**

Application A program, such as a word processor or spreadsheet, that performs a useful task by making calls to the operating system and by manipulating data.

Archiving Backing up data files, usually for long-term storage.

ARCnet A network architecture that employs a token-passing bus topology; usually connected using coaxial cable.

ASCII Acronym for the American Standard Code for Information Interchange. ASCII is the coding scheme used by most computers to represent numbers, letters, and symbols.

Asynchronous communications A transmission method in which bytes are sent one bit at a time. Each byte is transmitted with a start and stop bit to synchronize signals between the sending and receiving device.

Back up To make a copy of data files for safekeeping.

Bad block table A list maintained on a hard disk of areas physically unable to reliably store data.

Banner The first page generated by a print job on a network printer; usually contains information about who originated the job, the date and time of the job, and the print queue.

Baud rate The speed at which data is transmitted over a communications link. One character per second equals approximately 8 baud.

Bit   The smallest quantity that a computer can detect; corresponds to a binary digit represented by the presence or absence of voltage. One byte is composed of 8 bits.

Boot   To initialize a program, particularly the operating system. Derived from the expression "pull yourself up by your own bootstraps."

Bridge   A hardware-software combination that links two or more local area networks so that users of each network can access the resources available on the others.

Byte   The unit of measure used by computer memory and storage devices. One byte is composed of 8 bits and represents a single symbol, such as a number, letter, or special character.

Cache   A partitioned area of random-access memory that stores data so that the disk need not be accessed the next time the data is needed. Using the cache significantly increases file server speed.

Central processing unit   The component of the computer that contains the electronic circuitry designed to perform logical and arithmetic functions. Frequently referred to as the CPU.

Channel   A data communications path from an originating device to a destination.

Coaxial cable   A type of wiring frequently used as a network medium; contains a copper inner conductor surrounded by plastic insulation and then a woven copper or foil shield with an outer plastic covering.

Command   The instructions used to control the operating system or other software.

Communication medium   The physical vehicle, such as cables, microwaves, or lasers, for transmitting data from an origin to a destination.

Connection number   The number assigned by the file server to an attached station.

Console   The monitor and keyboard used to control file server activities.

Default drive   The drive automatically used by a computer. To use another drive, the user must specifically change drives.

Device driver   Software that translates operating system requests into a format appropriate for a peripheral device such as a printer or monitor.

Directory   A logical segment of a disk that is created and named by a user. Files are stored in directories for convenience. The directory structure can be hierarchical, with groupings of subdirectories within the directory.

Directory name   The name assigned by a user to a directory or subdirectory. The full directory name, or directory path (for example, FS1/SYS:\PRIVATE\GILLETT\WORDS), indicates the position of a file within the directory structure.

Directory rights   Security restrictions assigned to a specific directory. Directory rights override trustee rights for that directory.

Disk   A magnetically coated medium used to store electronic data files; used interchangeably to refer to both hard (fixed) disks and floppy (or flexible) disks.

Disk drive   The device that rotates a disk to allow data storage and retrieval.

Disk operating system   The operating system used to control the activities of a single computer, in contrast with the network operating system.

Drive   See Disk drive.

Drive letter   A letter used to designate a disk drive; represents either a local drive or network drive.

Effective rights The security rights that can actually be exercised by a user or group in a directory; determined by the trustee rights and the maximum rights mask for the directory.

Emulation The process of one computer imitating the functioning of another; for example, a microcomputer emulating a mainframe terminal.

Ethernet A local area network cable and access scheme originally developed by Xerox.

Extended memory Memory beyond 1 megabyte in a microcomputer running DOS.

File A collection of data stored on a disk or other storage medium.

File attributes Characteristics assigned to network files that determine how the files can be processed. File attributes include shareable, nonshareable, read-write, and read only.

File server The central computer in a local area network. The file server controls all network functions, including file sharing, security, and station-to-station communications.

File sharing The process of multiple users accessing the same file simultaneously.

Gateway A hardware and software combination that allows network users to access resources stored on mainframe and minicomputer hosts.

Hard disk A disk drive of high capacity (usually 10 megabytes or more) that cannot be removed from the computer's chassis; also referred to as a fixed disk.

Hardware The equipment that comprises a computer system, in contrast with computer software.

Host   The central computer, usually a mainframe or minicomputer, that runs applications or provides other services beyond simply storing or transmitting data. Sometimes the file server on a local area network is referred to as the host.

Internetwork   Two or more networks connected via a bridge; often referred to as an internet.

Internetwork packet exchange   A protocol designed to communicate packets of data on an internetwork; often referred to as IPX.

Kilobyte   A standard measure for computer storage; equals 2 to the tenth power, or 1024 bytes. Abbreviated KB.

LAN driver   Communications software that works in conjunction with the network operating system to transmit data between the network interface card and the operating system.

Local disk   A disk drive that is a component of the workstation, but that is not available for access through the network. Usually designated drive A, B, or C.

Log in   To establish a connection with the network. (Also called log on.)

Login script   The set of instructions that executes when a workstation logs in to the network.

Map   The assignment of a drive letter to a directory path.

Maximum rights mask   A component of NetWare security related to directories. Removing a right from a directory's maximum rights mask overrides any rights granted through trustee security.

Megabyte   One million bytes; abbreviated MB.

Microprocessor   An integrated processor (or chip) that contains the circuitry for performing calculations and communicating with other components of the computer.

Modem   An electronic device used to transmit electronic data over telephone lines; derived from modulator-demodulator.

Network   A group of computers connected together that can communicate with one another and share peripheral devices.

Network address   The unique identifier for each network on an internetwork.

Network interface card   A printed circuit board installed in a computing device that allows network stations to communicate with each other and with the file servers.

Network operating system   The program that controls the resources of a computer network and coordinates the transfer of information between devices.

Network operator   A network user granted special privileges to perform specialized functions such as operating a print queue.

Network station   A workstation, bridge, or server connected to the network by a network interface card.

Packet   A block of data transmitted over a network; contains the address of the origination and destination stations, error-control information, and a message.

Parallel communications   A communications technique that uses interconnected wires to send all 8 bits of a byte simultaneously; contrast with serial communications.

Parent directory   The directory one or more levels above a subdirectory.

Parity   A means of error checking during data transmission. A noninformation bit is added to each byte to make the sum of the bits always odd or always even.

Partition   A portion of a hard disk's storage space that is exclusively allocated to an operating system, such as DOS or NetWare.

Print server   A computer attached to the network that makes one or more printers available to network users.

Prompt   A request displayed on the screen asking the user to provide information or perform an action.

Queuing   A means of managing requests, such as print jobs, in the order that they are received while awaiting servicing.

Random-access memory   The internal memory used by the computer to store data and programs during task execution; frequently referred to as RAM.

Read   To retrieve data from a disk drive or other storage device.

Record   A collection of related data within a file that is addressed as a unit.

Remote communications   Communications between a network and a computer in another location that exceeds the distance permitted by the cabling limitations; usually occurs via telephone lines.

Rights   The privileges granted to a user (or group) by a system supervisor. Rights determine the functions that can be executed within a given directory. NetWare rights are open, read, write, parental, delete, create, search, and modify.

Read-only memory   The portion of the computer's memory that is permanently recorded; frequently referred to as ROM.

Root directory   The top directory in a multilevel directory structure.

Search drive   A network drive that is searched by the operating system for an executable file, or for a data file requested by an executable file, when the file is not in the default directory.

Security   The control implemented by a system supervisor to limit users' access to directories and files on the network; managed at four levels: login and password security, trustee security, directory security, and file attributes security.

Security equivalence   An aspect of NetWare security that permits a supervisor to grant a user or group the trustee rights assigned to another user or group.

Serial communications   A communications technique that transmits the 8 bits of a byte in sequence; contrast with parallel communications.

Server   A computer on a network that provides file, print, or communications functions to other network stations.

Sequenced packet exchange   A protocol, used in conjunction with the internetwork packet exchange, that communicates data across the network; frequently referred to as SPX.

Station address   A unique identifier assigned to every station on a network.

Stop bit   A signal used in serial communications to indicate the end of a character.

Subdirectory   A directory one or more levels below another directory in the directory structure.

Supervisor   The person assigned responsibility for maintaining the network. The supervisor is granted high-level security rights.

Synchronous communications   A transmission method that uses a clock signal to regulate data flow. Synchronous communications do not require start and stop bits.

Token ring   Refers to both the physical wiring and access scheme whereby packets of data are relayed from station to station in a logical ring configuration.

Topology The map of a network. Physical topology refers to the layout of the cables; logical (or electrical) topology refers to the manner in which the messages flow.

Trustee A user granted security rights to access a given directory or subdirectory.

Trustee rights The security rights assigned to a specific user permitting access to a given directory or subdirectoy.

Value-added process An application that connects to the network operating system to provide enhanced functionality, such as print server or database server software; frequently called a VAP.

Volume The highest level of a file server's directory structure. Hard disks can be divided into volumes of a predetermined size when NetWare is installed.

Wide area network interface module An interface board installed in a computer attached to the network to route communication transmissions.

Workstation A microcomputer attached to a network and used to perform user tasks.

Write To record data on a storage medium such as a hard or floppy disk.

X.25 An international communications standard for accessing packet-switched networks.

INDEX

A

access
to applications, 164–167
file, 171–177, 350, 390–395
programs for, 56–57
for supervisors, 137
access control rights, 391
access server, 307, 309–310
accounting information, 140, 234–236
addresses
adapter card, 276
file server, 85–86
network, 82–83
administration. *See* maintenance
Advanced NetWare 286 systems, 45,
75–85
ANSI.SYS file for message screens,
105–108, 156
antistatic measures, 66
AnyWare program, 306–308
application programs
accessing of, 164–167
loading of, 57, 132–133
printing from, 225
archive files, 350–351, 358–359
vs. backups, 284
for deleted users, 257
purpose of, 287–288
restoration of, 290–292, 297,
353–354, 364–365
utilities for, 288–297
ARCHIVE.LOG file, 292–294
archive-needed attribute, 393
ARCnet
bridges for, 21
data-passing scheme for, 31, 35
asterisks (*)
for script remarks, 151
for wildcards, 188
asynchronous bridges, 312
ATTACH command, 150, 334
attributes
character, 108
directory, 59, 189, 347–348

file, 59, 172, 186–189, 246, 345–346,
390–395
AUTOEXEC.BAT file, 108–112
automatic backups, 294–297
automatic logins, 104, 108–110

B

background color, 108
backups, 350–351, 358–359
and directory structure, 57
hardware and software for, 284–285
procedures for, 285–288
responsibility for, 283–284
utilities for, 288–297
base input/output address, 85
batch files
for backups, 294–297
for dynamic drive mapping, 164–167
for file deletion, 259
for login, 104, 108–110
for menus, 216
baud rate for serial printers, 68
bindery, 138
adding groups to, 143
backing up of, 285
and deleted users, 258
BINDFIX utility, 258
blinking characters, 107
booting
and automatic login, 108–109
disks for, 101
of file server, 92
from hard disks, 110–112
BREAK command, 150
BRGEN utility, 304
bridges, 20–24, 303–304, 312–314
BROADCAST command, 328, 335
buffers
communication, 82–83
memory, 77, 389
building of networks, 9
bus networks, 17–19, 35

C

cables, 16, 35–38
  in bus networks, 17, 19
  placement of, 47–48, 53
  in ring networks, 18, 20
  troubleshooting of, 276
  for workstations, 68–69
cache statistics, monitoring of,
      268, 271
CAPTURE command, 225,
      335–338, 345
Carbon Copy Plus program, 306
CASTOFF command, 247–248, 338
CASTON command, 247–248, 339
central processing unit, 5–6
channel numbers, 81
checklist, installation, 54–55
CHKVOL command, 329, 339–340
CLEAR STATION command, 328,
      340–341
Close-Up program, 306
cluster controllers, 26
coaxial cables, 36
coaxial SNA gateways, 317, 320
collisions, 31–32
color commands, ANSI, 108
COM1 port, 92
COMCHECK utility, 112–113
command line
  printing from, 228–229
  utilities for, 246–249
commands
  commonly used, 326–329
  formats for, 333–334
  listing of, 334–384
  login script, 149–151
  processor for, 150
  types of, 325–326
comments
  batch file, 109
  in login scripts, 151–152
COMMON directory, 127–128
  for file sharing, 172
  mapping drives to, 154
  monitoring of, 259
communications
  buffers for, 82–83
  networks for, 8
  non-network, 19–26

compression of files, 288
COMPSURF utility, 56, 86–88
computer requirements, 67–68
COMSPEC command, 150, 155
concurrent connections, limitation of,
      172, 174–175
CONFIG command, 326–327, 341
CONFIG.SYS file
  ANSI.SYS driver in, 105
  buffers settings in, 77
  device drivers in, 111
  files settings in, 77, 86, 89
  for IBM Token Ring, 101
  LASTDRIVE command in, 123
configuration
  of file server, 77, 82–83, 234
  of operating system, 55–56, 75–85
  of printers, 59–60, 202–205
  of shell files, 98–99
connections, monitoring number of,
      260–261
console
  commands for, 327
  and printer job deletion, 228
contention data-passing, 31–34
context-sensitive help, 145
COPY command (DOS), 101–102
copy inhibit attribute, 394
copying
  of files, 101–102, 246, 359–360
  of login scripts, 161–163
  of NetWare disks, 76
  of printer configuration, 203–204
courtesy screens, 104–108
CPU (central processing unit), 5–6
create rights, 173, 391–392
creation date of files, 246
current directory in prompt display,
      109, 156
Currently in-Use variable, 261
custom-level shell files, 98
custom login programs, 104–110,
      156–157

D

daily backups, 286
data
  passing of, 31–35
  transfer protocols for, 55, 68

See also files
date
    displaying of, 380
    setting of, 377
debugging, 272–278
    cable labeling for, 47
    error messages for, 153
dedicated power lines, 66
default drives
    changing of, 103, 239
    maps of, 124–125
default-level shell files, 98
default printer settings, 196–197
DEFAULTS directory, 127–128, 130,
        153, 173
delete inhibit attribute, 394
delete rights, 172–173, 391
deletion
    of drive maps, 238
    of files, 259, 371
    of printer jobs, 227–228
    of rights, 183–184, 372–375
    of users, 142, 257–258
destination computers, 32
device drivers in CONFIG.SYS
        file, 111
diagnosis of problems, 272–278
    file flag, 133
    tests for, 56, 112–113
dial-up lines, 310
digital leased lines, 311
DIP switches, interface card, 85–86
directories
    attributes for, 59, 189, 347–348
    changing of, 242
    creation of, 121–122, 127–130, 244
    displaying information about,
        242–244, 360–363
    listing of, 351–352
    loading files into, 130–133
    maintenance of, 262
    names for, 139, 373
    for network files, 141
    in prompt display, 109, 156
    restrictions to, 171–173
    rights to, 238–239, 375, 391–395
    search drive maps for, 152
    security for, 59, 126, 145, 177–186
    structure of, 57, 119–122, 126–130

user names for, 139
DISABLE LOGIN command, 326,
        328, 342
DISK command, 327, 342–343
DISKCOPY command (DOS), 76
disks
    cache statistics for, 271
    copying of, 76
    drivers for, 81
    duplexing of, 45
    letter assignment for, 57
    maintenance of, 255–259, 284
    master, creation of, 97–102
    mirroring of, 371–372, 381–382
    status of, 342–343
    See also drive maps
DISPLAY command, 150, 156–157
distributed star networks, 17, 19
documentation of cable layout, 69
DOS
    directory for, 127–128, 154, 172
    loading files for, 130–131
    menu execution from, 215
    network access to, 103
DOS command, 343–344
DOS BREAK command, 150
DOS SET command, 150
DOS VERIFY command, 150
DOWN command, 327, 344
DRIVE command, 150, 156
drive letters, assignment of, 57
drive maps, 122–126
    dynamic, batch files with, 164–167
    management of, 236–240
    modification of, 354–356
    setting up of, 152–155
drivers
    in CONFIG.SYS file, 111
    for file server, 80–81
    selection of, 99
dumb terminals, 6
duplexing, 45
duplicate files, monitoring of, 259
DXMA0MOD.SYS file, 101
DXMC0MOD.SYS file, 101
DXMT0MOD.SYS file, 101
dynamic drive mapping, 164–167
dynamic memory 1, 260–261
dynamic resource allocation, 389

E

ECHO OFF batch file command, 109
editing
   of login scripts, 162–163
   of printer options, 198–200
effective rights, 185–186
   displaying of, 375
   viewing of, 238–239, 393
efficiency, 8
   of data-passing schemes, 31–32
   of shared resources, 18–19
electrical interference, 35, 37–38,
   53, 66
electricity for file servers, 47, 53
electronic mail, 178
ellipses (...) in command formats, 334
ELS NetWare systems, 44–45
ENABLE LOGIN command, 326,
   328, 344–345
ENDCAP command, 225, 345
environment for file servers, 53, 65–66
environment variables, 150, 155–156
erase rights, 392
errors
   alert for, 150
   messages for debugging of, 153
Escape character, 106
Ethernet systems, 31, 34
EVERYONE group, 139, 143
execute-only attribute, 394
EXIT command, 150
expansion
   and cabling, 36
   of LAN-to-host communications,
      314–318
   of remote communications, 306–310
   of single-site communications,
      303–305
   of wide area networks, 310–314
extended memory, 77
external bridges, 21, 23, 304
external programs, inclusion of, 161

F

fans, cooling, 66
FAT (file allocation table), 263, 389

FCONSOLE utility, 260–261, 268,
   270–272
FDISPLAY command, 150
fiber-optic cable, 38
file allocation table, 263, 389
file scan rights, 392
File Server Disk Verification screen,
   89–90
File Server Information screen, 83–84
file servers
   booting of, 92
   commands for, 327–328
   configuration of, 77, 82–83, 234
   default, 234
   drivers for, 80–81
   environment for, 53, 65–66
   failures in, 263, 277–278
   hard disks for, 56
   list of, 378–379
   location of, 46–47, 65–66
   monitoring of, 260–261, 263,
      268, 272
   names for, 91, 358
   and network size, 45–46
   and network topology, 17–20
   new, building of, 396
   and printers, 48
   processor for, 67
   time and date setting for, 377
   version of, 366–367
FILER utility, 122, 240–246
   for directory attributes, 187, 189
   and maximum rights mask, 185
files
   accessing of, 350
   attributes for, 59, 172, 186–189, 246,
      345–346, 390–395
   compression of, 288
   CONFIG.SYS file setting for, 77,
      86, 89
   copying of, 101–102, 246, 359–360
   deletion of, 259, 371
   displaying information about,
      240–246, 360–363
   loading of, 130–133
   recovery of, 375–376
   restrictions to, 171–173
   sharing of, 132–133, 138, 172,
      187–188

shell, 97–102, 110
See also backups; printers; security
FIRE PHASERS command, 150
FLAG command and flags, 132–133,
    187–189, 345–346
FLAGDIR command, 189, 347–348
foreground color, 108
FORM command (PRINT), 328,
    367–368
forms, defining of, 200–201, 367–368
full name, user property for, 140, 142
functional groups, 138

G

games, interactive, 365–366
gateways, 21, 25–26, 317, 319–320
global security restrictions, 173–177
GRANT command, 348–349
greeting messages, 57–58, 105–108,
    156–157
ground wires, 66
groups
    creation of, 57–58, 142–144
    defining of, 138
    deletion of rights from, 372–375
    listing of, 234, 239
    messages for, 239–240
    and security, 145
    software for, 8
    trustee rights for, 178, 180–181
    user property for, 140
GROUPS directory, 127–130
GUEST user, 139

H

hard disks
    Advanced NetWare 286 support
        for, 81
    booting from, 110–112
    configuring operating system
        from, 77
    directory structure for, 119–122,
        127–129
    failures in, 277
    for file servers, 56
    preparation of, 86–88

hardware
    for backups, 284–285
    file server, configuration of, 82–83
    preparation of, 55, 66–68
    troubleshooting of, 273–278
help, online, 144–145
Hidden attribute, 189, 347, 394
hierarchical networks, 5–6
HOLDOFF command, 350
HOLDON command, 350
host hardware units, 6, 314–318
human networks, 8

I

IBM 3274 cluster controllers, 26
IBM Token Ring networks
    bridges for, 21
    data-passing scheme for, 31, 34–35
    device drivers for, 111
    interface cards for, 85
    supplemental file creation with, 101
IBM_PC long machine type, 102
IBM$RUN.OVL file, 213
identifier variables, 154, 166
IEEE data-passing standards, 34
IF...THEN command, 150
impedance, cable, 37
importing of printer definition files,
    197–198
INCLUDE command, 150
indexed attribute, 394
inherited rights mask, 393
installation
    and administration planning, 60–61
    checklist for, 54–55
    configuration of operating system,
        55–56, 75–85
    and directory structure, 57
    and login scripts, 57–58
    and menus, 60
    of network interface cards, 85–86
    of operating system, 88–92
    preparation for, 53
    and printers, 59–60, 69–70
    problems in, 112–113
    and security, 58–59
    of user access programs, 56–57
Installation Options screen, 89–90

Institute of Electrical and Electronics
   Engineers data-passing
   schemes, 34
INT2F.COM file, 97, 101
interface cards. *See* network
   interface cards
interfaces, terminal, 6
interference, electrical, 35, 37–38,
   53, 66
interleave factor, 87–88
intermediate-level shell files, 98
internal bridges, 21–22
interrupts, conflicting, 276
intruder detection, 175–176
IPX.COM file, 56, 97, 101–103

L

labels, mailing, 200–201
LAN.BAT file, 110
LARCHIVE command, 294–297,
   350–351
large networks, software for, 46,
   387–397
LASTDRIVE command, 123
leased lines, 311
less-than sign (<) for piping, 165
linear networks, 17–18
LISTDIR command, 130–131,
   351–352
%LMACHINE variable, 101
loading
   of applications, 57, 132–133
   of DOS, 130–132
local bridges, 21, 303–304
local drive maps, 123
lockout of intruders, 175–176
logic for directory structure, 126
LOGIN command, 352–353
LOGIN directory, 121, 154
LOGIN_NAME identifier
   variable, 154
login scripts, 57–58
   commands for, 149–151
   copying of, 161–163
   creation of, 104–110, 151–161
   types of, 149
logins
   disabling of, 342

enabling of, 344–345
initial, 102–104, 223–224
user properties for, 140
See also passwords
LOGOFF command, 353
logs, archive, 292–294
LONG MACHINE TYPE variable,
   102, 132
LPT1 port, 92
LRESTORE command, 294, 297,
   353–354

M

MACHINE NAME command, 150
MAIL directory, 121, 178
mailing labels, 200–201
mainframes, gateways to, 21, 25–26
maintenance
   of data, 8
   of disk space, 255–259, 284
   of file server, 260–261, 263
   planning for, 60–61
   of root directories, 262
   security check, 262
MAKE DIRECTORY command
   (DOS), 127–128
MAP command, 124–126, 151, 153,
   164, 354–356
   See also drive maps
MAP DISPLAY OFF command, 157
mapping, printer, 196
masks
   inherited rights, 393
   maximum rights, 184–185
master disks
   creation of, 100–102
   preparation of, 97–98
maximum rights
   displaying of, 243
   mask for, 184–185
Maximum variable, 261
MD command (DOS), 127–128
media defect record, 87–88
medium-sized systems, software for, 45
memory
   buffers for, 77, 389
   cache, monitoring of, 268, 271
   failures in, 277–278

with NetWare 386, 388–389
requirements of, 55, 67
MENU.EXE file, 212
MENUPARZ.EXE file, 213
MENUPARZ.HLP file, 212
menus
for application access, 164–167
creation of, 60, 214–216
planning of, 211–212
utility for, 60, 212–214
messages
blocking of, 338–339
error, 153
greeting, 57–58, 105–108, 156–157
for groups, 138
MONITOR, 357
packets for, 32–34
sending of, 138, 239–240, 247–248,
328, 335, 376
mirroring, 371–372, 381–382
miscellaneous information, user
property for, 141
modem sharing, 304–305
modify rights, 173, 392
modularity of networks, 9, 387
MONITOR command, 327, 356–358
monitoring
of disk space, 255–259
of file server, 260–261, 268, 272
of network use, 263
of system performance, 267–272
of workstations, 356–358
monthly backups, 287–288
MOUNT FORM command, 328

N

NACS (NetWare asynchronous
communications server), 304–305
NAME command, 327, 358
names
for directories, 139, 373
for file server, 91, 358
for supervisors, 137
for users, 139–140, 142, 159, 234
NARCHIVE command, 288–290,
358–359
NASI (NetWare asynchronous
interface) program, 304–305

NCOPY command, 359–360
NDIR command, 256–257, 360–363
NET3.COM file, 56
NET$BIND.SYS file, 289
NETBIOS.EXE file, 97, 101
NET$BVAL.SYS file, 289
NETGEN utility, 56, 75–85
for bridges, 304
directories created by, 121
NET$OS program, 56, 92
NETremote program, 306
NetWare 386 systems, 46
design philosophy of, 387–388
vs. earlier versions, 388–395
upgrading to, 395–397
NetWare 3270 Multi Workstation, 314
NetWare asynchronous
communications server, 304–305
NetWare asynchronous interface
program, 304–305
Network Configuration menu, 78–79
Network Generation Options menu,
78, 86–87
network groups. *See* groups
network interface cards, 16
installation of, 85–86
specifying of, 80
testing of, 56
network operators, 137–138
networks
adapter cards for, 275–276
address for, 82–83
benefits of, 8
building of, 9
drive maps for. *See* drive maps
topology of, 17–18
types of, 5–7
NETx.COM files, 97, 101–103
noise, electrical, 53, 66
nonshareable file attribute, 187–188
Normal subdirectory attribute, 347
NPRINT command, 228–229,
363–364
NRESTORE command, 288,
290–292, 364–365
NSNIPES command, 365–366
NSRO (nonshareable/read only)
files, 188
NSRW (nonshareable/read write)
files, 188

number of sequential passes
(COMPSURF setting), 87–88
number signs (#) for external
programs, 161
NVER command, 329, 366–367

O

OFF command, 327, 367
online help, 144–145
open files, monitoring of, 260–261,
268, 272
open rights, 173, 391
operating system, 17
configuration of, 55–56, 75–85
installation of, 88–92
NetWare as, 43
operators, network, 137–138
OSEXE-1 file, 92
OSEXE-2 file, 92
outages, power, protection from, 66

P

packet-switched networks, 310–311
packets, message, 32–34
parental rights, 172–173, 243–244, 391
parity for serial printers, 68
passwords, 59, 172
changing of, 223–224, 236, 248, 377
initial, 138
and intruder detection, 175–176
with NetWare 386, 390
SECURITY utility for checking
of, 262
user property for, 140–141
PATH command, modification of, 111
PAUSE command, 151, 157
PCCOMPATIBLE command, 151
PCONSOLE utility, 205–206,
225–228
PDN (public data networks), 21,
310–311
Peak Used variable, 261
peer networks, 7
percent sign (%) for identifier
variables, 154, 166
PERFORM utility, 267–270

performance, monitoring of, 267–272
peripheral devices, sharing of, 8,
18–19
personal computers and networks, 7
piping, 165
planning
for maintenance, 60–61
of menus, 211–212
of networks, 9
pointers, drive. *See* drive maps
ports, printer, 92
power supplies for file servers, 53
power surges, protection from, 66
PRINTCON utility, 202–205
PRINTDEF utility, 197–201, 328
PRINTER xx commands, 328,
367–370
printers
capturing data for, 335–338, 345
commands for, 328, 367–370
configuration of, 59–60, 202–205
default settings vs. customization,
196–197
displaying information about,
370–371
and file server location, 47
installation of, 69–70
location of, 48
with NetWare 386, 390
NPRINT command for, 228–229,
363–364
and operating system installation, 92
PCONSOLE utility for, 205–206,
225–227
preparation of, 68
PRINTCON utility for, 202–205
PRINTDEF utility for, 197–201, 328
protocols for, 55, 68
queues and servers for, 195–196,
227–228
PRINTQ_0 queue, 196
PRIVATE directory, 127–129,
173, 222
Private directory attribute, 189,
347–348
problems
and file flags, 133
installation, 112–113
troubleshooting of, 272–278
productivity benefits of LANs, 8

programs, user access, 56–57
  See also application programs
PROGRAMS directory, 127–129,
    153, 172
project groups, 138
PROMPT batch file command, 109
PROMPT environmental
    variable, 156
properties, user, 140–141
protocol engines, 32–34
protocols for printers, 55, 68
PSTAT command, 329, 370–371
public data networks, 21, 310–311
PUBLIC directory, 121
  commands in, 325
  for menu utility, 212–213
  search drive map for, 153
purge attribute, 394
PURGE command, 371

Q

queues, printer, 195–196, 205–206,
    225–228, 328
quotation marks ('') in messages,
    156–157

R

RAM disks, configuring operating
    system from, 76–77
RAM (random-access memory). *See*
    memory
read audit attribute, 394
read only file attribute, 172, 187, 395
read rights, 173, 392
read-write file attribute, 187, 395
receivers, 32
recovery of files, 375–376
regular users, 138
REMARK command, 151–152
REMIRROR command, 371–372
remote bridges, 21, 24, 312–314
remote communications, expansion of,
    306–310
remote-control software, 306
remote printers, 48

remote SNA gateways, 317, 319
REMOVE command, 372–373
rename inhibit attribute, 395
RENDIR command, 373
restoration of archived files, 290–292,
    297, 353–354, 364–365
restrictions, user, 171–177
REVOKE command, 374–375
REWIND command (PRINT), 328,
    368–369
rights
  deletion of, 183–184, 372–375
  effective, 185–186, 238–239, 375
  file, 172–173, 391–393
  for groups, 58
  parental, 172–173, 243–244
  trustee. *See* trustee security rights
RIGHTS command, 186, 375
ring networks, 18, 20
  See also IBM Token Ring networks
ROM addresses for file server, 85–86
root directories, maintenance of, 262
routing, network, 17–18

S

SALVAGE command, 375–376
satellite communications, 6, 311
scrolling of messages, 157
search drive maps, 124, 152
search modes, assignment of, 379–380
search rights, 173, 391
security
  and access server, 307
  attributes for. *See* attributes
  and backups, 289
  and commands, 325
  and definition of groups and
      directories, 145
  directory, 57, 126, 145, 177–186
  for EVERYONE group, 143
  and installation, 58–59
  login, 59, 173–177
  with NetWare 386, 390–395
  and operating systems, 44–45
  and software problems, 273–274
  strategy development for, 171–173

user property for, 141
See also passwords; rights; trustee
   security rights
SECURITY utility, 262
Select Disk Drivers screen, 81
Select LAN Drivers screen, 80
Selected Configurations screen, 83–84
semicolons (;) in messages, 156–157
SEND command, 138, 247–248,
   328, 376
serial printers, 55, 68, 92
SESSION utility, 236–240
SET command, 150, 155–156, 160
Set Operating System Options menu,
   78–79
SET TIME command, 327, 377
SETPASS command, 248, 377
SETTTS command, 378
SETUP program, 68
SFT disk, commands for, 371–372
sharable attribute, 395
sharing
   of data, 138
   of files, 132–133, 138, 172, 187–188
   of peripheral devices, 8, 18–19
SHGEN program, 56, 97–98
SHGEN-1 disk, 98
shell
   files for, 97–102, 110
   network, 16–17, 56
SHELL.CFG file, 101–102
shielded twisted-pair cable, 37–38
shutting down of system, 344
simplicity for directory structure, 126
simultaneous logins, limitations on,
   174–175
single-site communications, expansion
   of, 303–305
SLIST command, 378–379
small networks, software for, 44–45
smart terminals, 7
SMODE command, 379–380
SNA gateways, 26, 317, 319–320
software
   for backups, 284–285
   maintenance of, 8
   remote-control, 306
   troubleshooting of, 273–275
source computers, 32

square brackets ([ ]) in command
   formats, 333
SRO (shareable/read only) files,
   132, 188
SRW (shareable/read-write) files,
   132–133, 188
standalone computers vs. networks, 7
star networks, 17, 19, 35
START command (PRINTER),
   328, 369
static electricity, protection from,
   65–66
status information commands, 329
stop bits for serial printers, 68
STOP command (PRINTER), 328,
   369–370
subdirectories. *See* directories
submenus, 214
supervisor rights, 391
supervisors, 103, 137, 139
   commands for, 327
   and printer jobs, 197, 228
   and trustee rights, 178
supervisory rights, 392
support, user, 221–222
SUPPORT disk, 78, 86
surge protectors, 66
synchronization of passwords, 223
SYS directory, mapping drives to, 154
SYS drive, 90
SYSCON utility, 233–236
   for login scripts, 151–152, 159, 161
   for trustee rights, 178, 180
   for user changes, 138–139
SYS$ERR.DAT file, 213
SYS$HLP.DAT file, 213
SYS$MSG.DAT file, 213
system attribute, 395
SYSTEM directory, 121–122, 325
System Executive, 389
system login scripts, 149, 151–159
System subdirectory attribute,
   347–348
SYSTIME command, 380

T

T-1 service and bridging, 311,

314, 316
tape units for backups, 285, 287
telephone lines, 21, 36-37, 310
terminals, smart vs. dumb, 6-7
TESTFILE.PRN file, 257
testing
   of hard disks, 87-88
   of login scripts, 157-159
   by users, 221-222
time
   displaying of, 380
   restrictions on, 141, 172, 176-177
   setting of, 377
Time Restriction matrix, 176-177
TLIST command, 329, 381
token data-passing schemes, 31-35
Token Ring networks. *See* IBM Token
      Ring networks
topology, network, 17-18
training of users, 222
transaction tracking system,
      78-79, 378
transactional attribute, 395
transmitters, 32
troubleshooting, 272-278
   and file flags, 133
   for installation, 112-113
trunks, 17
trustee security rights, 59, 145
   assignment of, 348-349
   backing up of, 285
   deletion of, 183-184, 372-375
   displaying of, 243
   granting of, 177-183
   lists of, 381
   rescinding of, 374-375
   user property for, 141
TTS (transaction tracking system),
      78-79, 378
twisted-pair cables, 35-38
type-1, -2, and -3 cables, 36-37
types
   of commands, 325-326
   of login scripts, 149
   of networks, 5-7

U

uninterruptible power supplies, 66

UNMIRROR command, 381-382
unshielded twisted-pair cables, 36-37
UPGRADE utility, 396-397
upgrading, 395-397
uppercase letters for identifier
      variables, 154
UPS (uninterruptible power
      supplies), 66
user access programs
   creation of, 56-57, 97
   custom login, 104-110
   disk preparation for, 97-98
   hard disk booting, 110-112
   and initial login, 102-104
   and problem diagnosis, 112-113
   shell files for, 98-102
user groups. *See* groups
USER variable, setting of, 160, 166
USERLIST command, 248, 382
users
   addition and changing of, 138-142
   defining of, 137-138
   deletion of, 142, 257-258
   deletion of rights from, 182-184,
      372-375
   disk space for, review of, 257
   displaying information about, 249,
      383-384, 393
   listing of, 240, 248, 382
   login scripts for, 159-161
   names for, 139-140, 142, 159, 234
   preparation of, 221-223
   restrictions on, 171-177
UTIL directory, 127-128, 166, 172
   for menus, 213
   search drive map for, 153
UTILEXE-1 disk, 86
utilities, versions of, 383

V

VAP (value-added process), 19-20
variables in login scripts, 154, 166
VDISK.SYS file, 77
VERIFY command, 150
VERSION command, 383
versions
   of file servers, 366-367
   NetWare, 43-44

of utilities, 383
vertical bars (|) in command
  formats, 334
virtual disks, configuring operating
  system from, 76–77
VOLINFO utility, 255–256
volumes, 90–91, 120–121, 241–242,
  339–340, 388
VREPAIR utility, 263

W

weekly backups, 286–287
welcome messages, 57–58, 105–108,
  156–157, 224
WHOAMI command, 249,
  383–384, 393
wide area networks
  expansion of, 310–314
  interface modules for, 304–305, 307
wildcards with files, 188
wire closets, 47, 276–277
WNIM (wide area network interface
  modules), 304–305, 307

word length for serial printers, 68
work-group software, 8
workstations
  cabling of, 68–69
  clearing connection to, 340–341
  commands for, 326–328
  computers for, 67
  and file servers, 15–17
  and hardware problems, 273
  monitoring of, 356–358
  operating systems for, 17
  performance of, 268
  ROM addresses for, 85–86
  shell file generation for, 98–100
  testing of, 112
  user property for, 141
write audit attribute, 395
WRITE command, 151, 156–157
write rights, 173, 393

X

X.25 protocol, 310–315
XON/XOFF protocol, 68

TO JOIN THE SYBEX MAILING LIST OR ORDER BOOKS
PLEASE COMPLETE THIS FORM

NAME _____ COMPANY _____

STREET _____ CITY _____

STATE _____ ZIP _____

☐ PLEASE MAIL ME MORE INFORMATION ABOUT **SYBEX** TITLES

ORDER FORM (There is no obligation to order)

PLEASE SEND ME THE FOLLOWING:

TITLE	QTY	PRICE
_____	____	____
_____	____	____
_____	____	____
_____	____	____

TOTAL BOOK ORDER _____ $_____

CUSTOMER SIGNATURE _____

SHIPPING AND HANDLING PLEASE ADD $2.00 PER BOOK VIA UPS _____

FOR OVERSEAS SURFACE ADD $5.25 PER BOOK PLUS $4.40 REGISTRATION FEE _____

FOR OVERSEAS AIRMAIL ADD $18.25 PER BOOK PLUS $4.40 REGISTRATION FEE _____

CALIFORNIA RESIDENTS PLEASE ADD APPLICABLE SALES TAX _____

TOTAL AMOUNT PAYABLE _____

☐ CHECK ENCLOSED   ☐ VISA
☐ MASTERCARD   ☐ AMERICAN EXPRESS

ACCOUNT NUMBER _____

EXPIR. DATE _____ DAYTIME PHONE _____

CHECK AREA OF COMPUTER INTEREST:

☐ BUSINESS SOFTWARE

☐ TECHNICAL PROGRAMMING

☐ OTHER: _____

THE FACTOR THAT WAS MOST IMPORTANT IN YOUR SELECTION:

☐ THE SYBEX NAME

☐ QUALITY

☐ PRICE

☐ EXTRA FEATURES

☐ COMPREHENSIVENESS

☐ CLEAR WRITING

☐ OTHER _____

OTHER COMPUTER TITLES YOU WOULD LIKE TO SEE IN PRINT:

_____

_____

OCCUPATION

☐ PROGRAMMER   ☐ TEACHER

☐ SENIOR EXECUTIVE   ☐ HOMEMAKER

☐ COMPUTER CONSULTANT ☐ RETIRED

☐ SUPERVISOR   ☐ STUDENT

☐ MIDDLE MANAGEMENT   ☐ OTHER:

☐ ENGINEER/TECHNICAL   _____

☐ CLERICAL/SERVICE

☐ BUSINESS OWNER/SELF EMPLOYED

CHECK YOUR LEVEL OF COMPUTER USE

☐ NEW TO COMPUTERS

☐ INFREQUENT COMPUTER USER

☐ FREQUENT USER OF ONE SOFTWARE

   PACKAGE:

   NAME _____

☐ FREQUENT USER OF MANY SOFTWARE

   PACKAGES

☐ PROFESSIONAL PROGRAMMER

OTHER COMMENTS:

_____
_____
_____
_____
_____
_____
_____

PLEASE FOLD, SEAL, AND MAIL TO SYBEX

SYBEX, INC.
2021 CHALLENGER DR. #100
ALAMEDA, CALIFORNIA USA
                  94501

SEAL

SYBEX Computer Books
are different.

Here is why . . .

At SYBEX, each book is designed with you in mind. Every manuscript is carefully selected and supervised by our editors, who are themselves computer experts. We publish the best authors, whose technical expertise is matched by an ability to write clearly and to communicate effectively. Programs are thoroughly tested for accuracy by our technical staff. Our computerized production department goes to great lengths to make sure that each book is well-designed.

In the pursuit of timeliness, SYBEX has achieved many publishing firsts. SYBEX was among the first to integrate personal computers used by authors and staff into the publishing process. SYBEX was the first to publish books on the CP/M operating system, microprocessor interfacing techniques, word processing, and many more topics.

Expertise in computers and dedication to the highest quality product have made SYBEX a world leader in computer book publishing. Translated into fourteen languages, SYBEX books have helped millions of people around the world to get the most from their computers. We hope we have helped you, too.

For a complete catalog of our publications:

SYBEX, Inc. 2021 Challenger Drive, #100, Alameda, CA 94501
Tel: (415) 523-8233/(800) 227-2346   Telex: 336311
Fax: (415) 523-2373

WORKSTATION COMMAND-LINE UTILITIES

NPRINT *filespec* **[option …]**
>   Print files to a network printer.

NRESTORE
>   Restores files and NetWare attributes backed up with the NARCHIVE
>   command.

NSNIPES [*option*]
NCSNIPES [*option*]
>   Executes an interactive network game for one or more users. Use
>   NCSNIPES with a color monitor.

NVER
>   Displays the version number of NetBIOS, IPX, SP, the LNA driver, the
>   shell workstation operating system, and the file server operating system
>   currently running.

PSTAT [*option …*]
>   Displays information about network printers.

PURGE
>   Makes deleted files irrecoverable.

REMOVE ([USER] *user* | **[GROUP]** *group*) **[[FROM]** *path*]
>   Deletes a user or group from the list of trustee rights in a directory.

RENDIR *path* **[TO]** *directory*
>   Changes the name of a directory on a file server's hard disk.

REVOKE *option* … **[FOR** *path*] **TO ([USER]** *user* | **[GROUP]** *group*)
>   Rescinds trustee rights previously granted to users and groups.

RIGHTS [*path***]**
>   Displays a user's effective rights in a directory.